Pramatha Nath Bose

A History of Hindu Civilization during British Rule

Vol. 3

Pramatha Nath Bose

A History of Hindu Civilization during British Rule
Vol. 3

ISBN/EAN: 9783743370890

Manufactured in Europe, USA, Canada, Australia, Japa

Cover: Foto ©ninafisch / pixelio.de

Manufactured and distributed by brebook publishing software (www.brebook.com)

Pramatha Nath Bose

A History of Hindu Civilization during British Rule

A HISTORY

OF

Hindu Civilisation during British Rule

BY

PRAMATHA NATH BOSE, B.Sc. (Lond.), F.G.S., M.R.A.S.

AUTHOR OF "THE CENTENARY REVIEW OF THE RESEARCHES OF THE
ASIATIC SOCIETY OF BENGAL IN NATURAL SCIENCE."

IN FOUR VOLUMES

VOL. III

INTELLECTUAL CONDITION.

CALCUTTA: W. NEWMAN, & Co.
LONDON: KEGAN PAUL, TRENCH, TRÜBNER & Co.
BOMBAY: THACKER & Co. MADRAS: HIGGINBOTHAM & Co.
LEIPZIG: OTTO HARRASSOWITZ.

1896.

PRINTED BY R. DUTT,
HARE PRESS:
46, BECHU CHATTERJEE'S STREET, CALCUTTA.

The rights of translation and of reproduction are reserved.

TO

THE MARQUIS OF RIPON,

WHO, DURING HIS VICEROYALTY IN INDIA,
LABOURED, WITH A LOVING HEART,
FOR THE WELFARE OF MY COUNTRYMEN,
AND WHOSE NAME WILL EVER BE CHERISHED BY THEM
WITH GRATITUDE, I RESPECTFULLY
DEDICATE THIS VOLUME.

PREFACE.

I have attempted in this volume to give some idea of the nature and operation of the influences which have affected the Hindu intellect under British Rule. In doing this, I have indicated, in a general way, how these influences have moulded the modern literature of India. It is my intention to present in the next volume a more complete account of the present intellectual condition of the Hindus as reflected in literature. Considering the diversity of the vernacular literatures of India, I am probably showing more presumption than discretion in undertaking this task ; and, I must say, its execution will largely depend upon the co-operation I may be fortunate enough to secure from those parts of India with the literary history of which I cannot claim more than a very superficial acquaintance. I am glad to be able to state, that several gentlemen have already come forward with such assistance, and that several more have promised it. For the present, I desire to thank them collectively. My obligations to them individually will be acknowledged in the next volume.

DARJILING
November, 1895.

P. N. BOSE.

CONTENTS OF VOL. III.

INTRODUCTION.

SUBJECT	PAGE.
Decline of the Hindu intellect since the twelfth century	i
Chief cause of the decline : the caste-system	ii
Caste especially injurious to the cultivation of physical sciences	iv
Illustration how caste hindered progress	v
The anti-caste influence of the British contact : the doctrine of equality	viii
Influence of the doctrine of equality	x
Increased sense of individuality : its influence upon Hindu literature	xii
Superficial character of the recent renaissance of Hindu literature	xv
Causes of this superficiality : transitional state	xvi
Anomalous position of English among the literary languages of India	xviii
Consequences of this anomaly	xix
Poverty of the people	xxi
Its effect upon scientific progress	ib
Its influence upon general literature	xxiv

CONTENTS.

SUBJECT.	PAGE.
Standard of living	xxv
Influence of European luxuries	xxvi
Outer forms of European civilisation : the railways &c.	xxix
They do not indicate the progress of India	xxx
Educational and economic effects of Indian railways	xxxi
Influence of Indian railways upon Hindu progress not considerable	xxxvii
Reflections on the civilising methods of the Western nations	xxxix
The exclusive policy	xxxxii
Tranquillity maintained by British Rule favourable to progress	xxxxv
But to a small extent owing to its exclusive policy	ib
Present extent of the exclusion	xxxxvii
Alleged reasons for the exclusive policy	xxxxix
Depression of material condition, a consequence of the exclusion	li
Alleged indications of material prosperity—Expansion of trade	liii
Growth of population not a good test of material prosperity in India	lvii
Growth comparatively small	lviii
Partly due to improved enumeration	lix
Growth mainly in outlying parts of the country	ib
Taxation in India, why heavy	lx
Signs of material depression	lxii
Moral effect of the exclusive policy	lxiv
Present conditions on the whole unfavourable to sound intellectual development	lxvi

BOOK V.
INTELLECTUAL CONDITION
CHAPTER I.

A BRIEF SKETCH OF THE HISTORY OF THE HINDU INTELLECT FROM THE EARLIEST TIMES TO THE BRITISH RULE.

SUBJECT.	PAGE.
The Vedic Period :—	
The Rigveda	2
The Bráhmanas	3
Chhandas ; Siksha &c.	6
Astronomy	7
Geometry	8
The Buddhist-Hindu Period :	
High value set upon knowledge	8
Secularisation of knowledge	9
Science of language	10
Systems of philosophy: the Sámkhya	11
The Nyáya	12
The Vaisesika	13
The Púrva mímánsá and the Uttara mímánsá	14
The mathematical sciences	15
Medical sciences	17
Laws	20
General literature	22
The Puránic period :	
Mathematical science	24
General literature	28
Mahomedan influence upon Hindu literature	33
Rise of the vernacular literatures	38
Influence of Vaishnavism on vernacular literature	40

CONTENTS.

CHAPTER II.

INFLUENCE OF ENGLISH LIBERAMISM.

SUBJECT.	PAGE.
Liberalism in modern Europe	43
Liberalism in India since 1832	44
The Press	49
Spread of education since 1835 : influence of European democracy	52
Rise of political Associations under English influence : the British Indian Association &c.	58
The National Congress	60
District and Local Boards	69
Municipalities	71
The Indian Councils	72
Individuality as a developmental force in modern Hindu literature	74

CHAPTER III.

INFLUENCE OF ENGLISH INDUSTRIALSM.

Industrial condition of England and of India about the middle of the eighteenth century .	80
Industrial expansion of England in the beginning of this century	81
Effect of the expansion upon Indian industries	82
Recent growth of industrial enterprise and technical education	84
Difficulties of industrial progress .	85
Technical education	86
Industrial Schools	87
Art Schools	88
Institutions for higher technical education	90

CHAPTER IV.

INFLUENCE OF MODERN NATURAL SCIENCE.

Education in India until recently literary .	94
Difficulties of scientific progress among the Hindus	96
Recent progress of scientific education	103

CONTENTS.

SUBJECT.	PAGE.
Condition of general scientific education still unsatisfactory	105
Medical education	107
Engineering education	112
Forest School	114

CHAPTER V.

INFLUENCE OF THE ADMINISTRATIVE POLICY OF BRITISH RULE.

Tranquillity maintained by British Rule favourable to intellectual progress	117
Economic influence of British administration	118
Opinions about the impoverishment of India under British rule	120
Data for the ascertainment of the material condition of India not satisfactory	122
Hindu ascendency in pre-Mahomedan times	128
Hindu influence in Madomedan period	129
Intellectual effects of the exclusive policy in military and political departments	135
Exclusion in the civil departments	138
Policy of exclusion	139
Divergence of opinion with regard to the admission of Indians into responsible administration	140
Moral effect of the exclusive policy	148
The injurious effect of the exclusive policy upon intellectual progress	150

CHAPTER VI.

EDUCATION UNDER BRITISH RULE—ENGLISH EDUCATION.

High Education in pre-British times	154
Sanskrit influence upon British Scholars	158
Foundation of Sanskrit college, Benares	158
The educational minute of Lord Minto	159

CONTENTS.

SUBJECT.	PAGE.
The educational clause in the Charter of 1813	161
Establishment of Oriental Colleges of Calcutta, Agra and Delhi 1824-25	163
Sanskrit College of Puna 1821	164
Educational Policy of Elphinstone	165
Early educational measures in Madras	166
Indigenous efforts to spread English Education: Rám Mohan Ráya	166
The Hindu College of Calcutta	167
Early Missionary efforts to spread English education	169
The Elphinstone College of Bombay	169
The educational grant made by the charter of 1833	169
Controversy between the Anglicists and the Orientalists	170
The controversy terminated by the minute of Macaulay	173
The educational Resolution of Lord William Bentinck	174
Rapid spread of English education since 1835	175
Impetus to English education given by the discontinuance of Persian as official language about 1838	178
The Education Resolution of Lord Hardinge, 1844	178
Progress of English Education in Bengal 1844 to 1857	180
Progress of English Education in the Bombay Presidency to 1857	181
Progress of English Education in the Madras Presidency to 1857	182
The Education Despatch of 1854	183
Creation of Education Departments	184
The grant-in-aid system	185
Establishment of the Universities: the results of University education	185
High Class schools and Colleges under Hindu management	188

CHAPTER VII.

EDUCATION UNDER BRITISH RULE—VERNACULAR EDUCATION.

Indigenous Vernacular Education	190
Indigenous Vernacular schools about 1830	193

CONTENTS.

SUBJECT.	PAGE.
Spread of Vernacular education by Christian Missionaries	195
The Calcutta school Society	195
Committee of Public Instruction	196
Progress of vernicular education in Bengal 1835-1855	197
Vernacular education in the Bombay Presidency	197
Vernacular education in the North-West, 1845-1855	198
State of Vernacular education in 1859	198
Primary and Secondary education	200
Primary education in Bengal	201
In Madras	201
In Bombay	201
The Education Commission and Primary Education	202
Secondary Vernacular education	203

CHAPTER VIII.

EDUCATION UNDER BRITISH RULE—FEMALE EDUCATION.

Indigenous female education	205
Missionaries the pioneers in female education	206
The Bethune school	207
Progress of Female education in Bengal 1859 to 1893	208
Female education in Bombay, 1824 to 1892	209
Female education in Madras, 1841 to 1892	211
Female education in the North West, 1855 to 1892	213
Female education in the Punjab, 1855 to 1893	214
Female compared with Male literacy	215
Appendix A. Information concerning the study and practice of the Hindu system of Medicine	216
Appendix B. Extract from the evidence of Mr. A. O. Hume before the Public Service Commission	216
Appendix C. Some educational statistics	224

INTRODUCTION.

Decline of the Hindu intellect since the twelfth century.
Hindu intellect had been in a state of arrested development for nearly six centuries when the foundation was laid of the British Empire in India. During that long period, the Hindus had produced nothing of a strikingly original character. The last great name in the annals of Hindu philosophy was that of Samkaracháryya who lived about the ninth century; the last great name in Hindu mathematics was that of Bháscarácháryya who flourished about the middle of the twelfth century.

The decline was synchronous with the Mahomedan conquest and was no doubt facilitated by it. The depressing influence of foreign domination can never be otherwise than detrimental to healthy progress of a high order. But Hindu civilisation carried the germs of its decay within it. The Caste-system upon which it is based, rendered its continued development an impossibility, because it contravened the fundamental conditions of such development. It protected the different classes of Hindu society from the stress and strain of strenuous competition; but in doing so it rendered a halt in its onward march inevitable. It made life easy and contented; but it did so freeing it, to a considerable extent, from ceaseless struggle, the hard, inexorable condition of continued intellectual and industrial progress. It promoted spirituality and quietism, but it suppressed industrialism and combativeness which are among the principal motive forces of modern progress.

Chief cause of the decline: the Caste-system.

The Caste-system, however, does not deserve the large measure of odium which is usually cast upon it. It was probably the best solution possible, at the time it was formed, of the great social problem which is at present exercising the minds of Western philosophers, the problem, namely, how to distribute the good things of the world so as to liberate the lower classes from the vices and miseries of destitution. No such solution is possible now. The Western proletariat have been given political equality. But no steps have been taken to secure to them that measure of economic equality without which political equality is worse than meaningless—positively dangerous. The policy of *laissez faire* hitherto pursued by the most advanced nations of the West has landed them in a critical situation ; and some form or other of State Socialism is now being influentially advocated as a means out of it. Viewing the caste-system, as originally developed, in the light of recent Western developments and movements, we are inclined to think that it does credit to the head no less than to the heart of the Aryan sages of ancient India who conceived and constructed it, especially if we consider the condition of political morality which prevailed among the other civilised nations of the time. It is a system of organised inequality, but of inequality so adjusted as not to press very severely upon the classes affected by it. The dark-skinned aborigines of India were not made slaves ; but they were assigned a well defined position, though that position was the lowest in the society of the Aryan conquerors. The treatment which the Súdras received was no less humane, and infinitely less calculated to produce friction than the treatment which, at the present day, the "blacks" receive at the hands of the "whites" in parts of the United States after a century's war cry of "liberty, equality, and fraternity," and after so many centuries of the altruistic influence of Christianity.

The Bráhmans, as a class, did not seek material aggrandisement; government, trade, in short, every occupation calculated to further material interests they left to the lower classes, and thus they effectually secured themselves against the desire for encroachment. What they sought to restrict within the two highest classes, and especially within their own class, was spiritual and intellectual advancement; and that is of a nature which does not usually excite the jealousy of the mass of the people. This monopoly, however, was all the more detrimental to intellectual progress beyond a certain stage, because it was of such an immaterial character that the lower classes would not think it worth their while to contest. Competition artificially limited and secured within a well defined body restricted the range of favourable variation in intellectual development which was thus placed, to a great extent,

Caste specially injurious to the cultivation of physical sciences.

beyond the action of the law of natural selecticn—a law as supreme in the case of intellectual as in that of physical development. The isolation of the intellectual class was specially injurious to the progress of those branches of knowledge which increase the comforts, conveniences and luxuries of civilised life. The Bráhmans were averse to material progress. They looked down with undisguised contempt upon arts and manufactures, upon, in fact, all occupations which had not spiritual or mental culture as their primary object. Wrapped up in serene philosophic contemplation, taking but little interest in the struggles after material progress carried on by the lower classes whom they looked upon as the "vulgar herd," they carried mental science to a high pitch of perfection, while they neglected physical science to a most serious extent.

Illustration how caste hindered progress. Directly, the caste-system prevented, in course of time, the spread of knowledge beyond a small, privileged, hereditary class; and indirectly, it led to the neglect of the physical sciences. It is precisely because it did so, that the Hindu intellect has remained in such a condition of barrenness for so long a period, and the Hindu civilisation has remained stationary while other peoples, unhampered by caste restrictions, have been making rapid strides towards progress. The claim of Western civilisation to intellectual superiority over Hindu civilisation—in fact, over all ancient civilisations—rests upon the unrestricted diffusion of knowledge and upon the advance made in physical science. It rests upon the increased enlightenment of the race, not upon the increased intellectual capacity of the individual. Intellectual progress under modern civilisation has spread over a wider area; it covers a larger variety of subjects; but the mental power of the individual now is not higher than it was in ancient times. The great names in the intellectual world of the present day are no greater than the great names in the intellectual world of antiquity. The intellectual calibre of a Cuvier or of a Darwin cannot be said to be superior to that of a Kapila or of a Kanáda. The great men of the Western civilisation differ from the great men of the Hindu civilisation in the fact that the former represent the progress of a much larger body than the latter. The intellectual giants of the present day have been nourished not only by the accumulated knowledge of past civilisations,* but also by the acquired knowledge of the whole modern world. The sages

* "What the centuries have done for us" well observes Mr. Henry

of antiquity stand out as a few stupendous heights towering above a slightly elevated plain. But, the most prominent men of the present day are like peaks but slightly higher than innumerable other peaks surrounding them on all sides. True, to continue the metaphor, time will reduce -nay, plane away—many a peak that looks so majestic now. But, making all allowance for the destructive action of time, there can be no doubt, that the great men of the Western civilisation will, even after the lapse of many centuries, greatly outnumber the great men of the ancient civilisations. The eminent names that cluster round a single feat of the intellect at the present day are more numerous than all the eminent names connected with all the great intellectual efforts of ancient India. We can form some idea of the damaging influence of the caste-system upon Hindu progress, when we consider from what different ranks of the Western society have risen the men who have contributed to the building up or expansion of a modern scientific theory; how men who began life as indigent mechanics are ending it as great philosophers or honoured inventors; how the sons of parents altogether

George "is not to increase our stature, but to build up a structure on which we may plant our feet." ("Progress and Poverty" Book X, Ch. II).

unconnected with literature or science have risen to literary or scientific eminence.

<small>The anti-caste influence of the British contact; the doctrine of equality.</small>

The anti-caste influence of the British contact has given Hindu civilisation a fresh impetus to progress by relaxing the restrictions of the caste-system which, as we have just seen, was the primary cause of the halt which Hindu civilisation made about the time of the Mahomedan conquest. Foremost among the new forces which have come into play with the British rule is the doctrine of equality. It is no new doctrine. It is at least as old as Buddhism. But it is only in recent times that it has been endowed with sufficient vitality to be a motive factor in the world's progress. The tendency of legislation and of political movement in the West for the last century has been towards democracy. The goal has certainly not been reached. The greatest advance in political equality has so far only rendered more glaring the social inequality between the rich and the poor, the capitalist and the labourer. It should be observed, however, that the socialist agitation in the West, which is yearly gaining ground and attaining solidarity, will result sooner or later in new principles of progress. What these principles and their consequences will be no one can predict. But whatever they be, they will rest upon a broader basis of altruism than what modern civilisation rests upon. Progress has, in the past history of the world, often shifted its principal seat, from the East to the West; and, in the West, from one portion of it to another. But it has always added to the totality of its past acquisitions. Modern civilisation has not only retained the achievements of ancient civilisation, but has added to them considerably; and the civilisation of the future, wherever its centre * may be, is expected to do the same with regard to the civilisation of the present day. The altruism of the future civilisation is expected to be more real and more embracing than the altruism of the present civilisation.

* Mr. Pearson has indulged in a rather interesting speculation on this point. "The day will come," says he, "and perhaps is not far distant, when the European observer will look round to see the globe girdled with a continuous zone of the black and yellow races, no longer too weak for aggression or under tutelage, but independent, or practically so, in government, monopolising the trade of their own regions, and circumscribing the industry of the European. . . . . . . We were struggling among ourselves for supremacy in a world which we thought of as destined to belong to the Aryan races, and to the Christian faith; to the letters and arts and charm of social manners which we have inherited from the best times of the past. We shall wake to find ourselves elbowed and hustled, and perhaps even thrust aside by peoples whom we looked down upon as servile, and thought of as bound always to minister to our needs." ("National Life and Character," 1893, pp. 84-85).

Influence of the doctrine of equality.

The present state of inequality between the different classes of Western society is by no means of a very exceptional character. Such inequality has existed from the remotest antiquity. It is, however, now so keenly felt, and is fraught with so much danger to Western society, because the proletariat now claim equality as a matter of right, and consequently chafe under a sense of injustice if the conditions of existing society make the many starve while the few roll in wealth and luxury.* Industrial evolution on Western principles has not yet

---

* A revolution, however, is impending. Modern civilisation has been weighed in the balance and found wanting. "Even the best of modern civilisations" appeared to one of the greatest exponents of modern thought, "to exhibit a condition of mankind which neither embodies any worthy ideal nor even possesses the merit of stability. I do not hesitate to express the opinion, that, if there is no hope of a large improvement of the condition of the greater part of the human family; if it is true that the increase of knowledge, the winning of a greater dominion over nature which is its consequence, and the wealth which follows that dominion, are to make no difference in the extent and the intensity of want, with its concomitant moral and physical degradation, among the masses of the people, I shall hail the advent of some kindly comet, which would sweep the whole affair away, as a desirable consummation. What profits it to the human Prometheus that he has stolen the fire of Heaven to be his servant, and that the spirits of the earth and of the air obey him, if the vulture of pauperism is eternally to tear his very vitals and keep him on the brink of destruction?" Huxley, "Method and Results," p. 423.

proceeded far enough in India to produce such enormous economic inequality as is observable in Western society; and the Hindu community has not yet been permeated by aspirations for equality to such an extent as to feel the injustice of existing inequality. The spread of the doctrine of equality in India is confined as yet to the educated community who form an insignificant fraction of the total population. It has not yet led to any serious disturbance of social order, not even to a strike worth the name. The evils which are exercising the minds of philanthropists and philosophers in the West have not yet shown themselves among the Hindus. In politics, the democratic spirit of modern Europe has not yet gone further than strictly constitutional agitation by educated men for a moderate share in the administration of their country partly by representation on the Imperial and Provincial Legislative Councils and partly by admission into offices hitherto reserved for the British. In religion, it has led to movements like the Bráhma Samáj. In literature, it has wrested the monopoly of authorship from the hands of the Bráhmans; and writers of all castes from the highest to the lowest now join hands in literary comradeship. If the greatest novelist of modern Bengali literature is a

'Bráhman,* the greatest poet and the greatest dramatist are Káyasthas.† In this respect, however, the spread of Western ideas of democracy has only intensified the change set on foot by the Vaishnava Revolution a few centuries ago which, to a great extent, abrogated caste-distinction.

The progress of every community requires the suppression of individuality to some extent. But the ancient civilisations carried the suppression very far, and Hindu civilisation probably further than any other. The existence of the individual was made subservient to the existence of the community. Even in literature, the author often merged his individuality in his work. Huge works like the Mahábhárata, and many of the Institutes and the Puránas bear unmistakable evidence of being the compositions of numerous writers whose names even have not been preserved. The all but entire absence of historical literature in Sanskrit may be partly attributable to this suppression of the individual. When authors were so unmindful

Sidenote: Increased sense of individuality: its influence upon Hindu literature.

---

* Bankim Chandra Chatterji, born 1838, died, 1894. Several of his novels have been translated into English.

† Madhusudan Datta, (1824—1873) and Dinabandhu Mitra (1829—1873).

of the preservation of their own names, it is not to be wondered at, that they should have cared so little to transmit to posterity the lives of kings whose works must, in their estimation, have been of far less value than theirs; and the memory of kings was left to be preserved as best as it might be in the ballads of courtly bards, or, in more enduring form, in grants and inscriptions.

The wide prevalence which modern civilisation has given to the doctrine of equality has put the individual forward to an extent unknown in ancient civilisation. The tendency of the suppression of the individual encouraged by the latter has been to exalt authority, and to discourage originality. During the last seven centuries the best of Sanskrit authors, with but few exceptions, have ventured only to write commentaries. They followed the lead of some ancient work of authority, though some of them were endowed with the keenest intellect, and could have produced, if they chose to do so, original works of exceptional merit. On the other hand, though there is much that is objectionable, and worse, in the obtrusive self-assertiveness of the individual in modern civilisation, it has, nevertheless, furthered intellectual progress to no small extent. It has sapped the foundations of ancient authority, and relaxed the restraints of conventionalities sanctioned by immemorial usage. Ambition has a freer scope, and the intellect has been soaring into regions unknown in ancient civilisations. The Hindu intellect has ventured out of the accustomed and well-beaten paths of theology and metaphysics. Paths which had been used in ancient times, but which for centuries remained practically closed, have lately been not only reopened, but also widened and extended; and new paths have been coming into view which promise to lead in directions not even dreamt of by the sages of antiquity. The medical and mathematical sciences which had yielded such notable results to the ancient Hindus, but which received scarcely any attention, for nearly seven centuries preceding British Rule, are now being cultivated again on the improved methods of the West. History, biography, novel (in its modern forms), archæology, and the different branches of natural science are subjects almost entirely new in Hindu literature. It is true, the emancipated intellect has been producing much that is worthless and even mischievous; and the printing press makes such productions a source of positive danger to society. But evils like this are unavoidable under modern conditions of progress; and it would probably be no exaggeration to say, that the English influence, of which the sense of individuality fostered by aspirations for equality is one of the main factors, has caused a renaissance of Hindu literature.

Superficial character of the recent renaissance of Hindu literature. This renaissance is marked, however, rather by extent of surface than by depth. The range of vision of the Hindu mind has widened considerably. The works of the Hindus now treat of subjects which were beyond the conception of their forefathers. But, excepting a very few productions of genius, they are wanting in that depth and originality, that freshness and vigour of mind which always accompany healthly progress. The new life does not as yet appear to have acquired that strength which is essential for great works. To judge from the works that annually come out of the Indian press, there is undoubtedly an increasing amount of literary activity. But the activity is chiefly displayed in ephemeral tales and journalistic articles. Works with any prospect of occupying a permanent place in literature are very rare.

No doubt, in this dominant feature of superficiality, modern Hindu literature resembles, to a great extent, its prototype, the Western literature. The great majority of the books that appear in the West are also destined to live a short life. They are mostly written with the express purpose of affording amusement, of enabling the votaries of pleasure or of Mammon to while away an idle hour. But, there can be no denying the fact, that proportionately a great many more works of abiding interest appear in the West than in India.

Causes of this superficiality : transitional state.
One reason of this serious deficiency in Hindu literature is, no doubt, the transitional state through which the Hindus are passing at present. They must assimilate the progress made in the West during the stationary period of their civilisation, before they can produce anything of a strikingly original character. They must go over the ground already prepared by the Western intellect, before they can break new ground.

In the first stage of English education, its recipients showed, at least in Bengal, a marked and undiscriminating preference for Western habits and Western methods of progress. Everything Western was admired and adopted, and everything Eastern despised and rejected. In social polity, the tendency was observable in the aggressive attitude of the English-educated young men towards the social institutions of the country. In religion, it was manifested in the conversion to Christianity of some of the most promising among them. The Hindu intellect was emancipated from the bonds of Hindu tradition only to put on the shackles of Western custom. For a time there was irrational, nay slavish, imitation. It was forgotten, that the lasting progress of a community depends not upon wholesale change, but upon gradual adaptation to new environment, not upon the total extinction of the force of tradition, but upon such an adjustment between it and the desire for change, that the latter will only have a more predominant influence than the former. But, a reaction soon followed which showed that the internal forces of Hindu civilisation had only been dormant, but had not become extinct. They have, for sometime past, exerted a rather healthy conservative influence, which is indicated, among other things, by a more diffuse respect for Sanskrit literature. The Vedas, the Mahábhárata, the Rámáyana, the Bhagavatgítá, the works of Charaka and Susruta, and the systems of Hindu philosophy are now far more extensively read than before either in the original or in translations. The desire for change is now restrained by the conservative influence of Hindu, tradition. The efforts of the Hindu intellect are beginning to be directed more towards assimilation than towards imitation of Western thought. But the process of assimilation is always slow and tedious. Before the many things in Western civilisation that are fit for assimilation are found out by experiment, many more things that are unfit must be rejected. In an experimental or transitional state like this, perfected forms of intellectual work must be excessively rare.

The renaissance of Hindu literature, if it is due to one thing more than to another, is due to English education. Nearly all the Hindu writers of note within the last fifty years have been English-educated men. Purely vernacular, or purely Sanskrit education has done but little to enrich vernacular literature. Bengali literature which at the commencement of the present century was much poorer than Hindi, and scarcely as rich as Márâthi, is now the richest of all the vernacular literatures; and it is in Bengal that English education has been imparted longer than in any other part of India.

Anomalous position of English among the literary languages of India.

But English education has not made English the sole literary language of India. In English schools, English is studied as the principal language, and the vernacular or Sanskrit as the subordinate or second language. The educated Indians generally correspond in English. The work of the numerous political, social, and literary associations which have sprung up under English influence is usually carried on in English. Still, as a literary language, English holds a subordinate position. In the Bombay Presidency, there were published, in 1891, altogether 71 books in English, whereas the number of publications in Márâthi and Guzeráthi amounted to 223 and 297 respectively. In Bengal, during the same year, there were registered 1,347 publications in Bengali, and only 385 in English. Readers, especially the most educated portion of them, prefer to read English books, because a knowledge of English is the *sine qua non* of worldly advancement, and because English gives one the key to the intellectual treasures of modern civilisation. Writers, on the other hand, prefer to write in the vernaculars, because they can express themselves better in them than in a foreign tongue.

Consequences of this anomaly. One consequence of this anomaly is, that the number of authors is disproportionately great. There are not sufficient readers, especially of the cultured class, to support, appreciate, and honour them. The greatest and most popular of Indian novelists, Bankim Chandra Chatterji, who would hardly suffer by comparison with any European novelist of the present day, scarcely made more than two thousand rupees a year from his novels. Except a very few writers of school books, no Indian authors can earn a living by literary labour. They are either busy professional men or Government servants. Considering the enervating nature of the Indian climate, one can hardly expect from such men works requiring long-continued application and research. A leisured class of literary and scientific men such as we have in the West has not yet arisen in modern India. The learned Bráhmans, especially at the principal seats of Sanskrit learning, formed such a class in pre-British India. They were supported and honoured by the Hindu community. They pursued literature and science, undisturbed by the cares and anxieties of a living, and stimulated by the appreciation of pupils and fellow-Pundits who formed the little world in which they moved. Their number, glory, and influence have diminished to such an extent, that they may be said to be practically extinct, at least for all purposes of modern progress. But a new class has not yet taken their place; and the want of a well recognised literary language combined with the circumstances to be noted presently render the rise of such a class, at least in the near future, highly problematical.

The extreme poverty of the people is a serious obstacle to progress to an extent it is difficult to guage. True, they have always been poor. It cannot be established, at least conclusively, that they have become poorer under British Rule. But their civilisation was well adapted to the conditions which determined it. Arts and manufactures thrived upon small capital. Tuition was paid for or not according to the means of the pupils. Books and appliances had not to be bought, or if they had to be bought, they cost very little. The style of living was very simple. The community maintained the institutions which were designed for the spread of knowledge.

The extreme poverty of the people.

Now, the Hindus have been brought into competition with a people the richest in the world. Their average annual income, according to the highest official estimate, does not exceed £ 2; and they have to compete in the struggle for progress with a people whose average annual income is no less than £ 33. They are vastly poorer

Its effect upon Scientific progress.

than the poorest people in Europe. Yet, they must advance upon European conditions or they must retrograde, which means going backward to a position for worse than what they occupied during the stationary period of their civilisation before the establishment of British rule. They are required to run a race with one of the swiftest peoples of the modern world, on paths hitherto unknown to them but familiar to their foreign competitors, without the requisite equipment. Their arts and manufactures must perish, they must allow their country to be drained by foreigners, because they have not the capital and the enterprise of the latter. And their case appears to be hopeless under present conditions because their poverty will not certainly diminish as the drain goes on.

The general poverty of the people is also detrimental to higher intellectual work. Natural science is the intellectual speciality of modern civilisation. Its acquisition, however, is a matter of heavy expense. Well equipped laboratories are essential. But the people are too poor to afford them. The few that could endow scientific research do not do so, because they do not appreciate it. They would subscribe liberally to honour or to please high-placed British officials; but a cry for funds for the diffusion of scientific and technical education would be a cry in the wilderness. The private colleges have to adapt themselves to the means of the people and charge very low fees—in Bengal, generally, only three rupees a month for lectures on all subjects. They cannot provide the requisite means for effective scientific education. Until quite recently, the education in the Government colleges was of a literary character. It is only within the last decade that attempts have been made by Government to spread scientific and technical education. Even now, such subjects as Zoology and Botany which are of such vital importance in connection with Western thought, are taught in only one institution in the Bengal Presidency—the Medical College of Calcutta. There too the teaching is subordinated to the immediate professional requirements of medical students and is unaccompanied by laboratory work worth the name. There is only one institution in the Bengal Presidency—the Presidency College of Calcutta—where a chair of Geology has been in existence since 1892. Thus, the people are too poor to afford effective scientific education in the institutions directly supported by them ; and Government has hitherto been apparently too indifferent to place scientific education on anything like a sound basis. It cannot be said that

Government is not at all alive to the importance of natural science in modern civilisation. It has for sometime past carried on research by European agency in various branches of science. The educational or economic benefit of such research to the people of India has been so slight as to be almost inappreciable, compared especially to what it has cost them. It has benefited only a few members of the European community who can well afford its expense.

Poverty does not usually stand so much in the way of intellectual work of a purely literary character as it does in that of intellectual work of a scientific character. In India, however, it entails special disadvantages which are not felt in Europe. In European countries, there are rich libraries to which a poor man intent upon intellectual advancement can have easy access. In India, there are but few libraries worth the name. They are immeasurably inferior to the great libraries of Europe, and, besides, are not easily accessible.

<small>Its influence upon general literature.</small>

The national poverty of the Hindus also tells seriously upon their literary development in other ways. They are engrossed by anxious cares how to earn a bare living. They have neither the means nor the leisure to pursue or encourage higher intellectual work.

Intellectual work on modern conditions necessitates a much greater strain on the nervous system, and, therefore, requires a correspondingly greater amount of nourishing food than in ancient times. The high-pressure work of the present day is not possible upon such a simple style of living as the Hindus have been accustomed to hitherto. That style was no doubt adapted to their civilisation. It is, however, a distinct disadvantage to them now, whether in the higher or the lower forms of intellectual work, as they have to compete with a people with a very much higher standard of living. Work performed by a constitution nourished upon twenty rupees cannot generally be so efficient as work performed by a constitution nourished upon treble that amount. It is true, a slightly lower standard of living gives a people some advantage in competition. But, the difference in the standards of living must not be so great as what exist between the Hindus and the English. Efficiency and success, under present conditions, demand a rise in the standard of living of the Hindus, so that it may approximate, though not equal, that of the English with whom they have to compete. The necessity is felt by the Hindus. But the cost of living has immensely increased of late; not,

Standard of living.

however, the means to meet the increased cost. Work under new European conditions has to be performed upon such necessaries and conveniences of life as were suited to the old environment. The inevitable consequence of such an anomalous state of things is apparent in the rapid spread of such diseases as diabetes among those who have to live by brainwork in some shape or other.

<small>Influence of European luxuries.</small> It should be noted, however, that the tendency of the introduction of the outer forms, the luxuries and amusements, of European civilisation has been to intensify the effects of the national poverty of the Hindus. People are but little guided in their mode of living by philosophy. Fashion rules them. Even the most rational men are found among the most irrational votaries of fashion. The desire for show appears to be almost innate in all classes in all parts of the world; and the Hindus are no exception to the rule. Formerly, however, the gratification of this desire was determined by the indigenous standard of luxuries which was well adapted to their material condition. But, at the present day, there is a marked tendency among the upper classes to adopt the Western standard of luxuries. In the West, modern civilisation has raised the standard of luxuries considerably. There, the rise

has been attended by good as well as evil consequences. But, from the point of view of material progress, which is the special aim of Western civilisation, the former outweigh the latter. The multiplication of wants in the West has been partly the cause, and partly the natural outcome of the immense accumulation of wealth and of the remarkable progress in mechanical invention which have gone on there during the last fifty years. "In the atmosphere of luxury that increased wealth produces, refined tastes, perceptions of beauty, intellectual aspirations appear. Faculties that were before dormant are evoked, new directions are given to human energies, and, under the impulse of the desire for wealth, men arise to supply each new want that wealth has produced. Hence, for the most part, arise art and literature, and science, and all the refinements and elaborations of civilisation, and all the inventions that have alleviated the sufferings or multiplied the enjoyments of mankind."* All this is true in the West. In India, the spread of Western luxuries, without the previous accumulation of wealth or the preparation of mechanical talent as in the West, cannot imply progress, either present or prospective.

* Lecky, "Rationalism in Europe" Vol. II. pp. 366-367.

The Indians have neither the capital nor the mechanical knowledge and enterprise to compete successfully with the Western peoples. Free trade in their case means their exploitation by the West without any equivalent advantage to them. They do not even always enjoy an equality of opportunity. Anybody from the West, for instance, can establish himself anywhere in India and "develope" its resources or carry on trade as he likes. Such action, is, indeed, invited, encouraged, and even, to some extent, helped by Government. But, in English colonies in South Africa, Indians have recently been deprived of the rights which other British subjects exercise, and to which all subjects of Great Britain are entitled by international custom. In the case of the Europeans, their home markets failing to absorb their manufactures, and their own territories failing to afford sufficient scope for their ambition, energy, and the desire for the accumulation of wealth, they have for sometime past been subjugating weaker peoples outside Europe and annexing their territories—leaving, it should be observed by the way, the gospel of Equality and the banner of Liberty in their homes. In the case of the Indians, their industrial progress has not yet been sufficient to enable them to meet the demands of their own markets. And, under present conditions, there is hardly any hope that they will ever be able to do so : they have to run a race with a people who have had the start of a century, and who are armed with all the advantages of long experience, accumulated capital, and invigorating climate. The development of tastes for European luxuries in the Indians, in the present state of their industrial development, means in those few who can afford it the further enrichment of the already rich capitalist classes in Europe and the corresponding impoverishment of the already poor industrial classes in India ; and in the case of those who cannot afford such development, but are led to it by pressure of fashion—and they are by far the most numerous class—it means also embarrassment and possible ruin, the sacrifice of necessaries to luxuries, of substance to shadow.

<small>Outer forms of European civilisation : the railway &c.</small> The features which distinguish modern civilisation from the ancient, which, in fact, constitute that civilisation in the popular mind—the railway, the electric telegraph, and various other comforts and conveniences of modern civilised life—have been gradually introduced into India under British rule. There is one conclusion

sometimes drawn from the more striking among them which has only to be stated to show its fallacious nature. The rapid expansion of the railway system in recent times is not unoften pointed to as indicating the progress of India. A moment's reflection will show that it does not do so in any way.

All the railways have been surveyed and constructed by English Engineers; they are managed by Englishmen; the machinery and other plant required for their construction and maintenance almost entirely come from England. The captial, the enterprise and the education that are necessary for the construction and maintenance of the railways are all British. They loudly proclaim Western civilisation in India; but they do not indicate the progress of India in any way whatever. Not only so; their extension has, in one sense, been detrimental to the future progress of the Indians. The lines which are likely to be most remunerative have been constructed already. If Indians be ever able to undertake the construction of large railways themselves, they will find that the most promising outlets for their new-born enterprise have been closed already.

Do not indicate progress of India.

The railways have undoubtedly had some educational

value. "It is needless to point out," says Lord Ripon, "how

Educational and economic effects of Indian railways. improved communications and increased facilities for travel break down obstinate and long established prejudices and widen men's minds in a single generation ..... The introduction of railway travelling has had a direct and necessary influence in weakening and in certain respects overcoming the distinctions and prejudices of caste." *

Every word of this statement is perfectly true. By facilitating intercourse railways have certainly helped social and political progress of the Hindus to some extent. They have been of great use in transporting food to those parts of the country which are affected by famines. They have also by facilitating transport developed the export trade in raw produce. The wheat trade especially has undergone considerable expansion of late. But the cultivator, if he gains at all, does not gain to the extent it is generally supposed. The yield from his land has not been sensibly affected by the railways. It is the same now as it was in pre-railway times, or even less. He unquestionably gets better prices for his crops.

* *Paternoster Review*, October, 1890.

xxxii INTRODUCTION.

But a portion of his increased profits is consumed in enhanced rent. A portion also goes to pay enhanced wages for labourers, though, unfortunately, the enhancement is not in the same proportion as that of the prices of food-grains. The profits which he has left after meeting these charges may be considered to be only the equivalent of the grain he would have stored, had not the introduction of railways offered him tempting prices to sell it. Whether he is any gainer for having cash instead of a store of grain is a doubtful point, especially when we consider that the temptation to spend money, when one has it in hand, upon festivities and upon various European articles which the railway has brought to his doors is very great. The danger of these articles consists in their attractiveness and comparative cheapness. The cultivator and his family probably make a better show of respectability than they ever did before. But when famine threatens, they find they have little money and scarcely any store of grain to fall back upon.

In considering the effect of railways upon the economic condition of India it must be borne in mind, that they have, while facilitating the transport of food to famine-stricken districts, have also facilitated the transport of European manufactures and thus helped to destroy indigenous industries. The artisans whom these industries afforded occupation have been yearly swelling the number of needy peasants and labourers. No doubt, a portion of the artisan class finds employment in the railway workshops as smiths and carpenters; and many more find work as labourers in the mines, factories and tea-estates which the railways have helped to develop. Their number is estimated at one million and a quarter. This is no doubt a set-off against the heavy loss which the industrial people have suffered owing to the extension of railways. But the testimony of District officers is almost unanimous in showing that the greater majority of them are driven to be labourers or agriculturists. Large towns with urban populations have dwindled into inconsiderable villages. The increase of agricultural at the sacrifice of artisan population is certainly not advantageous for India. It is true the mass of her people must from time immemorial have been mainly agricultural. But there can be no doubt that a great portion of her wealth depended upon her mining and manufacturing industries, as indeed the wealth of every country must do. No country that is purely agricultural can ever be rich. Down to the early years of the present century, India did not export her food grains, but cotton, silk and various other manufactures. It was especially to participate in the trade of these manufactures that the Portuguese, the Dutch, the French and the English came to India. About the end of the last century (1798—99) the value of piece goods and Organzine silk exported from India to England amounted to over a million and a half pounds sterling. No cotton goods were then imported into India; iron and steel to the value of only £36,530 pounds were imported. Now the relations have been reversed. She sends abroad her spare food, and imports foreign manufactures. Her people are dependent upon Europe for most necessaries of life except food, not to speak of luxuries. The clothes they wear come from Manchester; the ploughs with which they till their land, the axes with which they cut their trees, are made of English iron; knives, scissors, cooking utensils, matches, in fact most of their household requisites are of European manufacture. The almost wholesale ruin of indigenous manufactures has directly and indirectly helped to produce a most serious state of congestion throughout British India.

It is true, handmade things such as those which the Indians used to make could not have long competed with machine-made articles. They might however, have gradually adapted to the new order of things. But cheap means of communication, amongst which railways are most prominent, did not give them the time. The present state of things in India is indeed very sad. No doubt, railways are not solely responsible for it. Free trade, which again, is one of the so-called benefits which have been conferred upon India, is also partly responsible. The Englishmen are now about the only people in the world who strictly follow the principles of free trade ; India (including Burma) is now the only extensive mart where English manufactures are admitted free of duty. The absence of a tariff combined with the extension of railways has helped to kill the indigenous industries, and has considerably handicapped the people in their endeavours to revive them.

We have already seen how railways have indirectly contributed to impoverish India by helping the substitution of foreign for indigenous manufactures. They have also done this directly, though to a very small extent. There are three kinds of railways in India : guaranteed, subsidised and State. For the guaranteed and subsidised railways, India has long had to remit to England a large amount as interest. "The country is too poor to pay for its elaborate railway system and irrigation projects, and, being compelled to borrow in England, has incurred an ever-accumulating debt at what has unfortunately proved to be an ever-increasing rate of interest."* This does not represent the entire drain. The superior management of all the railways is in the hands of the British; the savings out of the salaries of the Managers, Traffic Superintendents, and other superior Railway officers, swell the annual drain from India.

The Indian railways generally traverse tracts of deep alluvium subject to floods and require very high embankments to keep them above the flood-level. These embankments obstruct not only surface-drainage, but also subsoil percolation to some depth; and obstructed drainage must add to the insalubrity of a place.†

---

* H. J. S. Cotton, "New India," p. 61. "The railways, so far from being a commercial success, have entailed the heavy burden of over £47,000,000 on the Indian tax-payer . . . . The Indus Valley, and Sind-Punjab and Delhi railways are the most signal instances of bounty-supported lines, but to a less extent all the wheat-carrying lines are only worked by the help of the State."—Connell on "Indian Railways and Indian Wheat," *Statistical Journal*, 1885, pp. 244—253, quoted in Pearson's "National Life and Character" p. 98.

† "There is too much reason to believe," says Mr. H. J. S. Cotton, "that they (the Indian railways) have, by the obstruction to drainage

We have dwelt at some length upon the influence of the Indian railway, because it is usually and influentially held to be one of the most important developmental forces in the progress of India. It would probably be no exaggeration to say, that if the benefits conferred by the Indian railways be weighed against the evils attending them, it is doubtful which way the scale will turn. Their influence upon intellectual progress has been indirect, and, on the whole, not very considerable. It is true, without them such political movements as the National Congress would have been delayed. But we are not sure whether the delay would have done much, if any, harm; whether, in fact, slower development would not have afforded a firmer and sounder intellectual basis for these movements. Had railways been con-

Influence of Indian railways upon Hindu progress not considerable.

---

which they cause in some places, materially injured the general health of the population. The new lines now under construction and contemplation which, if I may use the metaphor, break up inferior soil, are naturally supported by the local officials, whose isolated position is ameliorated by railway extension, and by engineering authorities for whom the railways find employment. The promoters of these railways, who most loudly insist on the profitable character of their speculations, are not, however, really deceived, for they will not invest their money without a guarantee from Government and other substantial privileges. If they believed in their experiments they would proceed in them without Government assistance." "New India," p. 63.

structed and managed by indigenous agency they would have indicated progress, and would have been a developmental force of immense value. But constructed and maintained by foreign agency, with foreign material, they are not such incalculable benefits to India, as they are often asserted to be. The cool assurance and placid self-complacency with which such assertions are made would make one suspect a vein of irony in them, had it not been well known as a habit of thought with all powerful nations of the world, that what they consider to be good for themselves and for their country must be good for every other people and every other country, however divergent the circumstances may be. There are benevolent Englishmen who cannot conceive conditions under which the products of their civilisation can be anything but unmitigated blessings.*

* There are a few reflecting men among them who think otherwise. Frederick John Shore of the Bengal Civil Service, for instance, wrote long ago :—

" More than seventeen years have elapsed since I first landed in this country; but on my arrival, and during my residence of about a year in Calcutta, I well recollect the quiet, comfortable, and settled conviction which in those days existed in the minds of the English population, of the blessings conferred on the natives of India by the establishment of the English rule. Our superiority to the native Governments which we have supplanted; the excellent system for the administration of justice which we had introduced; our moderation; our anxiety to benefit the

Reflections on the civilising methods of the Western nations.

Any form of bureaucracy which determines and executes what is good for its subjects without consulting their wishes and taking their help, without, in fact, closely associating them with it, is not likely to succeed in its purpose. The failure becomes greater and more certain when the bureaucracy is a foreign one with a civilisation entirely different from that of the people. The truth of this proposition is so obvious, that it is incredible it should be so generally forgotten by the Western nations generally in their dealings with uncivilised peoples or peoples with civilisations different from their own, in Asia, Africa, and America; so incredible, indeed, that one cannot help suspecting the sincerity of their altruistic professions.* The methods of the political or

---

people—in short, our virtues of every description—were descanted on as so many established truths, which it was heresy to controvert. Occasionally I remember to have heard some hints and assertions of a contrary nature from some one who had spent many years in the interior of the country; but the storm which was immediately raised and thundered on the head of the unfortunate individual who should presume to question the established creed, was almost sufficient to appal the boldest."

* If the present aggressive policy continues, it is possible that the East would in the end be absorbed by the West. "There has been no period in history" observes Benjamin Kidd "when this ascendency [that of the Western peoples] has been so unquestionable, and so complete as in the time in which we are now living. No one can doubt that

commercial missionary of the West are such as may well create such suspicions and make the realisation of the dream of Peace descending in a "drapery of calico" dreamt of by the Manchester politicians as remote as ever. It is, indeed, strange that he should ever seriously think that he is civilising peoples while he is depleting their resources, giving them shadows while taking away their substance, or even striking at the very root of their existence.

Suppose you take possession of the estate of a man who is without your capital and your mechanical knowledge— we shall not inquire into the defensibility of the means. You effectively prevent thefts on the property, and develope its resources, taking the whole of its yield as the price of your labour and the interest of your capital, except the wage of the proprietor who works as your labourer. A good portion, if not the whole, of what is left after discharging the cost of his food, is spent upon clothing and little attractive fineries which are manufactured by sections of the community to which you

it is within the power of the leading European peoples of to-day—should they so desire—to parcel out the entire equatorial regions of the earth into a series of satrapies and to administer their resources, not, as in the past, by a permanently resident population, but from the temperate regions, and under the direction of a relatively small European official population."—" Social Evolution " Ch. X.

belong. You do not settle upon the estate, you do not in any way identify yourself with the community to which the owner belongs. All the wealth you acquire is spent in a way so as to benefit yourself and your community, except an insignificant fraction of it which is paid for the menial services of the members of the owner's community. You have, it is true, relieved him of the responsibility of defending what little property he can now call his own, and, even perhaps disburdened him of the arms he possessed. It is possible, that with your fineries, which it is your interest to sell him, he assumes a more " civilised" appearance than he ever did before. It is possible that he has, now and then, the comfort of a ride on a railway which you have built, and which you maintain with the proceeds of his estate. But, notwithstanding all this, can the condition of the owner be said to be better than when, though he had to defend his estate from occasional depredations with his own arms and the help of his own people, he had still all the actualities and all the possibilities of real ownership? Would it not be a mockery to tell him that he might compete with you if he liked, knowing very well that he has neither your industrial experience, nor your capital—augmented not a little, be it remarked, by the profits from his estate—nor the prestige and the numerous other advantages conferred by the possession and administration of his estate?

In one sense, it was no doubt advantageous to India that she came under British Rule just about the time when Europe was, so to say, modernised; for, she was thus brought under the renovating influence of modern civilization. In another sense, however, the circumstance was distinctly disadvantageous to her. As in the case of organisms, the union of highly specialised civilisations, if possible, is seldom fertile. Western civilisation is of a type markedly different from the Hindu civilisation. The discordance between the two is enormous; the former is as remarkably material as the latter is spiritual There can be but little real sympathy between them; and it still remains to be seen whether their union will lead to any abiding result, unless the character or structure of one or both undergo considerable modifications so as to diminish the amount of the existing specific difference between them. The British by getting out of the ancient into the modern stage of progress about the end of the last century, placed a gulf

The exclusive policy.

between them and the Hindus which it is difficult to bridge over. Had they advanced less along the path of modern material progress, there would have been greater sympathy. As it is, the Hindus have not yet been even partially assimilated into the British system of administration. The tendency of every civilised nation is to depreciate every other civilisation which is different from their own. The greater the difference, the greater is the depreciation. The inhabitants of the Celestial empire are not more dogmatic in considering all outsiders as barbarians than the inhabitants of modern Europe. Even such a cautious and thoughtful writer as Walter Bagehot considers the Western civilisation to have failed in producing a "rapidly excellent effect" in India, because it is "too good and too different."* Too different it undoubtedly is, but whether it is "too good" or not is at most a highly controvertible question. It is true, many of the British administrators are actuated by a noble sense of duty towards the dumb millions committed to their care. But, the altruistic development of Western civilisation does not appear yet to have proceeded far enough to invest the sense of duty with the motive force of living sympathy, and to

* "Physics and Politics," fifth edition, p. 145.

make it superior to self-interest. The British have always been credited with being an eminently " practical " people. Though this feature of their character has not been appreciated by some of their foreign critics, it has, no doubt, contributed largely to their national prosperity. But, success, such as it is usually understood, is certainly not in direct ratio to altruistic development, generally, indeed, it is securable by a process directly antagonistic to the ethical process, by a disregard, or, at least, by a not very scrupulous regard for the well-being or the rights of others. The ultimate question between every two nations, even more than between every two human beings still is, in the highly expressive, though somewhat exaggerated language of Carlyle : " Can I kill thee, or canst thou kill me ? "

These brief considerations afford, we believe, the explanation of the exclusive and unsympathetic policy of British Rule in India, though the reasons usually assigned for it are, as we shall presently see, somewhat different. The Mahomedans certainly had not such a high standard of administrative efficiency as the British have. But their civilisation was more akin to Hindu civilisation ; and the Hindus were consequently, more *en rapport* with their Mahomedan rulers, than they are with their British rulers. "In many respects," admitted Lord William Bentinck half a century ago, "the Mahomedans surpassed our rule; they settled in the countries which they conquered; they intermixed and intermarried with the natives; they admitted them to all privileges: the interests and sympathies of the conquerors and the conquered became identified. Our policy, on the contrary, has been the reverse of this, cold, selfish, and unfeeling."

The order maintained under British Rule throughout the length and breadth of India is undoubtedly favourable to progress. Its importance, however, as a condition of progress must not be exaggerated. As in the case of the individual, so in that of the nation, perfect tranquillity is not incompatible with a state bordering upon lifelessness, the negation, if not the reverse of what is usually understood by progress. The tranquillity maintained by a Government in which the people have a substantial share not only indicates advancement, but also aids it materially in various ways. But the tranquillity maintained by such an exclusive system of administration as the British in India can be neither indicative nor pro-

Tranquillity maintained by British Rule favourable to progress.

But to a small extent owing to its exclusive policy.

motive of progress, at least beyond a certain point. It is true, since the close of the last century, especially since the time of Lord William Bentinck, the British administration has been pervaded more or less by the liberal spirit of modern Europe. The statute of 1833 declared, for the first time, that no Indian " shall by reason of his birth, descent, colour, or any of them, be disabled from holding any place, office, or employment " under the British Government. The administration of Lord William Bentinck, who was Governor-General of India at the time, is memorable for a number of important steps taken by it in Indian interest, one among which was the admission of the Indians to posts of greater responsibility than what they had held till then, since the commencement of British Rule. The next decided step in this direction was taken in 1853, when the institution of an annual competitive examination in England for entrance into the Covenanted Civil Service opened it to the Indians. Since then, especially since the viceroyalty of Lord Ripon, a certain amount of local self-government has been granted, and quite recently steps have been taken to secure representation, though in a very restricted and obviously tentative form, in the Provincial as well as Imperial Legislative Councils.

PRESENT EXTENT OF THE EXCLUSION.

Even now, however, the British administration is practically exclusive to an extent which is seriously detrimental to progress.*

Present extent of the exclusion.

The people of India are entirely excluded from the Military and Political departments which are recruited by competition in England to which they are not eligible. The Covenanted Civil Service, or the Imperial

---

* The liberal spirit of modern civilisation appears just now to be diminishing instead of increasing in intensity, at least as regards its application to peoples outside Europe. The impulse given to liberalism by the democratic struggles in Europe in the beginning of the present century appears lately to have been losing its energy. It is but seldom that members of the Anglo-Indian bureaucracy give such free and bold expression to liberal sentiments as men like Macaulay did half a century ago. "Are we to keep these men [Indians] submissive?" urged Macaulay "or do we think we can give them knowledge without awakening ambition? or do we mean to awaken ambition and provide it with no legitimate vent? who will answer any of these questions in the affirmative? Yet one of them must be answered in the affirmative by every person who maintains that we ought permanently to exclude the people of India from high office. I have no fear, the path of duty is plain before us, and it is also the path of wisdom, of national prosperity, and of national honour." True there are at the present day a few statesmen of the stamp of Macaulay, at least in Europe. Humanity owes a large debt of gratitude to them. But theirs is a cry in the wilderness. It has not for sometime past led to any effective action. Forty years of agitation for even such a measure of bare and obvious justice as the holding of the open competition for the Civil Service of India in India as well as in England has not only come to nought, but principles are being laid down, and in part acted upon, which are undisguisedly antagonistic to the liberal spirit of the Charter of 1833, and of the Queen's proclamation of 1858.

Civil Service as it is sometimes called, is open to them. But, the fact of the preliminary competitive examinations being held in England acts as a very serious deterrent in their case. They do not certainly enjoy an equality of opportunity with the British subjects of Her Majesty. So serious and so obvious is their disadvantage, considering their extreme poverty and other circumstances, that Sir Stafford Northcote, who was for sometime Secretary of State for India said: "It seems a mockery to tell them to come and compete in Westminister if they like." The result is, that they are still practically excluded from the higher services the entrance to which lies through competition in England. In 1892, the Imperial Civil Service was composed of 939 members of whom only 21 were Indians.* From a parliamentary return issued in 1892, it appears, that the total amount, at that time, of annual allowances of not less 1,000 rupees for each person, of Europeans,

---

Indians, for instance, who entered the Public Works Department by passing examinations in India were formerly eligible, at least theoretically, to the highest grades. There was no distinction, at least theoretically, between them and those who entered the department by competition in England. Quite recently, however, the latter have been constituted into an Imperial Service with pay and prospects much higher than those of the former who would form only a Provincial Service.

* Strachey's "India," 1894, p. 58.

whether, resident or not resident in India, was about 170,000,000 rupees (taking payments in sterling at 1s. 1d. per rupee), nearly a fifth of the gross revenue of India. The fact is significant when it is remembered, that the total allowances received by the Indians in the service of their government do not amount to more than a fifth of the total allowances paid to the European servants of the Government.†

That the existence of a government is for the good of the governed is now a well recognised maxim of European politics. The validity of this principle even in the case of the Indian administration has long been admitted, at least since the time of Lord William Bentinck; and the exclusion of the Indians from responsible administration has hitherto been generally justified on the ground of their

Alleged reasons for the exclusive policy.

---

† Proceedings of the House of Commons Feb. 1895. The total amount of annual allowances to Europeans, at less than 1,000 rupees for each person, is not known. The late Secretary of State in the course of a debate in the House of Commons said, there were in the civil establishments of the Government 7,991 Europeans, 5347 Eurasians, and 119,514 natives. It was pertinently asked, however, "what do you pay to each?" The 119, 514 "natives" no doubt include the pettiest clerks, and probably even peons at Rs. 7 or 8 a month.

INTRODUCTION.

supposed unfitness.* Determination of fitness or unfitness can seldom be strictly impartial when it is left to the judgment of officials who have not much in common with, and are more or less prejudiced against, the parties to be judged, and who are themselves deeply interested in the result of their decision. The ground of unfitness is, however, not heard of so much now-a-days, except in the case of a few comparatively small departments the dark recesses of which have not yet been held up to the light of even such public opinion as there exists in India. The exclusion of the Indians is now usually justified upon the ground of policy. Sir John Strachey, for instance, says :—

"Let us give to the Natives the largest possible share in the administration. In some branches of the service there is almost no limit to the share of public employment which they may properly receive. This is especially true of the Bench, for the performance of the judicial duties of which Natives have shown themselves eminently qualified, and in which the higher offices are equal in importance and dignity and

---

* The Government has been likened to a "paternal" government looking after the people as a father looks after his children, keeping them off from the exercise of responsible functions of the State lest such exercise should do them any harm. The analogy scarcely holds. The great test of affection—and paternal affection is no exception to the rule—is self-denial. The father gives more to, than he takes from, his children. However, though the analogy does not hold, and is, perhaps, not meant seriously, it undoubtedly assumes the claim of the people to be governed in their own interest.

emolument to almost any of the great offices of the State. Even on the Bench, however, there are important administrative duties for which some degree of English supervision is necessary, nor would it be *politically wise* to place this great department of the government altogether in Native hands. Prejudices of race may be regretted, but they cannot be ignored, and it would be a dangerous experiment to give to native judges too wide a power of control over English Magistrates. Subject to these limitation, I would grudge to the Natives few judicial offices. *But let there be no hypocrisy about our intention to keep in the hands of our own people those executive posts*—and there are not very many of them —*on which, and on our political and military power our actual hold of the country depends. Our Governors of provinces, the chief officers of our army, our magistrates of districts and their principal executive subordinates ought to be Englishmen under all circumstances that we can now foresee."*

"The claim to a larger share of the highest offices" says Sir George Campbell "might be considered in the double aspect of the fitness of the literary native as compared to the European, and the political effect. Again we come to the question, do we desire to prepare the natives for political freedom ? And again we are not yet prepared to answer it."†

Depression of material condition, a consequence of the exclusion.

One of the consequences of the "unshared rule of a close bureaucracy from across the seas" as Sir C. Dilke designates British rule‡ has been to retard material development, and therefore indirectly, intellectual develop-

* "India," 1894, pp 389-390. The italics are ours.
† "The British Empire," p 84.
‡ "Problems of Greater Britain" P. 146. Sir W. Hunter writing in 1880 said: "I believe that it will be impossible to deny them [the Indians] a larger share in the administration. There are departments, conspicuously those of Law and Justice, and Finance, in which the natives will more and more supplant the highly paid imported officials from

ment as well. The British officers, while in active service, have to make large remittances home. While in retirement, large payments have to be made from the Indian revenues for their pensions in Europe. The drain on the resources of India due to these remittances is considerable, and repeated year after year must ultimately tell seriously on her material condition. The process of depletion is slow, but it is none the less sure. It is sometimes contended, that the drain is the price of the peace and tranquillity which India enjoys at present. Undoubtedly, it is so. But, the price is too high for the substantial benefits it secures, and is beyond the means of the people. The foreign element is reducible within much narrower limits than at present, and with it the drain it necessitates, without any serious detriment to Indian interests. But even if it were not, it would be better for the Indians if their Government

---

England. There are other departments, such as the Medical, the Customs, the Telegraph, and the Post Office, in which the working establishments now consist of natives of India, and for which the superintending staff will in a constantly increasing degree be also recruited from them." ("England's Works in India" Madras edition, pp 118-119), The course of events within the last fifteen years has not justified Sir William Hunter's belief.

were to conform its standard of "civilised" administration to their means.

What Sir George Cornewall Lewis wrote half a century ago holds good even at the present day; and he was not, it should be observed, a sentimentalist, or mere theorist, but a practical politician who had occupied high and responsible offices of the State: "It is lamentable to think how little good has hitherto resulted to them [the people of India] from the acts of a government which has of late years been, perhaps, the most benevolent which ever existed in any country."*

Alleged indications of material prosperity—Expansion of trade.

Tranquillity is only a subordinate condition of progress which, in the absence of other and more important conditions, can do but little good; and one of the most important antecedents of intellectual progress, especially on modern methods, is material progress. The importance of the subject demands our earnest attention.†

---

* "On the government of Dependencies" by Sir G. Cornewall Lewis (originally published in 1841). London, 1891, p. 265.

† The subject has been further treated of in Ch. V. of this volume. See also Introduction to Vol. I, and Book IV.

INTRODUCTION.

The great expansion of the trade of India in recent years is pointed to as irrefragable evidence of equivalent material development. The expansion when analysed is found to consist principally in the exports of food grains and in the imports of cotton and iron manufactures. With regard to the former, the production of land, acre for acre, has not increased; if anything, it has decreased.* Scientific agriculture has as yet made no progress. Its adoption is beyond the means of the people. The food grains that are exported are supposed to represent the suplus left after meeting the requirements of the country. "It may, however, be alleged with some truth, that if the whole population ate as much as they could, this surplus would not exist. The grain exports of India represent many hungry stomachs in India.......If all the poorer classes in India ate two full meals every day, the surplus for export would be much less than at present. That surplus only proves that the yearly supply of food in India is greater than the effec-

---

* "Wheat-land in the North-Western Provinces which now gives only 840 lbs. an acre, yielded 1140 lbs in the time of Akbar......The average return of food grains in India shows about 700 lbs per acre; in England wheat averages over 1700 lbs." Hunter "England's Work in India," Madras Edition, p. 88.

tive demand for it."* It is true, a good deal of land, which had either never been cultivated before or had run to waste during the troublous times consequent upon the disruption of the Moghul Empire, has recently been brought under cultivation. But the additional land thus cultivated is hardly sufficient to meet the demand of the additional population. Besides, already, "the clearing and cultivation of the jungles have been carried to such an excess in some parts of India as to seriously alter the climate. For forests, and the undergrowth which they foster, not only husband the rainfall, but they appear to

* Sir W. Hunter " England's work in India," pp. 75-76. A speaker in the course of a debate in the House of Commons last year observed :
" In the Colonies and in European countries there was an excess of imports over exports. In the United Kingdom for the past ten years— 1883 to 1892—the excess had been 32 per cent., in Norway it was 42 per cent., Sweden 24 per cent., Denmark 40 per cent., Holland 22 per cent., France 20 per cent., Switzerland 28 per cent., Spain 9 per cent., Belgium 7 per cent., and so on. Anyone with common sense would of course admit that if a quantity of goods worth a certain amount of money were sent out an additional profit is expected in return. If not, there could not be any commerce; but a man who only received in return 20 of the 100 sent out would soon go into the bankruptcy court.* * * * On the average of 10 years (1883 to 1892) India's excesses of exports every year, with compound interest, would amount to enormous sums lost by her. Could any country in the world, England not excepted, stand such a drain without destruction? They were often told they ought to be thankful, and they were thankful, for the loans made to them for public works; but if they were left to themselves to enjoy what they produced

attract it." "The pasture grounds of the villages have also, to a large extent, been brought under the plough and the cattle in many districts have degenerated from insufficient food. The same number of oxen can no longer put the same amount of work into the soil."*

The expansion of the import trade in cotton and iron manufactures can hardly be considered a gain to India, considering that they have displaced the indigenous cotton and iron manufactures without giving rise to any other manufactures to compensate for the loss. During the ten years 1883 to 1892, the exports of India averaged about 770,000,000 rupees per year; the annual average of imports, on the other hand, amounted, in round num-

with a reasonable price for British Rule, if they had to develop their own resources, they would not require any such loans, with the interest to be paid on them, which added to the drain on the country. Those loans were only a fraction of what was taken away from the country. India had lost thousands of millions in principal and interest, and was asked to be thankful for the loan of a couple of hundreds of millions. The bulk of the British Indian subjects were like hewers of wood and drawers of water to the British and foreign Indian capitalists. The seeming prosperity of British India was entirely owing to the amount of foreign capital. In Bombay alone, which was considered to be a rich place, there were at least £10,000,000 of capital circulating belonging to foreign Europeans and Indians from native States. If all such foreign capital were separated there would be very little wealth in British India." Dadabhai Naoroji, Proceedings of the House of Commons, August 14th 1894.

* Hunter *op cit* pp. 65-66.

bers, to 940,000,000 rupees. The result of this annual trade deficit of about 170,000,000 rupees is that a "large part of the increased production is not retained by the Indian peasant."*

Growth of population not a good test of material prosperity in India. It is true, the last census returns show a small increase of population. But, it should be observed, that in a country like India, where marriage is almost universal,† where multiplication far from being kept under prudential restraint is, on the contrary, considered by the greater portion of the people a sacred duty, and where easy climatic conditions render subsistence upon little food possible at least up to a certain point, the growth of population is by no means a good test of national prosperity. "Looking at the prevalence of marriage" says Mr. Baines, late Census Commissioner for India " it is clear that more than the existence of a

---

* Sir George Campbell "The British Empire" p. 70.

† "Of women in India between 15 and 25 years old, 87 per cent. are married; but in Europe the highest proportion, to the west of the Leith, is in France, where it is only 22. In the remaining period, from 25 to 40. the ratio of wives in India falls to 81 per cent., whereas in the West, it advances to about 70." The Census of India, 1891, General Report, p. 60.

few millions of widows more or less, is required to account for the comparatively slow growth of the population under the impetus of so enormous a number of births. The clue is to be found in the accompanying high mortality. The birth rate is, indeed, very far above that of any European country, if we except Russia, and reaches nearly 48 per mille on the whole country. But the death rate is equally abnormal, even if we omit the more frequent occurrence of famine and epidemic disease in India, and may be taken to reach, on an average, 41 per mille." *

Growth comparatively small. The increase is comparatively small, as will be seen from the following table:

	Country	Annual Increase per cent.		Country.	Annual Increase per cent.
1.	New South Wales	5·10	15.	Germany	1·07
2.	Queensland	4.39	16.	Canada	1·07
3.	Victoria	3.22	17.	Greece	1·05
4.	United States	2·48	18.	Belgium	0·99
5.	Saxony	2·00	19.	Denmark	0·99
6.	New Zealand	1·70	20.	India	0·93
7.	Algeria	1·56	21.	Austria	0·76
8.	South Australia	1·40	22.	Switzerland	0·64
9.	England and Wales	1·28	23.	Bavaria	0·65
			24.	Italy	0·62
10.	Egypt	1·25	25.	Norway	0.60
11.	Holland	1·18	26.	Spain	0·55
12.	Prussia	1·15	27.	Sweden	0·50
13.	Portugal	1·14	28.	France	0.06
14.	Hungary	1·08			

* "Census of India, 1891, General Report, p. 62.

A part of the increase shown by the last census is

Partly due to improved enumeration. due to improved enumeration. The total increase in Bengal is 7·3 per cent. "But," observes the Census Superintendent, "if we exclude that part of it due to more accurate enumeration, it probably does not exceed 6 per cent., and may be less."* The Census Superintendent of the Punjab says, "that a certain unknown proportion of the increase recorded is due to better enumeration."† Commenting upon the increase, the Census Commissioner for India observes: "It is indeed an open question whether the actual rate is not a little below this 9·3 per mille.) ...... There are persons especially amongst the forest tribes, who now appear for the first time in the return, though, no doubt they should have been in that of 10 years back also."‡

The increase has mainly been in outlying parts of the

Growth mainly in outlying parts of the country. country where the pressure of population is not felt as yet.

"With a few exceptions" observes the Census Commissioner, "such as the groups with a density of from 10 to 33 per cent. above

* "Census of India, 1891" Vol. III.
† "Census of India, 1891," Vol. XIX.
‡ "Census of India, 1891, General Report" p. 73.

the general mean, which contain several of the famine districts of Madras where the increase has been abnormal, the rate of increase varies with remarkable regularity inversely as the specific population. The most thinly-peopled tracts, such as those of Sindh, Lower Burma and the Assam Hills, show a rate nearly double the mean. This diminishes to about one and a half times that rate as the North-West and Central Province hills, the Western plains of the Punjab, and the Southern portion of the Brahmaputra valley in Assam, come on to the list; and here it remains, until the mean density is nearly reached. Just above that point, there is a drop, caused by the preponderance of the Berar districts with a few of those in the South of the North West Provinces. The fall continues through the next group, where the non-famine districts of Bombay are strongly represented. Then follows the rise consequent on the rebound from scarcity in Madras. The decline then continues, and takes a sudden drop again where the average density is 434. that of the water-logged tract of the North-West Provinces, where there has been a slight recession of the population."*

Taxation in India, why heavy. Taxation in India judged by the amount it realises is certainly not heavy; yet, the people of India are generally considered, even by high English officials, to have been taxed nearly to the utmost extent of their resources.† The taxation would

* Census of India, 1891, General Report p. 75.

† The contrary is sometimes asserted by people who ought to know better. But "all who are acquainted with Indian finance know" as Sir Auckland Colvin says "that the burden of taxation is in danger of be-

not have been such a drain upon their resources, and would not have been felt so heavy, had not such a large part of the revenue, the entire amount raised from those two objectionable sources—salt and opium—gone clean out of the country without any equivalent return. Had the revenue been spent in the country, the entire community, especially the industrial classes, would have been benefited in some way or another; and increased prosperity would have rendered enhanced taxation less burdensome and less exhausting.

It speaks well of the vitality of the civilisation of the Hindus, that they have stood so well as they have the domination of such an excessively industrial and exploiting community as the British. They have not become extinct, nor have they bordered upon extinction like savage races in a somewhat similar situation. It is true, in former times, hordes of barbarians, like those of Central Asia and Central Europe occasionally committed serious

coming excessive, and that the further margin of resource to which taxation can be applied is incredibly small, both in itself, and from pressure of political considerations." (Letter in the *Times* in reply to a speech delivered by Mr. Fowler on January 28th at the Northbrook Indian Club).

Lord Mayo said: "A feeling of discontent and dissatisfaction exists among every class, both European and Native, on account of the constant increase of taxation which has for years been going on. * * * * My belief is that the continuance of that feeling is a political danger, the magnitude of which can hardly be over-estimated."

depredations. But the depletion of weaker peoples accomplished by the nations of modern Europe is none the less serious, because it is effected more slowly and with civilised weapons. These weapons are none the less dangerous because they are usually not seen, and are wielded none the less effectively, because they are wielded by civilised and knowing peoples pleading the inexorable necessity of the sacrifice of the weaker peoples for the cosmic progress of the stronger.

There are already signs of exhaustion. Whatever test is applied, wheher it be the test of taxable income,* of trade, wage-rate,†

<small>Signs of material depression.</small>

---

* Mr. S. Smith M. P in moving for a full inquiry into the finances of India said (August, 1894) :

"Only one man in 700 comes within the category of £50 a year. I will make a further statement. The right hon. gentleman is well aware that in this country one penny in the income tax yields £2.000,000 sterling. In India it yields considerably less than £200,000. India cantains 220,000.000 of people under British rule. These people yield on the income tax less than one-tenth of what 38,000,000, yield in the United Kingdom. The meaning of that is that every million of the people in India yield just one-sixtieth of what a similar number yield in this country. If this is not conclusive of the poverty of the people, nothing will satisfy the most exacting mind. It is indeed difficult to realise the small amount of wealth that there is in India."

† Wages have risen in some places, but very slightly, certainly not in proportion to the rise in the prices of the staple food grain, see Book V, ch. V.

death-rate,* or increase of population, it will be seen that the material condition of the people of India is highly depressed at present; and the existing conditions leave but little room to hope for its prospective improvement. The British Government is no doubt very anxious to secure India against foreign encroachment, and the old natural frontiers have in recent years

* The following figures show the death-rate between 1880 and 1891 : 1880, 20'98; 1881, 24'05; 1882, 23'93; 1883, 23'17; 1884, 26'44; 1885, 26'12; 1886, 25 34; 1887, 28 35; 1888, 25'74; 1889, 27'98; 1890, 29'99; 1891, 28'09. This increase is all the more significant, as during the decade 1883 to 1892, there were no cases of widespread failure of crops. The death-rates in all the provinces were higher—and in the great majority of cases considerably higher—in 1894 than in the previous year, as will be seen from the following statement:—

	1894.	1893.
North-Western Provinces	42'51	24'10
Central Provinces	37'22	27 70
Punjab	36'52	28'18
Bengal	34 88	28'21
Bombay	36'26	27'20
Assam	30 69	30'28
Madras	20'0	19'3

It is true, the figures are not equally reliable for the different parts of India. But they may be supposed to represent the truth approximately, or else they would not be published by the Government.

The Commissioners of the Calcutta Municipality observe in their last annual report:

"The health officer attributes the increased mortality from fevers in Calcutta almost entirely to the defective state of the sewerage. But it is difficult to accept this explanation unreservedly as it will be observed, on a reference to the annual reports of the sanitary commissioner for Bengal, that there has also been a corresponding rise in the death-rate from

been greatly extended. But all such extension adds to the exhausting drain from India. The good is prospective and problematical, the evil is present and certain. It is hardly any advantage to a man to have the most effective means for securing his property against possible depredation, if it means the certain diminution of the property to an amount which it is not worth securing even against more imminent danger.

The British administration is no doubt pervaded by the humane impulses of a civilised government. But, the measures taken by it to alleviate misery or promote happiness have somewhat the effect, so pithily expressed by a Bengali poet of "sprinkling water on the top of a tree while it is being cut away at the root."

Moral effect of the exclusive policy.
The exclusive policy of British Rule has been no less unfavourable to progress morally than it has been economically. Its tendency has been to add to the enervating influence of a tropical climate and foster mental passivi-

---

fevers in other parts of Bengal during the same period, and that being so, it is only reasonable that the increased mortality is in part to be attributed to some other cause of a general character, applicable alike to Calcutta and the country around rather than to any local peculiarities."

ty. "The nation as a whole, and every individual composing it, are without any potential voice in their own destiny. They exercise no will in respect to their collective interests. All is decided for them by a will not their own, which it is legally a crime for them to disobey. What sort of human beings can be formed under such a regimen? What developmet can either their thinking or their active faculties attain under it? * * * A person must have a very unusual taste for intellectual exercise in and for itself, who will put himself to the trouble of thought when it is to have no outward effect, or qualify himself for functions which he has no chance of being allowed to exercise. * * * * * The public at large remain without information and without interest on all the greater matters of practice; or if they have any knowledge of them, it is but a *dilettante* knowledge, like that which the people have of the mechanical arts who have never handled a tool. Nor is it only in their intelligence that they suffer. Their moral capacities are equally stunted * * * * Leaving things to the Government, like leaving them to Providence, is synonymous with caring nothing about them, and accepting their results when disagreeable, as visitations of nature. * * It is an inherent condition of human affairs, that no intention, however sincere, of protecting the interests of others, can make it safe or salutary to tie up their hands. Still more obviously true it is, that by their own hands only can any positive and durable improvement of their circumstances in life be worked out." *

We have nothing to add to these forcible words of one of the greatest thinkers of modern Europe to show their application to the case of the Indians. Some of the new conditions introduced by British Rule are as unmistakably favourable to progress as there are others antagonistic to it. The more notable among the former are the diffusion of Western education and of the doctrine of equality along with it, and the tranquillity which pervades the length and breadth of India. Among the adverse conditions we have noted the transitional state through which Hindu society is passing at present; the present anomalous position of English among the literary languages of India; the excessive poverty of the Hindus as compared with the people with whom

Present conditions on the whole unfavourable to sound intellectual development.

---

* "Considerations on Representative Government" by John Stuart Mill, Ch. III.

they have to compete ; the great discordance between the Hindu and the English civilisations, which has given rise to want of sympathy between the rulers and the ruled ; and the exclusive policy of British Rule. So long as the influence of the unfavourable conditions is not minimised, so long sustained intellectual efforts of a very high order must be very rare.

The present depressed state of the Indian mind—a state which is always unfavourable to sound intellectual development—may be realised by reversing the existing conditions.

"Let us conceive the leading European nations to be stationary, while the Black and Yellow Belt, including China, Malaysia, India Central Africa, and Tropical America is all teeming with life, developed by industrial enterprise, fairly well administered by native governments and owning the better part of the carrying trade of the world. Can any one suppose that, in such a condition of political society, the habitual temper of mind in Europe would not be profoundly changed ? Depression, hopelessness, a disregard of invention and improvement would replace the sanguine confidence of races that at present are always panting for new worlds to conquer. Here and there, it may be, the adventurers would profit by the tradition of old supremacy to get their services accepted by the new nations, but as a rule there would be no outlet for energy, no future for statesmanship. The despondency of the English people, when their dream of conquest in France was dissipated, was attended with a complete decay of thought, with civil war, and with a standing still, or perhaps a decline of population, and to a less degree of wealth. The discovery of the New World, the resurrection of old literature, the trumpet of the reformation scarcely quickened the national pulse with real life till the reign of Elizabeth. Then, however there was revival because there were possibilities of golden conquest in America, speculative treasures in the reanimate learning of Greece, and a new faith that seemed to thrust aside the curtain drawn by priests, and to open heaven. But it is conceivable that our later world may find itself deprived of all that it valued on earth, of the pageantry of subject provinces and the reality of commerce, while it has neither a disinterred literature to amuse it, nor a vitalised religion to give it spiritual strength."*

* C. H. Pearson, " National life and Character," 1893, pp. 130-131.

BOOK V.
INTELLECTUAL CONDITION.
CHAPTER I.

A BRIEF SKETCH OF THE HISTORY OF THE HINDU INTELLECT FROM THE EARLIEST TIMES TO THE BRITISH RULE.

The intellectual life of a community, like that of an individual, passes through youth and manhood to old age. These three stages in the history of the Indo-Aryan intellect are roughly marked by the three periods* into which we have found it convenient to divide Hindu history previous to the British rule. In the Vedic period we find the Indo-Aryans in all the simplicity, the vigour, and the credulity of adolescence. In the next period they show the robustness, and the philosophical spirit of matured manhood. The last period exhibits them in the decay and decrepitude of old age.

* Vedic, Buddhist-Hindu, and Puránic, Vol. I. p. 1.

The Vedic Period—The Age of Belief.

The Rigveda. The Rigvedic Aryans, like many other peoples in their intellectual infancy, looked upon the striking phenomena of nature with awe, and worshipped them as gods. To them there was divinity in the storm "causing the earth, the mountains, and both the worlds to quake"; in the fire consuming and blackening the woods with his tongue; in the sun "standing on his golden chariot," the soul of all things moving or stationary; in the Dawn chasing away darkness and awakening all creatures to cheerfulness. The Indo-Aryans invoked these and various other deities in songs which have been preserved in that remarkable collection, the Rigveda. In some of them we detect poetic powers of no mean order. In others, again, we discover the inquisitive mind and the generalising spirit which are among the most important antecedents of intellectual progress. One of the bards boldly speculates about creation: "when earth was not, and the far stretching sky was not, what was there that covered? which place was assigned to what object? Did the inviolate and deep water exist?—Who knows truly? Who will describe? When were all born? Whence were all these created?" "Sages" says another bard "name variously that which is one; they call it Agni, Yama, Mátarisvan." "In the beginning" says a third "there arose Hiranyagarbha—He established the earth and this sky—He is alone God above all gods."

But the philosophical spirit discernible in these and similar passages in the Rigveda did not bear any fruit until the very close of the vedic period. For some centuries subsequent to the composition of the hymns of the Rigveda, the works produced by the Indo-Aryans were chiefly manuals for the proper performance of sacrifices. The chanting of the hymns to the vedic deities was accompanied by sacrifices—offerings of grain, milk, animals, and soma-juice. The sacrificial portion of the worship appears at first to have been of a very simple character. Gradually, however, it increased in complexity until the poetical Nature-worship of the Rigvedic Aryans was practically replaced by a dry creed of sacrifice and penance. There arose different classes of priests who performed different duties at sacrifices. One class prepared the ground and the altar, got the sacrificial requisites ready, and immolated animals; another was entrusted with the duty of singing; a third with that of reciting hymns; and the fourth class of priests was charged with general superintendence. It was provided, that every hymn must be recited in a particular manner—nay, every word, every syllable must be pronounced in a prescribed way. The minutest rules were framed for penance not only for mistakes committed and observed during a sacrifice, but also for hypothetical mistakes which might have escaped the observation of the priests.

The Bráhmanas.

When the hymns of the Rigveda were composed, the Aryans lived in the Punjab or its immediate vicinity.

For some centuries subsequently, the great majority of them were busily occupied with extending their territories eastward and southward; and there arose powerful kingdoms like those of the Videhas, the Kosalas, and the Kásis. During this period of warfare and expansion, the task of preserving the vedic hymns naturally fell to a limited section of the Aryan community. There were several circumstances which favoured this restriction of vedic knowledge within a small class. The hymns, over a thousand in number, were transmitted orally from generation to generation. With the gradual expansion of the Aryans territorially and numerically, it became impossible for the great majority of them to preserve so many hymns in their memory, especially as the language of the hymns tended to become, in course of time, obsolete. There were many in out of the way places who could not even have access to the possessors of vedic lore. There must have been others again who were too busily occupied with the struggle for life to afford time for instruction. But the Aryans had great veneration for the hymns. It was these which had led their ancestors to victory and prosperity. The greater their ignorance, the greater and more superstitious was their veneration. A halo of sanctity spread round the hymns. The families which preserved them, which furnished men to recite them, and to perform the sacrifices accompanying them, gradually formed the priestly class (the Bráhmans). Monopoly produced its inevitable consequences. The Bráhmans having it all their own way, not unnaturally tried to increase the influence of their class by increasing the number and complexity of the functions upon which that influence was based. As vedic specialists, they not unnaturally attached an exaggerated importance to the subjects which formed their lifelong study. They dissected the hymns, and studied their metres, their words, nay even the syllables, as histologists of the present day would study the minute constituents of the animal or vegetable tissues. As they displayed their analytic ability in the study of the vedic hymns, so they also exhibited their synthetic powers in building up vast and complicated systems of sacrificial ceremonies. It is highly probable that in doing so they were not unmindful of the material interests of their order ; and increase in the wealth of the Aryan community consequent upon territorial acquisitions enabled its well to do members to celebrate sacrifices and make gifts to the priests upon a scale of grandeur and munificence unknown in previous times.

After a time, however, towards the close of the vedic period probably about B. C. 1000 * after the Aryans had settled down in their newly acquired territories and got time for reflection, an important movement, in which the Kshatriyas, the next caste, took the leading part, began in reaction against the dogma of the efficacy and importance of sacrifice. The ascendency of the Bráhmans was based upon this dogma ; and to question it was to strike at the very root of that ascend-

* It need scarcely be observed, that the dates given are only very roughly approximate.

ency. The spirit of inquiry of which we have faint glimmerings in the hymns of the Rigveda now began to shine in the Upanishads. They put forth the doctrine of the superiority of spiritual knowledge to sacrificial ceremonies. "The wise who perceive him [supreme spirit] within their self" says one Upanishad " to them belongs eternal happiness, not to others." "Those who imagine," says another, "that oblations and pious gifts are the highest object of man are fools ; they do not know what is good." With the movement initiated by the Upanishads commenced the age of enquiry which we shall find at its culmination in the next period.

That the superstitious veneration in which the hymns of the Rigveda came to be held in time and the gradual complication of the sacrificial ceremonies and the extravagant importance attached to their proper performance was productive of some good, there can be no doubt. The mystical virtues assigned in the Bráhmanas* to the different metres of the Rigveda led to their systematic study under the title of Chhandas or Prosody. The minutest rules were framed for the proper pronunciation and accentuation of the hymns; and these rules under the title of sikshá or Phonetics were probably appended at first to some of the Bráhmanas. But they

<small>Chhandas ;
Siksha' &c.</small>

---

* He who wishes for beauty and wisdom should use the Gáyatri hymn. One who wishes for long life should use Ushnish verses. He who desires wealth and glory should use Brihati verses : and so on ; (Haug's Aitareya Bráhmana, ii, pp. 12 ff. c.f. Satapatha Bráhmana quoted in Muir's Sanskrit Texts iv. p. 123)

were soon superseded by systematic treatises, the latest editions of which have come down to us under the title of Prátisákhyas.* Elaborate lists were made of vedic words; and they were explained and commented upon by a class of writers, the Nairuktas, the latest and most celebrated of whom was Yáska.†

Astronomy. The superstitious belief in the importance of performing sacrifices at auspicious moments gave rise to the science of astronomy, just as the superstitious belief in the mystic virtues of the vedic hymns favoured the growth of the science of language. In the Bráhmanas there are frequent allusions to astronomers or astrologers. In the third book of the Aitareya Bráhmana there is a passage of considerable interest in connection with astronomy which has been thus rendered by Dr. Haug : " The sun does never set nor rise. When people think the sun is setting (it is not so). For having arrived at the end of the day it makes itself produce two opposite effects, making night to what is below and day to what is on the other side. When they believe it rises in the morning. (This supposed rising is thus to be accounted

---

* Prof. MaxMüller considers the Prátisákhyas to be more ancient than Pánini's grammar. Prof. Goldstücker however, holds the latter to be more ancient.

† Yáska lived probably before the 7th century B. C. He is referred to by Pánini (Goldstücker's "Panini" pp. 224 ff). "I doubt" says Prof. MaxMüller "whether even at present with all the new light which comparative philology has shed on the origin of words, questions like these [whether all nouns are derived from verbs] could be discussed more satisfactorily than they were by Yáska." (Hist. A. S Lit. pp. 168-169).

for). Having reached the end of the night it makes itself produce two opposite effects, making day to what is below and night to what is on the other side. In fact, the sun never sets." *

Geometry. The science of Geometry arose out of the rules for the construction of altars at sacrifices. The altars were of very various shapes square, triangular, oblong, circular, falconshaped, heron-shaped &c. " Squares had to be found which would be equal to two or more given squares, or equal to the difference of two given squares; oblongs had to be turned into squares, and squares into oblongs; triangles had to be constructed equal to given squares or oblongs; and so on. The last task and not the least, was that of finding a circle, the area of which might equal as closely as possible that of a given square." † These operations necessitated a series of geometrical rules which were collected under the title of the Súlva sútras dating from the 8th century B. C.

THE BUDDHIST-HINDU PERIOD THE AGE OF REASON.

High value set upon knowledge. The seed of rationalism sown by the Upanishads yielded a rich harvest in the next period. A high value was set upon knowledge and wisdom. In one of

---

* "Aitareya Bráhmana," ii, p. 242.

† Thibaut, Journal, Asiatic Society of Bengal, 1875, p. 227. See R. C. Dutt, " Civilization in Ancient India " Vol. I p. 270.

the works of the period, seniority among the Bráhmans is declared to be according to their knowledge. The ignorant Bráhman is compared to a wooden horse or an antelope made of leather, which has nothing but the name. The measure of greatness is declared to be neither age, nor birth, nor wealth, but knowledge and wisdom. It is stated, that no good whatsoever results from presents made to ignorant Bráhmans. The right of keeping a treasure if found is claimed for a learned Bráhman only.*

Secularisation of knowledge. In the Vedic period, there was no knowledge apart from religion. Grammatical, metaphysical, or astronomical speculations formed only subsidiary portions of the works appended to the Vedas, the Bráhmanas, and the A'ranyakas, and were ancillary to the great objects of sacrifice. The first step towards the secularisation of knowledge was the composition of concise manuals on some of these subjects under the title of Sútras, like the Prátisákhya sútra dealing with phonetic rules and the Súlva sútra treating of geometrical principles. In their style and mode of treatment, they contrast favourably with the Bráhmanas. They too, however, were mere appendages of the different Vedas, and thus restricted research within a narrow groove.

---

* Manusamhitá, II. 154-158, III. 142. Though, in its present form one of the latest works of the period we are treating of, there are reasons to believe, that the Manu-Samhitá is based upon one of the earliest, the Mánava Dharmasútras.

Science of language

Knowledge was, however, soon freed from the bonds of religion, and for nearly fifteen centuries led a glorious career of independence. The first start of the Indo-Aryan intellect was, as we have seen already, in the direction of the science of language. To Yáska and a number of grammarians whose names alone have been preserved succeeded the great Pánini who lived probably about the seventh or eighth century, B. C.* "Panini's grammar" says Weber "is distinguished above all similar works of other countries partly by its thoroughly exhaustive investigation of the roots of the language, and the formation of words; partly by its sharp precision of expression, which indicates with an enigmatical succinctness whether forms come under the same or different rules. This is rendered possible by the employment of an algebraic terminology of arbitrary contrivance, the several parts of which stand to each other in the closest harmony, and which, by the very fact of its sufficing for all the phenomena which the language presents, bespeaks at once the marvellous ingenuity of its inventor, and his profound penetration of the entire material of the language." † Since the time of Pánini the most important contributions to the science of language have been made by Kátyáyana who lived a few

---

* Panini's date is still one of the many disputed points in the history of ancient India. See Goldstücker's "Panini" pp. 129-141, 224-227; Weber, "History of Indian Literature" (translation, pp. 217 ff: Max-Müller, "History of ancient Sanscrit Literature" pp. 163 ff

† Weber, *op cit.*, p. 216.

centuries after Pánini, Pátanjali who flourished about the second century B.C., and by Amara Sinha whose date has been assigned to about the 6th century A. D.

Systems of philosophy: the Sámkhya. The rationalistic spirit was nowhere better exhibited than in several of the systems of philosophy. Of these the Sámkhya is the oldest,* as it is certainly the boldest. Kapila, the author of this system, starts with denying the efficacy of the Vedic rites. Herein he was not singular, as several of the Upanishads had also done the same before him. But he went further. He would admit nothing that could not be known by the three kinds of evidence recognised by him—perception, inference, and testimony. And he would not admit the existence of a Supreme Being as it could not be proved by such evidence. Kapila derives everything except Soul from matter; the five elements, the sense organs, the organs of action, intellect, consciousness, and mind are all derived from Prakriti, or the eternal primordial principle. The five grounds given by Kapila for this conclusion are very remarkable. First, specific objects are finite in their nature and must have a cause. Secondly, different things have common properties, and must be different species of the same primary genus. Thirdly, all things are in a constant state of progression and shew an active energy of evolution which must have been derived from a primary source. Fourthly, the existing

* Weber, *op cit* p. 235. For analyses of the Sámkhya and other systems of philosophy referred to here, see Colebrooke, "Miscellaneous Essays."

world is an effect, and there must be a primary cause. And fifthly, there is an undividedness, a real unity in the whole universe which argues a common origin. "The latest German philosophy" says Mr. Davies "is a reproduction of the philosophic system of Kapila in its materialistic part, presented in a more elaborate form, but on the same fundamental lines. In this respect the human intellect has gone over the same ground, that it occupied more than two thousand years ago; but on a more important question it has taken a step in retreat. Kapila recognised fully the existence of a soul in man, forming indeed his proper nature—the absolute ego of Fichte—distinct from matter and immortal; our latest philosophy, both here and in Germany, can see in man only a highly developed physical organisation. 'All external things' says Kapila 'were formed that the soul might know itself and be free.' "'The study of psychology is vain' says Schopenhauer, 'for there is no Psyche.'" *

The Nyáya. The Nyáya as a philosophical system is based upon the Sámkhya, and differs from it mainly in admitting the existence of a supreme soul and in recognising analogy as a kind of evidence in addition to the three kinds—perception, inference, and testimony—admitted by the Sámkhya. The speciality of the Nyáya is the development of dialectical method. It discusses methods of reasoning with the greatest subtlety. It starts with sixteen topics for discussion which leave nothing to be desired to the

* "Hindu Philosophy," Preface.

most contentious dialectician. First of all, there is the proof and the thing to be proved. Then follow doubt, motive, instance, determined truth, argument or syllogism, confutation, ascertainment, controversy, jangling, objection, fallacy, perversion, futility, reasoning. The Nyáya syllogism consists of five parts—the proposition, the reason, the instance, the application of the reason, and the conclusion. The following is a generally quoted instance of Nyáya syllogism :

1. The hill is fiery (Proposition).
2. For it smokes (Reason).
3. Whatever smokes is fiery, as a kitchen (Instance).
4. The hill is smoking (Application of the reason).
5. Therefore it is fiery (Conclusion).

The Vaisesika. The fundamental principles of the Vaisesika philosophy of Kanáda are that all material substances are aggregates of atoms, and that as such aggregates they are perishable though the atoms themselves are eternal, invisible, and intangible. Kanáda recognises seven categories : substance, quality, action, community, particularity, coherence, and nonexistence. In the first of these categories are included earth, water, light, air, ether, time, space, soul, and the internal organ. Quality comprises colour, savour, odour, tangibility, number, extension, individuality, conjunction, disjunction, priority, posteriority, intellection, pleasure, pain, desire, aversion and volition. Action comprises upward and downward movement, contraction, dilation, and general motion. Community denotes qualities common to a number of objects. Particularity denotes simple objects devoid of community. Coherence is constant relation, such for instance, as subsists between yarn and cloth.

These three systems of philosophy—the Sámkhya, the Nyáya, and the Vaisesika are among the grandest monuments of the Indian period of philosophical inquiry.

The Pu'rva mi'-ma'nsa' and the uttara mi'ma'nsa'.

In them we find anticipated some of the most important scientific truths of the present day. There is scarcely any trace of dogmatism or superstition in them. Discussions are conducted with a closeness of reasoning and are pursued to their logical conclusions in a manner such as we would expect in any philosophical work of the present day. But side by side with the heterodox rationalistic schools, there were two orthodox systems the Púrva Mímánsá, and the Uttara Mímánsá. The former endeavoured dogmatically to maintain the absolute authority of the Vedas (comprising the Bráhmanas) which it holds to be eternal and revealed. Its conception of duty is the performance of sacrificial ceremonies prescribed by the Bráhmans. The Uttara Mímánsá or Vedánta of Vyása Bádaráyana is based upon the Upanishads and inculcates pantheism. It is a protest against the heterodox rationalistic systems one of which—the Sámkhya—did not recognise a Supreme Soul, and the others, though they admitted it, considered it to be distinct from the individual soul. The protest, however, was well worthy of the age which produced it. It is more a system of religion than of philosophy as generally understood, but of religion probably the most philosophical that the world has yet seen. The manner in which the pantheism of the Upanishads is systematised in the Vedánta, shows how the rationalistic spirit of the age had influenced religion. It would probably be no exaggeration to say, that the Vedantic conception of the Supreme Spirit is the loftiest that humanity has yet been capable of. "The supreme Being is one, sole existent, sempiternal, infinite, ineffable, invariable, ruler of all, universal soul, truth, wisdom, intelligence, happiness." He is the first cause. "All this universe is indeed Brahma ; from Him does it proceed ; into Him is it dissolved ; in him it breathes." "The sea is one, and not other than its waters ; yet, waves, foam, spray, drop, froth, and other modifications of it differ from each other." "Like sun and other luminaries, seemingly multiplied by reflection though really single, and like space apparently subdivided in vessels containing it within limits, the supreme light is without difference or distinction."

The mathematical sciences, like the mental and natural sciences, were also liberated from sacerdotal influence during the period under review, and were pursued to a very high state of development. The earliest Indian mathematicians whose works are still extant are the compilers of the old Siddhántas, Parásara, Garga &c. The dates of these works are a century or two before Christ. After them comes A'ryyabhata who was born in A.D. 476. The motion of the solstitial and equinoctial points was

The mathematical sciences.

noticed by him. He was also acquainted with the true theory of lunar and solar eclipses, as well as with the diurnal revolution of the earth on its axis. The ratio of the diameter to the circumference was given by him as 3·141, which is as near an approximation to modern calculations as we could reasonably expect. Before the close of the seventh century, there arose two other mathematicians of note, Varáhamihira and Brahmagupta. The former is known as the author of the Panchasiddhántiká (a compilation from five older astronomical works) and the Brihatsamhitá. The latter, which has been translated by Dr. Kern, is a work of great magnitude dealing not only with subjects strictly appertaining to astronomy, but also with various miscellaneous matters such as portents, gardening, house-building, precious stones, furniture &c. &c. Brahmagupta who wrote about A. D. 628 is best known as the author of the Brahmasphutasiddhánta. It comprises twenty-one chapters; "of which the first ten contain an astronomical system consisting (1st and 2nd) in the computation of mean motions and true places of the planets ; 3rd, solution of problems concerning time, the points of the horizon, and the position of places ; 4th and 5th, calculation of lunar and solar eclipses: 6th, rising and setting of the planets ; 7th, position of the moon's cusps ; 8th, observation of altitudes by the gnomon ; 9th, conjunction of the planets; and 10th, their conjunction with stars. The next ten are supplementary, including five chapters of problems with their solutions ; and the twenty-first explains the principles of the astronomical system in a compendious treatise on spherics, treating of the astronomical sphere and its circles, the construction of sines, the rectification of the apparent planet from mean motions, the cause of lunar and solar eclipses, and the construction of the armillary sphere." *

Medical sciences. The progress of the medical sciences kept pace with that of the others. The oldest writer whose works have come down was Charaka. He is referred to by Serapion, one of the earliest of the Arab physicians as well as by Avicenna and Rhazes.† Avicenna acknowledges his obligations to Indian authorities. Numerous drugs of Indian origin are noticed by the Greeks previous to the Arab authors. It is even supposed that Hippocrates derived assistance from the Hindus. Prof. Dietz has shewn that the Arabians were familiar with the Hindu medicaments, and extolled the healing art as practised by the Indians, quite as much as that in use among the Greeks; that a variety of treatises on medical science were translated from the Sanskrit into Persian and Arabic, particularly the more important compilations of Charaka and Susruta ; and that Manka and Saleh, the former of whom translated a special treatise on poison into Persian, held appointments as body physicians to Harun-al-Rashid [eighth century A. D.].‡

* "Algebra &c. of Brahmagupta and Bhascara" by H. T. Colebrooke, 1817, pp. xxviii.-xxix.
† Dr. Royle's "Essay on the antiquity of Hindu Medicine" p.p. 37-38."
‡ Royle's "Antiquity of Hindu medicine," p. 64.

Chemistry forms one of the eight divisions in which the treatise of Charaka is divided. There can be no doubt that the Arabians derived their knowledge of this subject from the works of the ancient Hindus; and as the originals were unknown in Europe they got the credit of being the discoverers.* The chemical skill of the Indo-Aryans was peculiar and remarkable. They knew how to prepare muriatic, nitric and sulphuric acids. "The number of metals which the Hindus" says Royle "were familiar with, and their acquaintance with the various processes of solution, evaporation, calcination, sublimation and distillation, prove the extent of their knowledge of chemistry, and the high antiquity of some of the chemical arts, such as bleaching, dyeing, calico-printing, tanning, soap and glass-making."

"The oxides of several metals as of copper, iron, lead, tin and zinc, they were well acquainted with and used medicinally. Of lead, we find mention of both the red oxide and of litharge. With the sulphurets of iron, copper, antimony, mercury, and arsenic, both realgar and orpiment, they have long been familiar. Among the salts of the metals, we find the sulphates of copper, of zinc, and of iron, and of the latter the red distinguished from the green: the diacetate of copper, and the carbonates of lead and of iron, are not only mentioned in their works, but used medicinally."†

Medicines were derived by the Hindus from the

---

* Royle's "Antiquity of Hindu medicine," p.p. 40 ff.
† Royle's "Antiquity of Hindu medicine" pp. 43-44.

vegetable and animal, as well as the mineral kingdom. Susruta describes a very large number of medicines prepared from plants. Various animals and animal substances were utilised as medicines: skins, nails, hair, blood, flesh, bones, fat, marrow, bile, milk, urine, dung, &c. The Hindus were perhaps the first who had the boldness to apply mineral drugs internally. Among the minerals used in medicine are mica, diamond, precious stones, brimstones, ammonia &c. The metals employed by physicians of the time of Susruta were gold, mercury, silver, copper, lead, tin, zinc, antimony, iron and arsenic. The doctrine of antidotes is treated of by both Charaka and Susruta.

Surgery had early attained a high stage of development. The ancient Hindus were bold and expert surgeons, and performed some of the most difficult operations, such as lithotomy, extraction of the dead fœtus, paracentesis, thoracis and abdominis, &c. The great variety of surgical instruments, as well of astringent or emollient applications, bandages, &c., proves the nicety and care which they displayed in this branch of the medical science.*

The subjects treated of in the works of Charaka and Susruta are much the same; but surgery is the speciality of the latter as medicine is that of the former. The work of Susruta is divided into six books each of which is subdivided into various chapters. The first book treats principally of preliminary matters such as the requisites for

---

* Wise's "commentary on the Hindu system of Medicine" pp. 157 ff.

surgical practice, the mode of visiting and observing the sick, and the classifications of diseases and of medicines. The second book deals with the diseases of the nervous system, hæmorrhoids, calculus in the bladder, fistula in anus, skin diseases, urinary disorders, Erysipelas, Elephantiasis &c. The third book treats of the anatomy of the human body, the management of pregnancy and parturition, the treatment of infants &c. In the fourth book, such matters as inflammation, wounds, ulcers, stone in the bladder, lithotomy and diabetes are dealt with. The fifth book treats of the preservation of food and drink from poison ; the vegetable, animal and mineral poisons ; snake-bites, and bites of dogs, jackals and of insects, &c.*

Laws. The laws of a people are a good index of their intellectual condition. The laws of the period under review as preserved in the Manusamhitá show a great advance upon those of the Vedic period as preserved in the Bráhmanas, or even in the Dharma Sútras.† Trial by ordeal prevailed in Vedic times. "They bring a man hither whom they have taken by the hand, and they say : 'He has taken something, he has committed theft.' (When he denies

---

* A very small portion of the Susruta Samhitá (the greater part of Book I) has been translated into English. Bibliotheca Indica, Calcutta 1883.

† The existing *Dharma Sútras* belong to the very close of the Vedic, or the commencement of the Rationalistic period. The date of the Manusamhitá may be approximately given as about a century or two before or after Christ.

they say); 'Heat the hatchet for him.' If he committed the theft, then he grasps the heated hatchet, he is not burnt, and he is delivered."* Though this barbarous form of trial appears to have been abolished by the close of the Vedic period, the judicial procedure appears still to have been very rude. In the Dharma Sútras of Gautama, the thief is directed to appear before the king with flying hair, holding a club in his hand and proclaiming his deed. If the king pardons him and does not slay him or strike him, the guilt falls on the king.

But in the Manusamhitá the forms of judicial procedure are laid down in a manner such as to extort the admiration even of James Mill who was prejudiced to a degree against everything Hindu. "They display," says Mill, "a degree of excellence not only far beyond itself in the other branches of law, but far beyond what is exemplified in more enlightened countries."† One of the most important objects which the judicature should have in view is the avoidance of delay ; and this object is secured by a number of wise regulations.‡ Cases brought before a tribunal are to be thoroughly investigated. A plaintiff who having knowingly called a witness disclaims him, or who consciously, contradicts himself, who does not prove what he has alleged, or who declines answering a question properly put is declared to be

* Chhandogya. VI. 16.
† "History of British India." I.
‡ Manu, VIII, 58 ff.

nonsuited. The witnesses are to be assembled in the middle of the court-room, and the judge is to examine them after having addressed in the following manner: "What ye know to have been transacted in the matter before us, between the parties reciprocally, disclose at large and with truth." A scale is laid down for the punishment of perjured witnesses. If a witness speaks falsely through covetousness or terror or friendship, he is to be fined 1000 *panas* ; if through distraction of mind, 250 ; if through lust, 2500 ; if through wrath, 1500; if through ignorance, 200 ; if through inattention 100.*

The civil laws indicate, on the whole a high stage of intellectual progress. They are treated under twelve heads : non-payment of debts, deposits and pledge, sale without ownership, partnership, resumption of gifts, non-payment of wages, non-performance of agreements, rescission of sale and purchase, disputes between owners of cattle and servants, disputes about boundaries, altercation between husband and wife, and inheritance.† The idea of property and the different modes of its acquisition by possession, by purchase, contract, labour, donation, and inheritance, are clearly comprehended.

General literature. The general literature of the period boasts of names quite as great as any connected with the sciences. It is noteworthy, however, that poetry and fiction flourished towards the

---

* Manu VIII, 120-121.
† Manu VIII. 4-7.

close of the period after the sciences had attained maturity, in fact while they (with the single exception of mathematics) were either stationary or already on the decline. Kálidása, Bháravi, Bhartrihari, Dandin, Bánabhatta, Bhavabhúti, all wrote between the sixth and the eighth centuries. That the Rámáyana and the Mahábhárata existed in crude forms long before the Christian era, there can be no doubt. But they received their final touches probably not long before the commencement of that era. The fact that poetry and fiction were carried to a high stage of development, during the last two or three centuries of the period under review, without any corresponding progress in those branches of literature which call for a sustained exercise of the reasoning faculties, shows, we venture to believe, that Hindu civilization was already on the wane. One reason of such high development of Sanskrit poetry during that period probably is, that it was then that Hindu mythology such as we know it now took shape; and Hindu mythology is the perennial source from which our great poets, ancient as well as modern, have drawn their subjects. Ráma and Sitá, Nala and Damayantí, Mahádeva and Umá who are among the heroes and heroines of Kálidása, Bhavabhúti and other great poets are scarcely known in the Vedic, or the earlier part of the philosophical period; or, if known, the beautiful legends associated with them had not yet sprung up. The Vedic cults, Bráhmanism and Vedantism, were ill calculated to inspire poetry, because the former was a dry creed of rites and ceremonies, and the latter, though far nobler and far more philosophic, was, nevertheless, an equally dry creed of salvation by meditation. The rationalism of the earlier portion of the philosophical period, while it furthered the development of the sciences, retarded the growth of *belles lettres*. Poetry began to shine forth in all its glory, as modern Hinduism arose with its myths and legends about gods and goddesses. The very fact of the supersession of an essentially non idolatrous creed like that of Vaidikism by an essentially idolatrous creed like that of modern Hinduism argues a decline of mental vigour. And this decline is apparently reflected in the literature of the closing century of the Buddhist Hindu period ; for while remarkably rich in works of poetry, in epics, dramas and novels, it is as remarkably poor in scientific works. Philology and medical and mathematical sciences became more or less stereotyped about the close of the seventh century soon after the time of Varruchi, Amara Simha, Susruta, Varáhamihira and Brahmagupta.

THE PURÁNIC PERIOD – THE AGE OF DECAY.

The decay of Indo-Aryan intellect began with the ninth century, and was accompanied by important political and religious revolutions. The Rajputs who had hitherto been but little known now rose into prominence. They overthrew the older dynasties and established their rule over nearly the whole of Northern and Western India. Those were troublous times not only in politics, but also

Mathematical science.

in religion. Buddhism was extirpated ; and modern or Puránic Hinduism was firmly established. The decay was hastened by another revolution three centuries later—the establishment of the Mahomedan Empire. Before the close of the twelfth century Sanskrit works appeared from time to time which bore the stamp of originality. There was the great mathematician Bháscaráchárya, who wrote his masterpiece, the *Siddhánta Siromani*, about the middle of the twelfth century. Bháscara dealt with such subjects as interest, permutation and combination, progression, indeterminate problems and mensuration of surfaces and solids. The rules are exact, and nearly as simple as in the present state of analytical investigation. Algebra was carried to a high degree of perfection.* The points in which the Hindu Algebra of Brahmagupta and Bháscara, appears distinguished from the Greek are besides a better and more convenient algorithm :—

(1) The management of equations involving more than one unknown quantity.

(2) The resolution of equations of a higher order in which if the Hindus achieved little, they had at least the merit of the attempt.

(3) General method for the solution of indeterminate problems of the first and second degrees, in which they went far beyond Diophantus and anticipated discoveries of the modern algebraists.

---

* Colebrooke in his "Algebra from the Sanskrit of Brahmagupta and Bháscara," has shewn that the Arabians borrowed their Algebra from the Hindus.

4) The application of Algebra to astronomical and geometrical demonstrations, in which they also hit upon some matters which have been reinvented in more modern times.*

The *Siddhánta Siromani*† of Bháscara treats of the general view of the sphere, cosmography, the principles of the rules for finding the mean places of the planets, the construction of an armillary sphere. the cause of eclipses of the sun and moon, the principles of the rules for finding the times of rising and setting of the heavenly bodies, the use of astronomical instruments &c.

Since the time of Bháscara India has produced only one astronomer of distinction—Raja Jay Sing of Amber who flourished during the first half of the eighteenth century.

"Jay Sing went deep, not only into the theory, but also the practice of the science, and was so esteemed for his knowledge, that he was entrusted by the emperor Mahomed Shah with the reformation of the calendars. He had erected observatories with instruments of his own invention at Delhi, Jeypoor, Oojein, Benares, and Mathura, upon a scale of Asiatic grandeur; and their results were so correct as to astonish the most learned. He had previously used such instruments as those of Ulug Beg (the royal astronomer of Samarcand, which failed to answer his expectations. From the observations

---

* Colebrooke *op. cit.* p. xvi.
† It has been translated into English by L. Wilkinson and Bápudeva Sástri.

of seven years at the various observatories, he constructed a set of tables. While thus engaged, he learned through a Portuguese missionary, Padre Manuel, the progress which his favourite pursuit was making in Portugal, and he sent several skilful persons along with him to the court of Emanuel. The king of Portugal despatched Xavier de Silva, who communicated to the Rajpoot prince the tables of De la Hire. 'On examining and comparing the calculations of these tables (says the Rajpoot prince) with actual observation, it appeared there was an error, in the former, in assigning the moon's place of half a degree; although the errors in the other planets was not so great, yet the times of solar and lunar eclipses he found to come on later or earlier than the truth by the fourth part of a ghurry, fifteen puls (six minutes of time).' In like manner, as he found fault with instruments of brass used by the Toorki-astronomer, and which he conjectures must have been such as were used by Hipparchus and Ptolemy, so he attributes the inaccuracies of De la Hire's tables to instruments of inferior diameters. The Rajpoot prince might justly boast of his instruments. With that at Delhi, he, in A.D. 1729, determined the obliquity of the ecliptic to be $23° 28'$; within $28''$ of what it was determined to be the year following by Godin. His general accuracy was further put to the test in A.D. 1793 by our scientific countryman, Dr. W. Hunter, who compared a series of observations on the latitude of Oojein with that established by the Rajpoot prince. The difference was $24''$; and Dr. Hunter does not depend on his own observation within 15″. Jey Sing made the latitude 23° 10′ N., Dr. Hunter 23° 10′ 24″ N. From the results of his varied observations, Jey Sing drew up a set of tables, which he entitled Zeij Mahomedshahi, dedicated to that monarch; by these all astronomical computations are yet made, and almanacs constructed. It would be wrong,—while considering these labours of a prince who caused Euclid's Elements, the treatises on plain and spherical trigonometry, Don Juan Napier on the construction and use of logarithms, to be translated into Sanskrit,—to omit noticing the high strain of devotion with which he views the wonders of the "Supreme Artificer," recalling the line of one of our own best poets:

"An undevout astronomer is mad." *

General literature. In the field of general literature, there were Mágha, the author of *Sisupálabadha*, who lived in the eleventh century; Sríharsha, the author of *Naishadha*, Jayadeva, the author of *Gitagovinda*, and Somadeva, the author of *Kathásaritságara* all of whom flourished before the close of the twelfth century. These were men far inferior to the great men of the last period. But even such as they were, they have not had their equals since. The history of Sanskrit literature from the thirteenth century is almost a blank. Sanskrit learning flourished at a few places, such as Mithila, Benares and Nadiyá; and there arose from time to time eminent scholars such

---

* Tod's " Rajasthan "—Annals of Amber, Chapter II.

as Raghunáth, Raghunandan and Sáyanácharya,* who have left their mark behind. But they were few and far between, and they showed at best the possibilities of the Hindu intellect during a period of decay and degeneration.

Thenceforth mathematics and medicine, in which the Hindus had probably made more progress than any other nation of antiquity, were gradually reduced to empiric arts, by which impecunious astrologers and needy quacks earned a bare living. The last great name in the annals of Hindu science was that of Bháscarácharya. The last great name in the annals of Sanskrit poetry was that of Jayadeva. The last great name in the history of Sanskrit prose was that of Somadeva. The few courts of Hindu kings, such as that of Bijaynagar in Southern India, which escaped the grasp of the Mahomedans, still fostered Sanskrit learning; it was also kept up at such places as Benares and Nuddea. But during the five centuries and a half of Moslem supremacy, Sanskrit literature can boast of only a few commentators, such as Sáyanáchárya, of Bijaynagar, and Raghunandan, of Naddia, and Sanskrit science of only one astronomer, Rájá Jay sing of Jaypur.

The fact of the decline of Hindu civilization being

---

* Raghunáth flourished at Nadiyá (in Bengal) about the end of the fifteenth century. He wrote various works on the Nyáya philosophy and was the founder of a distinct school of that philosophy. Raghunandan lived during the first half of the sixteenth century. He wrote extensively on Smriti (Hindu law and ritual). Sáyanácharya was the great commentator of the Rigveda.

nearly synchronous with the Mahomedan Conquest, has led to the assumption of an intimate connection of the one with the other. That the Mahomedan Conquest is, to a certain extent, responsible for Hindu degeneracy, admits of no question. Alberuni, who wrote half a century before the invasion of Shahabuddin Ghori, referring to Sabuktagin and his son Mahmud, who made frequent incursions into Hindusthan, between (A. D. 976 and A. D. 1026)* says :—

"God be merciful to both father and son! Mahmud utterly ruined the prosperity of the country, and performed those wonderful exploits by which the Hindus became like atoms of dust scattered in all directions, and like a tale of old in the mouth of the people. Their scattered remains cherish, of course, the most inveterate hatred towards all Muslims. This is the reason, too, why Hindu Science has retired far away from those parts of the country conquered by us, and has fled to places which our hand cannot yet reach, to Kashmir, Benares, and other places."

The Mahomedan conquest, as we have already observed, was, no doubt, partly responsible for the decadence of Hindu literature and Hindu science. But the caste-system was equally, if not in a greater degree, responsible for this decadence. Hindu literature and Hindu science before the thirteenth century meant Sanskrit literature and Sanskrit science. In pre-Mahomedan times, at least since the Vedic period, the cultivation of literature and science was practically confined to the Bráhmans. The great poets, the great mathematicians, the great doctors, the great writers of

---

* Alberuni's India, translated by E. C. Sachau. Vol. I, p. 22.

fiction, were all Bráhmans, just as the great warriors were all Kshatriyas. The mass of the people had as little to do with learning as they had to do with war. They were debarred from the study of the sacred books. Alberuni says : " Hindus differ amongst themselves as to which of these castes is capable of attaining to liberation ; for, according to some, only the Bráhmana and Kshatriya are capable of it, since the others cannot learn the Veda."* From this passage it appears that the Vaisyas, who had formerly enjoyed the right of studying the sacred books, had lost it by the middle of the 12th century, if not earlier. Together with the Súdras, they must then have greatly out-numbered the higher classes, as they do now. Amongst the names that adorned the Courts of Bhoja of Dhar, or of Vikramáditya of Ujjain, we do not find a single Súdra or Vaisya. The vernacular dialects, the dialects in which the mass of the people spoke, had not yet been developed. Sanskrit was still the language in which books were written. These books could have had but an extremely small cirle of readers, and that only amongst the Bráhmans and the Kshatriyas. To the Vaisyas and the Súdras, who formed the great mass of the people, these books were as good as sealed. Their authors lived under the patronage of Hindu kings, not by the sale of their books. When the Mahomedans swept away the courts of these kings, Sanskrit leanring fled, as Alberuni says, to such places as Benares and Kashmir. The downfall

* *Op. cit. p.* 104.

of the kings meant the ruin of the learned Bháhmans whom they patronised; and the ruin of the learned Bráhmans meant the ruin of Hindu literature and Hindu science, just as the overthrow of the Kshatriya Rajputs meant the destruction of Hindu independence.

Till the time of the Mahomedan occupation, the Bráhmans reigned supreme in the intellectual world of India. At one time, during the period when the Upanishads were composed, their right to intellectual supremacy had been disputed by the millitary caste. But they emerged from the struggle victorious, and in the earlier Puránic period, the brightest period of Hindu civilization, they were certainly the sole possessors of the field of literature and science. They had no equals, certainly no superiors, amongst any other caste. They always led; they had never been led. They came to believe, as Alberuni says,* "that there is no country but theirs, no nation like theirs, no religion like theirs, no science like theirs." They are by nature niggardly in communicating that which they know, and they take the greatest possible care to withhold it from men of another caste among their own people, still much more, of course, from any foreigner. According to their belief, there is no other country on earth but theirs, and no created beings, besides them, have any knowledge or science whatever. Their haughtiness is such that, if you tell them of any science or scholar in Khorasan and Persia, they will think you to be both an ignoramus and a liar.

* *Op. cit.* vol. I. p. 22.

If they travelled and mixed with other nations, they would soon change their mind, for their ancestors were not as narrow-minded as the present generation is." Alberuni, an accomplished and sympathetic Mahomedan, found it very hard to pursue his studies in Hindu science, though, as he says, he had a great liking for it, in which respect he was quite alone in his time, and, though he spared neither trouble nor money in collecting Sanskrit books from places where he supposed they were likely to be found, and in procuring for himself, even from remote places, Hindu scholars who understood them and were able to teach him.*

<small>Mahomedan influence upon Hindu literature.</small>

At the Mahomedan Conquest, the haughty Bráhmans, for the first time, had to regard as masters, men whom they had hitherto looked upon as impure, foul-feeding, barbarians (*Mlechhas*). They were no longer courted, no longer venerated by high officials; their counsels were no longer sought after by kings. Hitherto, throughout the entire length and breadth of India, in the north as well as in the south, they had possessed the greatest influence. The favours bestowed by kings must have hitherto acted as a great stimulus for the acquisition of knowledge. But now strangers filled the thrones from which kings had smiled upon them—strangers who generally regarded them somewhat as Europeans generally regard them now. Such of the Bráhmans as could afford to do so, fled to Kashmir,

---

* *Op. cit.* vol. I. p. 24.

Benares, and other places. "And there," says Alberuni, "the antagonism between them and all foreigners receives more and more nourishment, both from political and religious sources."* At such places as Benares and Nadiyá, Sanskrit learning was kept up by a few Bráhmans. But the great majority of them gradually became more and more immersed in ignorance. The line of demarcation between them and the lower classes gradually became less and less sharp. To the Mahomedans, Bráhmans, Vaisyas and Súdras were all *kafirs*. The Bráhmans still received the customary homage from the lower classes. But they had no longer the strength of intellect which is begotten of self-confidence; they had no longer the originality which is the sure indication of intellectual progress. The Bráhmans were the greatest sufferers by the Mahomedan invasion. The lower classes continued to pursue their occupations as they had pursued them for ages. Even the Kshatriyas found employment in the armies of Mahomedan kings. But the occupation of the Bráhmans, if not quite gone, lost all its lustre and dignity. They were utterly neglected, nay humiliated. They must have considered themselves disgraced. No wonder that they retired into obscurity in moody silence, or devoted their energies to the composition of frivolous stories about gods and goddesses. The lower classes were now almost their only customers. The Súdras and the Vaisyas now fed and clothed them. They, therefore, not

* *Op. cit.* vol. I. p. 22.

unnaturally, did what pleased their customers best. During the five and a half centuries of Mahomedan regime the best of them could produce only a few commentaries or compilations. They had all along pandered more or less to the superstitions of the mass of people, who were mostly non-Aryans. Hinduism was the result of a compromise between the non-idolatrous worship of the Aryans, as presented in the Rig-Veda, and the idolatry and fetishism of the non-Aryans; and this compromise was, at least partly, the work of the Bráhmans.

With the Mahomedan Conquest the Bráhmans lost the patronage of enlightened Hindu kings, and became more dependent than ever for their living on the gifts of the lower castes with whom the superstitious part of Hinduism was most popular. The Bráhmans had now to please the mob more than ever. The most enlightened amongst them were, no doubt, monotheists, pantheists, or atheists, as they still are. But they never expected, probably they never wanted, the mob to be what they were. Three centuries previously to the Mahomedan occupation, Sankarácháryya had expressly preached one creed (pantheism) for the philosophic few, and another (Saivism) for the ignorant many. Now the number and influence of the philosophic few were greatly reduced, while that of the ignorant and credulous many remained, and increased and throve. The influence which produced the sublime in Hindu works vanished; the influence which produced the superstitious and the ridiculous in them, gradually increased. The science of astronomy, for instance, ceased to have any higher interest than that which it had for astrologers for the purpose of ascertaining which dates are propitious for certain purposes and which dates are not; on which dates and at what hours the festivals of the people are to be held; on which dates certain kinds of food are to be eaten, and on which dates they are not to be eaten. All that was grand and noble in the Indo-Aryan literature and science gradually disappeared; all that was base and degrading, or at best indifferent, remained and flourished.

But the Mahomedan Conquest was by no means an unmixed evil. It did some good. Hindu civilization hitherto had been mainly Aryan civilization, the civilization chiefly of the two upper classes, the Bráhmans and the Kshatriyas. To the lasting honour of the Bráhmans be it said, they spread their civilizing influence throughout India. It was they that lifted up the aborigines, taught them to lead a settled life, made them more humane, in one word, more civilized than they had been before. This the Bráhmans did, not by brute force, but by sheer force of character and intellect. To conquer a country with the idea of civilizing it, seldom entered their heads. They penetrated to the remotest south, to the north, and to the east; and wherever they went, they carried the light of civilization. Whether it be the Drávidians of the south or the mountainous tribes of the north, their traditions, their religions, their dialects, their manners and customs, all bespeak Bráhmanical influence. The aborigines were admitted within the pale of Hinduism, though on the condition that they would form the lowest class in Hindu society. The low caste people were considered beings inferior to the Bráhmans. They could never aspire to rise to the social status of the Bráhmans. It was otherwise with the Mussulmans. The meanest peasant amongst them could rise to the rank of the greatest nobleman. The lowest Mussulman had a right to read the Koran and to pray in the mosque. Not so with the Hindus. "Every action," says Alberuni,* "which is considered as the privilege of a Bráhman, such as saying prayers, the recitation of the Veda, and offering sacrifices to the fire, is forbidden to him [Súdra or Vaisya] to such a degree, that when e. g. a Súdra or a Vaisya is proved to have recited the Veda, he is accused by the Bráhmans before the ruler, and the latter will order his tongue to be cut off." It was chiefly the influence of Mahomedanism with its doctrine of the brotherhood of man that produced that succession of earnest reformers who shed such lustre on India from the commencement of the fourteenth century to the beginning of the sixteenth. Rámánanda, Kabir, Nának, and Chaitanya were certainly influenced by the tenets of Mahomedanism. They all preached the unity of the Godhead; they all protested against caste; they all denounced idolatry. Kabir, Nának, and Chaitanya founded large sects which have survived to the present day. Rámánanda chose his disciples from among the lowest castes.

* *Op. cit.* Vol. II.-p. 136.

He had even a leather dresser amongst them. The most distinguished of his disciples was Kabir, a weaver. Kabir, Chaitanya and Nának, all admitted Mahomedans into their sects. There were Moslems who regarded Kabir as one of their own.

The impetus which the reformers gave directly and indirectly, to the progress of the vernacular literatures, was very great. In Northern India the teachings of Kabir and Chaitanya were embodied by their followers in voluminous works, which enriched the vernacular literatures. They preached to the people in the languages of the people. Their adoption of the vernaculars as their literary languages was a protest against the exclusiveness of the orthodox Bráhmans, a small number of whom still clung to the carcase of Sanskrit. Sanskrit had no longer any life in it ; it was now dead. If it was ever a spoken language—and on this point eminent scholars are still divided—it ceased to be such about the time of the Mahomedan Conquest. The books written in it were not understood by the people : they were not meant for the people. Now the people had books written in their vernaculars, books which, if they could not read themselves, they could at least understand if read to them. It was about the time of the Mahomedan Conquest that the Indian vernaculars, the Hindi, the Bengali, the Uriya, and the Marathi, began to be developed. This development was not the direct work of the Mahomedan occupation. Long before that time, even centuries before the Christian era, the mass of the Hindus spoke

Rise of the vernacular literatures.

RISE OF THE VERNACULAR LITERATURES.

in Aryan dialects, which were called Prákrits. Varruchi, the earliest Prákrit grammarian, enumerates four classes of these in the sixth century A.D.—Mahárástri, Sauraseni, Mágadhi, and Paisáchi. The vernaculars of India were gradually evolved from these dialects. They must have been in process of evolution long before the Mahomedan Conquest.

But the Mahomedan Conquest hastened the development of the vernacular literatures, as it also hastened the decay of the Sanskrit literature. Sanskrit was destined to die a natural death. It was artificially kept alive by a small band of intellectual Bráhmans. With the ruin of the Hindu Courts at the time of the Mahomedan Conquest, these Bráhmans dispersed, and gradually dwindled in numbers. The vernacular literatures would have sprung up in the natural course, because, they were the literatures of the mass of the people. But the Mahomedan Conquest helped their development in two ways. First by lowering the status of the Bráhmans and the Kshatriyas, it indirectly tended to elevate that of the lower classes. Secondly, the close contact of Mahomedanism influenced the Hindu mind so that it revolted against the inequality of the caste-system, and the domination of a hereditary priesthood. That such reformers as Kabir, Chaitanya, and Nának were at least partly the products of Mahomedan influence, there can be no doubt ; and however they might differ in details, they all denounced caste, and they all preached the unity of the Godhead. The preachings of the reformers stimulated the progress of the vernacular literatures in a most marked manner. The works of the Kabir-panthis (the sect founded by Kabir) formed the greater portion of the early Hindi literature, and the contributions of the followers of Chaitanya swelled the mass of early Bengali literature.

Influence of Vaishnavism on vernacular literature

That the first great impulse to vernacular literatures was given by the Vaishnava Reformation which was carried on from the thirteenth to the sixteenth century by Rámánanda, Kabir, Chaitanya and a number of other reformers, is shown by the facts that with the exception of some Hindi ballads in Rájputáná, vernacular literatures have scarcely anything to shew before the thirteenth century,* and that the earliest writers were

---

* The Tamil is excluded from this generalisation. Its development was earlier than that of the other vernaculars. The Tol-káppiyam the oldest extant Tamil work, is believed to have been written a few centuries before the birth of Christ. It is still the greatest authority on Tamil grammar. "Whatever antiquity" says Caldwell "may be attributed to the Tol-káppiyam, it must have been preceded by many centuries of literary culture. It lays down rules for different kinds of poetical compositions, which must have been deduced from examples furnished by the best authors whose works were then in existence...... In endeavouring to trace the commencement of Tamil literature we are thus carried further and further back to an unknown period." ("Comparative grammar of the Dravidian Languages," 1875, pp. 127-128). "With the exception of a few works composed towards the end of the twelfth century, nearly all the Telugu works that are now extant appear to have been written in the fourteenth and subsequent centuries, after the establishment of the kingdom of Vijaynagara; and many of them were written in comparatively recent times." (Caldwell *Op. cit.* p. 123). The most ancient and esteemed grammar of classical Canarese, that

mostly Vaishnavas. In northern India, besides the reformer Kabir, the two great Hindi writers previous to the eighteenth century were Sur Dás, and Tulsi Dás ; * and they were both earnest Vaishnavas. The earliest Bengali authors from the fourteenth to the sixteenth century were enthusiastic worshippers of Krishna, the most notable among them being Bidyápati and Chandi Dás.† No Maráthi writer of any note is known

by Kesava, was written about 1170 A.D. The oldest extant work in Malayálam is "Rámcharita" which was written about the thirteenth century A.D.

* Sur Dás flourished about the middle of the sixteenth century. "He and Tulsi Dás" says Mr. Grierson "are the two great stars in the firmament of Indian vernacular poetry. Tulsi was devoted to Rám (*ekánt Rám-sebak*) while Sur Dás was devoted to Krishna (*ekánta Krishna-sebak*), and between them they are said to have exhausted all the possibilities of poetic art." (Journ. As. Soc. of Bengal pt. I for 1886, special number, p. 21. Tulsi Dás flourished about the commencement of the seventeenth century. For his life see Grierson, *op. cit.* p. 42 *et seq.*, and Growse's "Rámáyana of Tulsi Dás," Introduction. In Northern India, the Rámáyana of Tulsi Dás is "in everyone's hands, from the court to the college, and is read or heard, and appreciated alike by every class of the Hindu community, whether high or low, rich or poor, young or old."

† Bidyápati flourished about the commencement of the fifteenth century. "Bidyápati's influence on the history of the literature of Eastern Hindustán" says Mr. Grierson "has been immense. He was a perfect master of the art of writing those religious love sonnets which have since become in a much degraded form the substance of the Vaishnava bibles." (Grierson *op. cit.* p. 11). Chandi Dás was a contemporary of Bidyápati. For his life, see R. C. Dutt's "Literature of Bengal," 1895, p. 26.

before the thirteenth century and the greatest poets of Maháráshtra, Tukárám, and Sridhar were Vaishnavas.*

* Tukárám died in 1649. He was an ardent worshipper of Vithoba (Vishnu) "He is," says Mr. Acworth "the most original of all Máráthi poets, and his work is remarkable for a high and sustained level of religious exaltation." Sridhar died in 1728. He rendered the Rámáyana and the Máhábhárata into Máráthi. "There is no Máráthi poet who equals Sridhur in the acceptance he obtains from all classes In every town and village in the Deccan and Konkan, especially during the rains, the pious Márátha will be found enjoying with his family, and friends the recitation of the Pothi of Sridhar and enjoying it indeed. Except an occasional gentle laugh, or a sigh, or a tear, not a sound disturbs the rapt silence of the audience, unless when one of those passages of supreme pathos is reached which affects the whole of the listeners simultaneously with an outburst of emotion which drowns the voice of the reader." "Ballads of the Máráthas" by H. A. Acworth, Introduction.

CHAPTER II.

Influence of English Liberalism.

Liberalism in modern Europe. The foundation of the British empire in India was laid just about the time when Europe was on the verge of a revolution, probably the most important, politically, intellectually, and socially, which the world has ever seen. It was during the last half of the eighteenth and the first half of the nineteenth century that modern Europe sprung up with its democratic governments, its natural science, its steam engine and electric telegraph, and its innumerable labor-saving appliances. It would probably be no exaggeration to say, that the Europe of the present century is more different from the Europe of the seventeenth, than the Europe of the seventeenth was from the Europe of the first century. The Congress of Vienna did its best to restore to Europe the political arrangements which had existed before the rise of Napoleon.

But the Powers did not see, or they ignored the new political forces which had come into existence towards the close of the eighteenth century; and the political equilibrium which they thought they had established did not endure long. The interest of the political history of Europe for sometime after the Vienna Congress was centred in the struggles of the people for liberty and self-government. In 1820, Spain rose in rebellion against her king and secured a constitution of which universal suffrage was the principal feature. Shortly after, Greece threw off the tyrannical yoke of the Turks. In July 1830, the French people tried conclusions with the forces of absolutism for the second time; and their success gave a fresh impulse to democratic ardour in nearly every state in Europe. In England, various restrictions which weighed heavily upon the people were removed, and the Reform Bill which made the representative system more a reality than a name was passed in 1832.

The wave of liberalism which passed through England affected even her distant administration of India, though of course to a very small extent. The people of India were too far off from Europe, and were too deeply imbued with the old-world ideas of government to be moved by the new idea of government for the people and by the people which electrified modern Europe. They submitted to the despotism of the British as quietly and as resignedly as they had submitted to the despotism of any Hindu or Mahomedan Power; and the Government of the

Liberalism in India since 1832.

East India Company had nearly until the close of the eighteenth century been a despotism with scarcely any mitigating features to compensate for the loss of the manifold advantages of a native rule. All that the Company had till then cared for was money; all that their servants in India had till then striven for was to secure a dividend for their masters, and to secure as much as they could for themselves either in the shape of gain or perhaps also of fame. But since then, especially since 1832, the year in which the Reform Bill crowned the cause of democracy in England, the British-Indian administration has been pervaded, to however small an extent, by the spirit of modern Europe. Since then, the benefit of India has generally been urged, at least by English statesmen, as the main object of the retention of India;* and though in practice that object has not often been kept in view, its theoretical recognition bespeaks the liberal spirit of modern Europe. It is this spirit which, notwithstanding the frequent advocacy of narrow-minded views of coercion and repression by influential organs of the Anglo-Indian world has kept Anglo-Indian bureaucracy from sinking into unmitigated absolutism.

It was in 1833 that a statute was passed which provi

---

* Mr. Gladstone said on one occasion: "The question is not whether we are justified in the acquisition or not of India; the question is not whether our hands were clean or not in that acquisition; the question is what obligations we have contracted towards the nearly 200 millions of people under our rule in India, and towards the God who cares for that people as much as for us." "Essays political, social, and religious, India" by R. Congreve, 1874, pp. 78-79.

ded that no native of India, "nor any natural-born subject of His Majesty resident therein, shall, by reason only of his religion, place of birth, descent, colour, or any of them, be disabled from holding any place, office, or employment under the said Government."

It was in the same liberal spirit that the court of Directors issued their despatch of the 10th December, 1834.

"It is fitting that this important enactment should be understood in order that its full spirit and intention may be transfused through our whole system of administration.

" . . . . . The meaning of the enactment we take to be that, there shall be no governing caste in British India; that, whatever other tests of qualification may be adopted, distinctions of race or religion shall not be of the number; that no subject of the King, whether of Indian, or British, or mixed descent, shall be excluded either from the posts usually conferred on our Uncovenanted Servants in India, or from the Covenanted Service itself, provided he be otherwise eligible, consistently with the rules and agreeably to the conditions observed and enacted in the one case and in the other. . . .

"Certain offices are appropriated to them (the Natives), from certain others they are debarred; not because these latter belong to the Covenanted Service, and the former do not belong to it, but professedly on the ground that the average amount of Native qualifications can be presumed only to rise to a certain limit. It is this line of demarcation which the present enactment obliterates, or rather, for which it substitutes another, wholly irrespective of the distinction of races. Fitness is henceforth to be the criterion of eligibility."

The administrative policy of the Government had hitherto been to exclude Indians from all responsible posts. In the executive Government the only Indian officer entrusted with any power was the Police Daroga with a salary of twenty-five rupees a month.

In the judicial department the highest officer was the Munsiff who could try civil cases involving only petty amounts. While European judges could in the ordinary course of promotion rise up to two thousand and five hundred rupees a month, the Munsiff had no pay whatever, but was left to get what he could by a small commission on the value of suits. The fatal effects of this unjust and shortsighted policy soon made themselves apparent. In the words of Trevelyan, " the wheels of Government soon became clogged; more than half the business of the country remained un-performed; and at last, it became necessary to abandon a plan, which, after a fair trial had completely broken down."*
It was left to Lord William Bentinck one of the few liberal-minded and large-hearted statesmen that India has seen, to carry out the principles of the despatch of 1834; and for the first time in the History of British Rule, Indians were appointed to posts of any responsibility.

The noble sentiments of the despatch of 1834 have been reiterated over and over in official documents of which the most authoritative is the proclamation issued by Her Gracious Majesty the Queen in 1858 when she assumed the direct Government of British India :

" We hold ourselves bound to the Natives of our Indian territories by the same obligations of duty which bind us to all our other subjects; and those obliga-

---

* Trevelyan, "Education of the People of India." p. 156.

tions, by the blessing of Almighty God, we shall faithfully and conscientiously fulfil. . . .

"And it is our further will that, so far as may be, our subjects, of whatever race or creed, be freely and impartially admitted to offices in our Service, the duties of which they may be qualified by their education, ability, and integrity, duly to discharge."

A great deal has been done to give effect, to these liberal principles. But, a great deal more still remains to be done. Until 1853, appointments to the Covenanted services of the East India Company were made by the Directors by nomination. In that year, the Covenanted Civil and Army Medical Services were thrown open to public competition in England, to which all British subjects were to be eligible. This was certainly a gain for the people of India who had hitherto been entirely excluded from those services. But, the gain was small considering their poverty and other circumstances which stood in the way of their sending their boys to a distant country on the mere chance of a competitive examination; and a great meeting was held in Calcutta in 1853 at which one of the speakers said :

"True it may be said that as the competition is to be "unlimited," the natives may send their children to England to pass through Haileybury or Addiscombe to qualify them for one or other of the branches of the Service, but am I to be told that with the mere chance of obtaining appointments, natives are to send their children to England, without their families around them, without their friends to guide them, to be left there in the midst of strangers?" *

* "Speeches of Rámgopál Ghose," p. 8.

Indians form only an insignificant fraction of the candidates who go up for the Imperial Civil Service. In 1892 this service was composed of 939 members of whom only 21 were Indians.* After forty years of agitation (always confined as yet to the press and the platform in India), a Resolution was passed by the House of Commons in 1893 in favour of holding simultaneous examinations in India and in England for the Imperial Civil Service. But the resolution has hitherto remained inoperative owing to the opposition of the Indian authorities. We shall, in a subsequent chapter, see to what a large extent the British administration is still exclusive, and how depressing the effect of such an administration has been upon the intellectual development of the Hindus.

The Press.
Lord William Bentinck initiated a measure for granting freedom to the Press. It was, however, left to his successor, Lord Metcalfe, to carry the measure into execution. The first newspaper ever printed in an Indian vernacular was issued in Bengali by the Christian Missionaries at Serampore, on the 31st May, 1818.† It was called the *Samáchár-Darpan* or the "mirror of news." Its appearance rather alarmed the Anglo-Indian officials, but the then Governor-General, Lord Hastings, encouraged it by allowing its

---

* Strachey's "India," 1894, p. 58.
† "The Life and Times of Carey, Marshman and Ward," Vol. II, (1859), p. 163

D

circulation at one-fourth the ordinary rate of postage. He showed the same liberal spirit towards the English press, and notwithstanding the determined opposition of his council removed the censorship which Lord Wellesley had imposed upon it. In deference, however, to the despotic feeling which pervaded the Indian bureaucracy, he "laid severe restrictions on the editors regarding the subjects or personages they were allowed to touch, any infraction of which was to be visited by an indictment in the Supreme Court or by the penalty of deportation. But the Supreme Court, on the occasion of the first application,* refused to grant a criminal information, and Lord Hastings was unwilling to inflict the odium of banishing an editor on his administration. The restriction, therefore, fell into abeyance, and the press became practically free. In replying to an address from Madras, Lord Hastings embraced the opportunity of vindicating his policy by stating that he was in the habit of regarding the freedom of publication as the natural right of his fellow-subjects, to be narrowed only by special and urgent cause assigned..........Further, he said, 'it was salutary for supreme authority, even when its intentions are most pure, to look to the control of public opinion.' "

Entire liberty to the press however, was not granted until 1835, when the power of deporting offending

---

* In the case of the *Calcutta Journal* of which the Proprietor and Editor was Mr. J. S. Buckingham, "a gentleman permitted to reside in Calcutta by special license." (Mill and Wilson's " History of British India" Vol. VIII, p. 415).

journalists was taken away from the Government of India.* The vernacular Press act passed by Lord Lytton imposed restrictions of a rather severe nature upon the vernacular press. They were, however, removed by his successor, Lord Ripon. In 1881-82, the number of Bengali newspapers and periodicals was thirty-eight of which six were daily, twenty-eight weekly, two fortnightly, and two monthly papers. Of the daily papers, not one had a circulation of much above 600. Of the weekly papers, two had a circulation of 4,000, one of 2,000, seven of between 500 and 1,000, and the rest of less than 500; the two fortnightly papers had a circulation of 600 between them; and of the monthly papers, one had a circulation of 2,100, and another of less than 200. In 1891-92, there were 41 Bengali papers, of which seven were monthly and fortnightly, one trimonthly, twenty-seven weekly, and six daily. The increase in the number of newspapers within the decade was small, but their circulation increased immensely. Of the daily papers, one had a circulation of 1,500, another of 1,000. Of the weekly papers, one is said to have had a circulation of 20,000, one of 8,000, one of 4,000, two of 3,000 each, and three between 1000 and 3,000. The number of vernacular newspapers in the Bombay Presidency in 1890 numbered 158. In the Madras Presidency the number was 100 compared with 87 in 1888. Of these 51 were classed as "general and politi-

* The Metcalfe Hall in Calcutta testifies to the gratitude of the people for the measure which was carried out by Sir Charles Metcalfe, who was Governor-General from 1835 to 1836.

cal," 19 as "educational and literary," and 30 as "religious." The largest circulation (5,500 copies) was enjoyed by a Christian religious monthly paper in Tamil. The total number of newspapers in the North-West Provinces and Oudh was 104, of which 24 were monthly, 61 weekly, and 3 daily.* About the middle of this century there were edited by Hindus only two English weekly newspapers in Bengal, the *Hindu Patriot* and the *Hindu Intelligencer*; one in Madras, the *Madras Rising Sun*; and one in Bombay, the *Hindu Harbinger*. Now there are under Hindu Editorship, in Bengal alone, three daily newspapers besides a dozen or so of weekly ones.

The charter of 1813 had for the first time forced the East India Company to spend a sum of not less than one lakh of rupees upon educational purposes. The charter of 1833 raised the amount ten-fold; and the administration of Lord William Bentinck is memorable for the vigorous steps which were taken for the dissemination of English education. The intellect of the Hindus has been most remarkably influenced by English education in various ways. In ancient times they had come into close contact with the Greeks; and it is probable that for their progress in architecture and in astronomy,†

Spread of education since 1835; influence of European democracy.

---

* "Moral and material condition of India for 1889-90."

† It is only in Gándhára and the Punjab, however, that the general architecture bears a Greek character. In the vast continent of India itself, the architecture shows but little trace of any foreign influence. (R. C. Dutt's " Civilization in ancient India,'' 1893, Vol. II. p. 63).

they were to some extent indebted to the Yavanas. But the exchange of ideas between them and the civilized nations of antiquity was such as takes place at the present day among the civilized nations of the West ; and the Hindus probably gave more than they took. The medical science of the Greeks and several of the systems of their philosophy testify to undoubted Hindu influence. But down to the eleventh century, that is, during the entire period when their civilization was on the whole progressive, their literature does not bear any trace of foreign influence to speak of. They thought, they observed, they expressed in their own way. In nature, close interbreeding leads to degeneration, and one of the causes of the decay of the Hindu intellect was the restriction of its culture to one caste, the Bráhmans. There was not only no admixture of foreign blood, but even an admixture of such closely related blood as that of two classes of a community was prevented when the caste-system was firmly established. Hindu thought became at first stereotyped, then lost all its vigour and gradually decayed. The Mahomedan contact introduced foreign blood ; and partial regeneration of the Hindu intellect in the thirteenth and subsequent centuries was largely owing to this influence. One of the important features of this revival was the recognition by its leaders of the equality of man which is one of the fundamental tenets of the Mahomedan religion. Kabir in Northern India, Chaitanya in Bengal, Eknáth in Maháráshtra and Nának in the Punjab all denounced caste.* For the first time in the history of the Hindus, earnest attempts were made to popularise knowledge. The Rámáyana and the Mahábhárata which had hitherto been sealed books to the people were rendered into all the important vernaculars.† The greatest Hindu poets during the Mahomedan period all wrote in the vernaculars which the people could understand; and they were mostly Vaishnavas who, to a great extent at least, ignored caste-distinction. But this democratic tendency in Hindu literature was confined to religious and socio-religious subjects, as indeed it was bound

* The work of Kabir, Nának, and of Chaitanya has already been referred to. Eknáth, a Márathi poet of note, was a Bráhman. He not only preached against caste and other social disabilities, but "boldly carried his principles into practice. On one occasion one of his audience, a pious and intelligent Mahar [one of the lowest castes whose very touch would be pollution to a high caste man] asked Eknáth, while he was urging his usual views, whether he would be an examplar of the principle that before God a Bráhman and a Mahar are equal, by dining at his house. The poet had the courage of his opinions, and next day he went to the house of the man who had questioned him, and there publicly partook of food prepared by the Mahar's wife." (Acworth "Ballads of the Marathas" p. xxv). Many stories are current of the persecution which Eknáth suffered at the hands of the Bráhmans. On several occasions he was excommunicated, and once his works were publicly thrown into the Godávari. He lived about the end of the sixteenth century.

† Sridhar, who rendered the Rámáyana and the Mahábhárata into Márathi early in the eighteenth century, says in the preface to one of his works: "The Pandits should not neglect this poem because it is written in the Prákrit (popular) language; where the subject treated of is the same, whether written in Márathi or Sanskrit the meaning must be the same ... ... Women do not understand Sanskrit, and in this respect, their helplessness may be likened to that of a weak person distressed with thirst standing at the side of a deep well."

to be, the literature treating almost exclusively of such subjects. The Mahomedan literature, which the Hindus studied largely especially from the time of Akbar when Persian was made the official language, did not differ in its character much from the Hindu literature. Besides astronomy and mathematics, they both dealt chiefly with religious, social and moral subjects. It is true the Mahomedan literature possessed histories, which the Hindu literature may be said to be almost devoid of. But the histories are not so much histories of the people or of the most advanced sections of them, as narratives of the deeds of kings and the members of their courts, of bloodshed and intrigue. Nowhere in the east the people have ever had any political power such as several of the most advanced nations of the West have acquired for themselves. Their political history is consequently a blank.

English education first initiated the Hindus into a historical literature which showed how the people had come to be a great political power among several of the most civilized nations of the West; how they had wrested important privileges from unwilling tyrants; how they had risen against despots, deposed them, nay even executed them and established republican forms of government. The Hindus had known of kings wading to the throne through blood even of near relatives, they had known of conspiracies among highplaced officials to depose or kill tyrannical or otherwise obnoxious sovereigns, but they had never known the people to have been associated with any political movement of importance. It is true they had long been familiar with representative government ; but it was strictly of a local character. The jurisdiction of the village or caste *punchayet* never extended far beyond the limits of the village. It was with English education, that the Hindus imbibed the idea of a national representative government. They came to know that the sovereign of the great British Empire could not get a single penny unless the representatives of the people voted it ; that the great Englishmen, who in India set up or deposed, rewarded or punished kings ruling over large territories were accountable for their deeds to those representatives, and that one of those magnates had actually been arraigned before a tribunal of justice for his misdeeds in India. They had known of emperors summarily punishing erring governors ; but the idea of the people or their representatives having any voice in such matters was quite new to them. The growth of democracy in the West was quite a revelation to them ; and it made a powerful impression. Hitherto politics had among the Hindus been almost entirely disassociated from literature; the literary men had scarcely ever been known to take part in political movements or concern themselves about the political rights of the people. There were writers like the Maráthi Eknáth who advocated the equality of man in religion, and who denounced social disabilities ; but equality in political matters and representative form of government were new ideas introduced by English education, and they made a deep impression upon the Hindu intellect. Soon after the establishment of English schools, there grew up men like Harish Chandra Mukherji and Rámgopál Ghosh* who ably advocated the cause of the people and agitated for their rights. Writing as early as 1838, twenty years after the establishment of the first English school in Bengal, Sir C. Trevelyan recognised in the educated youth of that province a strong desire for representative form of Government. Some of his observations in this connection are so suggestive and are made in such a sympathetic spirit that they may be aptly quoted here. Coming from the North-Western Province to Bengal, he was struck by the remarkable difference in the political altitude of the better class people in the two provinces. In the former, where English education had scarcely penetrated yet, the people had no other idea of political betterment than the absolute expulsion of the English; in Bengal, on the other hand, where English education had already made some progress, some form of representative national assembly was held up as the

* Harish chandra Mukherji was born in 1824. He was the editor of the *Hindu Patriot* newspaper from 1853 until his death in 1861. He warmly advocated the cause of the ryots oppressed by the Indigo planters. He was prosecuted by the planters for the charges he had brought against them in his journal. The planters got a decree, and his house was attached and auctioned of. Those who accuse the educated Indians of apathy to the interest of the lower classes will do well to bear this fact in mind.

Rámgopál Ghose was born in 1815. He took a very prominent part in the politics of his day. His speech on the Charter act of 1853 was spoken of by the *Times* as a "masterpiece of oratory." He died in 1868. His speeches were published in a collected form in Calcutta

ideal. "No doubt, both the schemes of national improvement [the sudden and absolute expulsion of the English, and the gradual formation of a national representative assembly]," says Trevelyan, "suppose the termination of the English rule; but while that event is the beginning of the one, it is only the conclusion of the other. In one, the sudden and violent overthrow of our Government is a necessary preliminary: in the other, a long continuance of our administration, and the gradual withdrawal of it as the people became fit to govern themselves, are equally indispensable."*

With the progress of English education, the idea of representative government has taken deep root into the Hindu mind. It has been fostered not only by the spirit of English literature with its Milton, Burke and Mill, but also by the living sympathy of a few noble-minded Britons,† who have cordially helped or guided the political aspirations of educated Hindus. Political Associations have sprung up in various parts of India, some of the more notable among which are the British Indian Association and the Indian Association in Bengal,

Rise of political Associations under English influence; the British Indian Association &c.

---

* Trevelyan, " On the Education of the people of India" (London, 1838), p. 200.

† Among these mention may be made of George Thompson, Allan O. Hume and Sir William Wedderburn. George Thompson a distinguished orator, came to India in 1833. It was with his active co-operation that the Landholders' Association (which was afterwards converted into the British Indian Association) was established. The active part taken by Mr. Hume and Sir William Wedderburn in the National Congress is well known to need any mention here.

RISE OF POLITICAL ASSOCIATIONS.

the Bombay Presidency Association and the Puná Sárvajanik Sabhá in Bombay, and the Mahajana Sabhá in Madras. The oldest of these, the British Indian Association of Calcutta, came into existence in the year 1851. It is an association of recognized influence, and its opinion is sought for by government on all legislative measures of importance. From its foundation it has counted among its members, the pick of the landed aristocracy of Bengal. Kristodás Pál,* one of the greatest journalists that India has produced, was its Secretary from 1879 to 1884. The Indian Association of Calcutta was established in 1876. The Puná Sárvajanik Sabhá was started in 1870 with the object of affording "facilities to the people for knowing the real intentions and objects of Government as also adequate means for securing their rights by making timely representations to Government of the real circumstances in which they are placed." The Journal of the Sabhá often contains matter of considerable value. The Bombay Presidency Association was founded in 1889. The East

---

* Kristodás Pál was born in the year 1838. He was Editor of the *Hindu Patriot* from 1861 till his death which occurred in 1884. He was for sometime, member of the Imperial Legislative Council and his services were thus acknowledged by Lord Ripon : "By this melancholy event, [the death of Kristodás Pál,] we have lost from amongst us a colleague of distinguished ability, from whom we had on all occasions received assistance, of which we readily acknowledge the value . . . . Mr. Kristodás Pál owed the honorable position to which he had attained to his own exertions. His intellectual attainments were of a high order, his rhetorical gifts were acknowledged by all who heard him, and were enhanced, when addressing this Council, by his thorough mastery over the English language."

Indian Association was founded twenty years ago "for the independent and disinterested advocacy and promotion, by all legitimate means, of the public interest and welfare of the inhabitants of India generally."

Unquestionably the most important political movement of modern India is what is known as the National Congress. It has brought the political aspirations of educated Indians to a focus. The Congress came into existence in the year 1885. Since then, it has met annually at some important place in India. Delegates from every part of India representing many important interests attend its meetings.* The following statement exhibits the number of delegates who attended the last five sessions of the Congress :—

The National Congress.

Year.	Place.	Number of Delegates.
1890	Calcutta	677
1891	Nagpur	812
1892	Allahabad	625
1893	Lahore	867
1894	Madras	1163

* Writing about the National Congress, Sir Richard Garth, late Chief Justice of Bengal, says : "I am aware that amongst many of our countrymen, and by a certain section of the Press, both here and in India, these Congresses have been regarded with disfavour. Their motives have been impugned, their proceedings ridiculed, and attempts have been made to depreciate their importance, by disparaging the rank and position of the delegates who composed them. All this seems to me very much to be regretted. It is unjust, ungenerous, and impolitic......It is undoubtedly the fact, that the gentlemen who attended these Congresses are for the most part in high social position, and the recognised leaders of native thought and opinion ; and if in their honest endeavours to correct abuses, and to bring about what they believe to be wholesome reforms, they are treated unfairly by the English Press, what wonder is it that the crowd of disaffected scribblers, who write in the native papers would vent their

A large proportion of the delegates belong to the legal profession. But other occupations are also well represented. Among those who attended the last congress, there were present: zamindars or landholders, 275; merchants, bankers and contractors, 167; teachers, 68; editors and managers of journals, 34; doctors, 11. Besides committees in all parts of India, the Congress has a committee in England which reckons among its members several members of the House of Commons. The organ of the Congress is a monthly journal called "India" published in England. The following resolutions were passed by the last Congress which met at Madras in December, 1894, under the presidency of Mr. Alfred Webb M. P.: —

I. (a) That this Congress respectfully enters its emphatic protest against the injustice and impolicy of imposing excise duty on cottons manufactured in British India, as such excise is calculated to cripple seriously the infant mill industry of this country.

(b) That this Congress puts on record its firm conviction that in proposing this excise the interests of India have been sacrificed to those of Lancashire, and it strongly deprecates any such surrender of Indian interests by the Secretary of State.

(c) That in case the Excise Bill becomes law this Congress earnestly prays that the Government of India will without delay seek the sanction of the Secretary of State to exercise the powers which the Bill confers on Government to exempt all cottons from 20th to 24th from the operation of the Act.

(d) That the President be authorised to telegraph the above Resolution to the Government of India and to the Secretary of State.

---

spleen and indignation in the only way open to them, by abusing the British Government." "A few plain Truths about India" pp. 10-11.

II. (a) That this Congress desires to express the profound alarm which has been created by the action of Government in interfering with the existing Permanent Settlement in Bengal and Behar (in the matter of Survey and other cesses) and with the terms of sanads of permanently settled estates in Madras; and, deeming such interference with solemn pledges a national calamity, hereby pledges itself to oppose in all possible legitimate ways all such reactionary attacks on permanent settlements and their holders and resolves to petition Parliament in that behalf.

(b) That this Congress regrets extremely that the Government of India have not only failed to carry out the pledges (given by the Secretary of State in his despatches of 1862 and 1865) for permanent settlement in the Provinces in which it does not exist, but have also failed to give effect to the policy of granting modified fixity of tenure and immunity from enhancement laid down in 1882 and 1884 by the Government of India and approved by the Secretary of State; and this Congress hereby entreats the Government of India to grant a modified fixity of tenure and immunity from enhancement of land tax for a sufficiently long period (of not less than sixty years) so as to secure to landholders the full benefits of their own improvements.

III. That this Congress, concurring in the views set forth in previous Congresses, affirms:

That fully fifty millions of the population, a number yearly increasing, are dragging out a miserable existence on the verge of starvation, and that in every decade several millions actually perish by starvation.

And humbly urges, once more, that immediate steps be taken to remedy this calamitous state of affairs.

IV. That this Congress considers the Abolition of the Council of the Secretary of State for India, as at present constituted, the necessary preliminary to all other reforms; and suggests that in its place a Standing Committee of Members of the House of Commons be appointed.

V. That this Congress, while thanking Her Majesty's Government for the promise they have made to appoint a Select Committee of Members of Parliament to enquire into the financial expenditure of India, regards the enquiry with so limited a scope as inadequate, and is of opinion that if the enquiry is to bear any practical fruit it must include an enquiry into the ability of the Indian people to bear their existing financial, burdens and the financial relations between India and the United Kingdom.

VI. That this Congress expresses its deep sense of disappointment at the despatch of the Secretary of State supporting the views of the Government of India on the question of Simultaneous Examinations, and this Congress hereby places on record its respectful but firm protest against the despatch as, among other things, introducing a new principle inconsistent with the Charter Act of 1833 and the Proclamation of the Queen of 1st November, 1858, (the solemn pledges contained in which the Secretary of State and the Government of India now seek to repudiate) by creating a disability, founded upon race; for the despatch lays down that a minimum of European officials in the Covenanted Service is indispensable.

That in the opinion of this Congress the creation of the Provincial Service is no satisfactory or permanent solution of the problem, as this Service, constituted as it is at present, falls short of the legitimate aspirations of the people; and that the interests of the subordinate service will not suffer by the concession of Simultaneous Examinations.

That no attempt has been made to make out a case against the holding of Simultaneous Examinations for the recruitment of the engineering, forest, telegraph, and the higher police service examinations, and the Congress regrets to notice that the despatches of the Secretary of State, the Government of India and the various local Governments are absolutely silent with regard to this aspect of the Resolution of the House of Commons.

That this Congress respectfully urges on Her Majesty's Government that the Resolution of the House of Commons of 2nd June, 1893, on the question of Simultaneous Examinations should be speedily carried out as an act of justice to the Indian people.

VII. That this Congress views with great dissatisfaction the system of recruiting the higher Judicial Service of the country, and is of opinion that provision should be made for proper Judicial training being given to persons who are appointed to the place of District and Sessions Judges and that the higher Judicial Service, in Bengal, the North-West Provinces and Oudh, Bombay and Madras, and the Judicial Service generally in other parts of the country, should be more largely recruited from the legal profession than is now the case.

VIII. (*a*) That this Congress is of opinion that the present constitution of the higher Civil Medical Service is anomalous, indefensible in principle and injurious in its working, and unnecessarily costly; that the time has arrived when, in the interests of public medical education and the advancement of medical service and of scientific work in the country as also in the cause of economic administration, the Civil Medical Service of India should be reconstructed on the basis of such service in other civilized countries, wholly detached from, and independent of, Military Service.

(*b*) That the very unsatisfactory position and prospects of members of the subordinate Civil Medical Service (Assistant-Surgeon and Civil Hospital Assistants) compared with members of similar standing in other departments of the Public Service require thorough investigation and redress, and we pray that Government will grant for the purpose an open enquiry by a mixed Commission of official and non-official members.

(*c*) That whilst this Congress views with satisfaction the desire of the Imperial Government to reorganise the Chemical Analyser's department with a view to its administration as an independent scientific department, it earnestly hopes that Government will not fail to recognise the responsible and meritorious work of Assistants, or as they in reality are, Government Chemical Analysers, and place them on the footing of Specialists.

IX. *(a)* That this Congress, in concurrence with the preceding Congress, considers that the creation of a Legislative Council for the Province of the Punjab is an absolute necessity for the good government of that Province, and, having regard to the fact that a Legislative Council has been created for the N.-W. Provinces, requests that no time should be lost in creating such a Council for the Punjab.

(b) That this Congress, in concurrence with the preceding Congress, is of opinion that the rules now in force under the Indian Councils Act of 1892 are materially defective, and prays that His Excellency the Viceroy in Council will be pleased to have fresh rules framed in a liberal spirit with a view to a better working of the Act and suited to the conditions and requirements of each Province.

X. That this Congress wishes to express its respectful condolence, and sympathise with the Royal Family of Mysore in their recent sad and sudden bereavement, and at the same time to testify to its deep sense of the loss which has been sustained in the death of the Mahárájá of Mysore not only by the State over which he ruled with such wisdom and ability, but also by all the Indian peoples to whom his constitutional reign was at once a vindication of their political capacity, an example for their active emulation, and an earnest of their future political liberties.

XI. *(a)* That, in the opinion of the Congress, the time has now arrived when the system of trial by Jury may be safely extended, in cases triable by Sessions Courts, to many parts of the country where it is not at present in force.

(b) That, in the opinion of the Congress, the innovation made in 1872 in the system of trial by Jury, depriving the verdicts of Juries of all finality, has proved injurious to the country, and that the powers then, for the first time, vested in Sessions Judges and High Courts, of setting aside verdicts of acquittal, should be at once withdrawn.

(c) That, in the opinion of this Congress, it is extremely desirable that the power at present vested in Government to appeal against acquittals be taken away.

XII. That this Congress having till now appealed, though in vain, for many successive years to the Government of India, and also to the Secretary of State, to remove one of the greatest defects in the system of administration, one fraught with incalculable oppression to all classes of people throughout the country, and having noted with satisfaction the admission of the evil by two former Secretaries of State (Lord Kimberley and Lord Cross) and being of opinion that reform is thoroughly practicable, as was shown by Messrs. R. C. Dutt, M. M. Ghose, and P. M Mehta, entreats the Government of India to direct the immediate appointment in each province of a Committee (one-half at least of whose members shall be non-official natives of India qualified, by education and experience in the workings of various Courts, to deal with the question) to prepare each a scheme for the complete separation of all Judicial and Executive functions in their own province with as little additional cost to the State as may be practicable, and the submission of such schemes with the opinions of the several Governments at an early date.

XIII. That this Congress affirms the opinion of the preceding Congress that the time has now come to raise the status of the Chief Court of the Punjab to that of a Chartered High Court in the interests of the administration of justice in that Province.

XIV. That having regard to the fact that the embarrassed condition of the finances of the country has been giving cause for grave anxiety for some years past, this Congress records its firm conviction that the only remedy for the present state of things is a material curtailment in the expenditure on the Army Services and other Military expenditure, Home Charges, and the cost of Civil administration, and, in view of the proposed appointment of a Parliamentary Committee to investigate the subject, this Congress strongly recommends that the Standing Congress Committees of the several Presidencies and Provinces should, so far as practicable, make arrangements to send to England at least one well qualified delegate from each Presidency or Province to urge such reduction before the Committee.

XV. That this Congress is emphatically of opinion that it is inexpedient, in the present state of education in the country, that Government grants for higher education should in any way be withdrawn, and, concurring with the previous Congresses, affirms in the most emphatic manner the importance of increasing public expenditure on all branches of education, and the expediency of establishing Technical Schools and Colleges.

XVI. That this Congress concurs with its predecessors in strongly advocating:

(a) The reduction of the Salt duty by at least the amount of its latest enhancement:

(b) The raising of the Income Tax taxable minimum from five hundred to one thousand rupees;

(c) The persistent pressure by the Government of India on all provincial administrations to induce them to carry out, in its integrity, the excise policy enunciated in paragraphs 103, 104, 105 of the despatch published in the *Gazette of India* of March, 1890, and the introduction of a simple system of local option in the case of all villages:

(d) The introduction into the Code of Criminal Procedure of a provision enabling accused persons in warrant cases to demand that instead of being tried by the magistrate they may be committed to the Court of Sessions;

(e) The fundamental reform of the Police Administration by a reduction in the numbers and an increase in the salaries and in the qualifications of the lower grades, and their far more careful enlistment: and by the selection for the higher posts of gentlemen of higher capacities more in touch with the respectable portions of the community and less addicted to military pretensions than the majority of existing Deputy Inspectors-General, Superintendents, and Assistant-Superintendents of Police are at present;

(f) A modification of the rules under the Arms Act so as to make them equally applicable to all residents in, or visitors to, India without distinction of creed, caste, or colour; to ensure the liberal concession of licenses wherever wild animals habitually destroy human life, cattle, or crops; and to make all licenses, granted under the revised rules, of life-long tenure revocable only on proof of misuse, and valid throughout the provincial jurisdiction in which they are issued;

(g) The establishment of Military Colleges in India whereat natives of India, as defined by statute, may be educated and trained for a military career as commissioned or non-commissioned officers (according to capacity and qualifications) of the Indian army;

(h) The organising throughout the more warlike races of the Empire of a system of militia services, and

(i) The authorising and stimulating of a widespread system of volunteering, such as obtains in Great Britain, amongst the people of India;

(j) The discontinuance of the Exchange Compensation allowance granted to undomiciled European and Eurasian *employés* of Government, involving an annual expenditure of over a crore of rupees while the Exchequer is in a condition of chronic embarrassment;

(k) The giving effect to the report of the Parliamentary members of the India Office Committee on the subject of the Rules, Orders, and Practices in Indian Cantonments with regard to Prostitution and Contagious Disease, and endorsing their conclusions:

(i) That the system and incidental practices described in that report and the statutory rules, so far as they authorised or permitted the same, did not accord with the plain meaning and intention of the resolution of the House of Commons of June 5th, 1888; and

(ii) That the only effective method of preventing these systematic malpractices is by express legislation.

XVII. That this Congress hereby empowers its President to convey to the Government of India its opinion that the powers proposed to be conferred on District Magistrates by amendments and additions to section 15 of Police Act V. of 1861, with respect to the levy of the costs of punitive police and of granting compensation, are of a most arbitrary, dangerous, and unprecedented character.

XVIII. That this Congress records its deep-felt gratitude to the Government of India for its circular resolution No. 22 F, published in the Supplement to the *Gazette of India*, dated 20th October 1894, and its appreciation of the generous principle which it enunciates of subordinating fiscal interests to the needs and agricultural interests of the rayat population in the management of forests ;

And would further represent that in forests falling under classes 3 and 4 of the said resolutions, fuel, grazing concessions, fodder, small timber for building houses and making agricultural implements, edible forest products, etc., may be granted free of charge in all cases, under such restrictions as to quantity, etc., as the Government may deem proper; and that wherever hardship may be felt under present conditions, the policy of the said resolution may be carried out with reference to existing forest areas and existing reserve boundaries so adjusted as to leave a sufficiently large margin to facilitate the enjoyment by the agricultural population of their communal rights without molestation and annoyance by the minor subordinates of the department.

XIX. That this Congress being of opinion that the Government of India's notification of 25th June, 1891, in the Foreign Department, gagging the press in territories under British administration in Native States, is retrograde, arbitrary, and mischievous in its nature, and opposed to sound statesmanship and to the liberty of the people, most respectfully enters its emphatic protest against the same, and entreats its cancellation without delay.

XX. That this Congress views with apprehension the arbitrary policy of the Government with regard to the imposition of water-cess, introducing as it does a disturbing element in taxation, and suggests that the imposition of the said cess be regulated by certain defined principles, affording security to the rights of landowners and of persons investing money on land.

XXI. That this Congress earnestly entreats Her Majesty's Government to grant the prayer of Her Majesty's Indian subjects resident in the South African colonies by vetoing the Bill of the Colonial Government disfranchising Indian subjects.

District and Local Boards. The principle of representation has received some application in Indian administration within the last quarter of a century, especially since the viceroyalty of Lord Ripon. The Local Self-government act of 1885 provided a District Board for every district; and the Local Government may, by notification, establish a Local Board in any one sub-division or in any two or more sub-divisions combined. Two thirds of the members of Local Boards in the more advanced districts are elected; and Local Boards are entitled to elect such proportion of the members of the District Boards as Government may from time to time direct. The Local Board is presided over by a chairman who is elected by the members from among their own number. The Vice-chairman of a District Board is always elected; but the Chairman has hitherto been appointed by the Local Government, though the Act provides that, should the Government in any case so direct, he may be elected by the members of the District Board from among their own number.

The following statement shows the constitution of the District and Local Boards in 1891-92 : *

---

*" Moral and Material Progress and Condition of India 1891-92," p. 115

Province.	Class of Board.	Total number of Members.	By Qualification.		By Employment.		By Race.	
			Nominated	Elected.	Officials.	Non-Officials.	Europeans, &c.	Natives.
Madras*	District	654	377	277	226	428	118	536
	Local	1,141	1,141	—	317	824	65	1,076
Bombay	District	503	277	226	139	374	78	425
	Local	2,984	1,642	1,342	661	2,323	122	2,862
Bengal	District	790	481	309	253	537	197	593
	Local	1,248	778	469	154	1,094	105	1,143
N.-W. Provinces	District	1,561	277	1,284	266	1,295	56	1,595
	Local	1335,	863	472	245	1,090	89	1,246
Punjab	District	1,584	595	989	89	1,496	11	1,573
	Local	1,132	241	891	109	1,023	17	1,115
Central Provinces	District	371	224	147	61	310	130	241
Assam†	District	128	32	96	16	112	5	123
Berar	Local	306	105	201	24	282	—	306
India	District	6,474	2,772	3,702	1,305	5,169	690	5,784
	Local	7,263	4,262	3,001	1,245	6,018	303	6,960

* Excluding Unions. † Figures for 1890-91.

MUNICIPALITIES.

Forty years ago Municipal administration was confined to the three Presidency towns. The local affairs of every large town are now managed by its Municipality, the majority of the members of which are elected by the townspeople. The following table exhibits the growth of the elective system between 1882 and 1892:*—

Province.	Total Members of Municipalities		Nominated.		Elected.		Official.		Non-official.		European, &c.		Natives.	
	1881-82.	1891-92.	1881-82.	1891-92.	1881-82.	1891-92.	1881-82.	1891-92.	1881-82.	1891-92.	1881-82.	1891-92.	1881-82.	1891-92.
Madras	804	906	650	409	69	497	355	216	449	690	289	169	515	737
Bombay	2,590	2,493	1,839	1,529	48	964	919	708	1,671	1,785	407	222	2,183	2,271
Bengal	2,372	2,208	1,814	1,004	85	1,204	621	387	1,751	1,821	543	218	1,829	1,990
N.-W. Provinces & Oudh	1,460	1,555	328	319	694	1,236	477	287	983	1,268	347	156	1,113	1,399
Punjab	2,171	1,050	1,497	851	28	805	692	314	1,479	1,342	400	125	1,771	1,531
Central Provinces	640	634	8	193	397	441	230	157	401	477	139	51	501	583
Assam	100	126	70	75	—	51	47	50	53	76	37	25	63	101
Lower Burma	97	321	65	210	—	111	43	84	54	237	52	74	45	247
Berar	97	128	60	38	—	90	50	36	47	92	37	17	60	111
Coorg	49	53	32	45	—	8	17	17	32	39	7	6	42	47
TOTAL	10,380	10,080	6,363	4,673	1,321	5,407	3,460	2,256	6,920	7,824	2,258	1,063	8,102	9,017

* "Statement exhibiting the Moral and Material Progress and Condition of India," 1891-92 p. 94.

There were in 1892 all over India 755 municipalities, with a population within municipal limits of 15,742,581 and a revenue of Rs. 33,955,940.

The Indian Councils. The Indian Councils Act of 1892, though it did not come up to the expectations of the Indian National Congress was unquestionably an important step towards the growth of the elective system in India. It carried the principle of representation in Indian administration, though in a tentative and therefore imperfect form, from the local to the imperial stage. The Legislative Council of the Governor General has been "expanded by four additional members to be nominated under rules framed by him, with the approval of the Secretary of State, with a certain latitude of interpellation. To a considerable extent, the representative principle has been recognised in respect to the nominations both to the Council of the Governor General and to those of the Councils of Madras, Bombay, Bengal, and the North-West Provinces. The large municipalities, for instance, groups of Local Boards, Chambers of Commerce, Senates of the Universities, and wherever such classes exist, bodies of influential landholders, or others of undoubted rank, whose interests are fairly homogeneous and are bound up with those of a considerable portion of the rural population, all these can be called upon to elect the representative whom they respectively propose for nomination. In the case of the remaining seats, which, so far as the non-official members are concerned, are the minority, the rules provide for the nomination of such persons as the Local

'Governments think will best represent the views of branches of the community not possessing sufficient power of combination to recommend a man of their own choice."*

The introduction of the elective principle into local as well as the imperial administration, in its present restricted and experimental form, is evidently a step towards an end. What that end is to be cannot even be guessed now. But, in this connection it would be interesting to read the following passage from the writings of one of the most thoughtful of Englishmen that India has ever seen :—

"This class [the English-educated] is at present [1838] a small minority, but it is continually receiving accretions from the youth who are brought up at the different English seminaries. It will in time become the majority ; and it will then be necessary to modify the political institutions to suit the increased intelligence of the people, and their capacity for self-government. The change will thus be peaceably and gradually effected : there will be no struggle, no mutual exasperation ; the natives will have independence, after first learning how to make a good use of it : we shall exchange profitable subjects for still more profitable allies. The present administrative connection benefits families, but a strict commercial union between the first manufacturing and the first producing country in the world, would be a solid foundation of strength and prosperity to our whole nation."

* " Statement exhibiting the Moral and Material Progress and Condition of India, 1891-92." p. 68.

"From being obstinate enemies, the Britons soon became attached and confiding friends; and they made more strenuous efforts to retain the Romans, than their ancestors had done to resist their invasion. It will be a shame to us if, with our greatly superior advantages, we also do not make our premature departure be dreaded as a calamity. It must not be said in after ages, that the "groans of the Britons" were elicited by the breaking up of the Roman empire; and the groans of the Indians by the continued existence of the British."*

Individuality as a developmental force in modern Hindu literature.

The underlying principle of the democratic movement of modern Europe is the sense of individuality, which, instilled into the Hindu mind under English influence, has greatly influenced Hindu literature. Among the Hindus, the individual has ever been more or less merged in the community. There has never been any restriction upon thought; and while civilization was progressive, the Hindus displayed considerable individuality in their literature and science. But, with the decay of civilization, Hindu thought practically restricted to the Bráhman caste, began to run in a narrow groove. Since the fourteenth century some of the great writers, like the great reformers, have shown much originality and independence of thought. The very fact that they wrote in the vernaculars which the learned steeped in

---

* Trevelyan "Education of the people of India," (1838) pp 194-197.

Sanskrit lore heartily despised, shows that they could think for themselves. But scarcely any of them ever went beyond Hindu mythology either for their subjects or for their conceptions of character; and none of them ever attempted to be rid of the fetters of rhyme. Ráma, Krishna, Siva or his consort, Umá, with the legends which had gathered round their names in the course of centuries are the principal figures in their compositions. Between the thirteenth and eighteenth centuries Hindu thought scarcely ever ventured beyond the well-beaten tracks of religion and morality. There were numerous writers both in Sanskrit and vernaculars. But either commentary on some ancient philosophical or religious work, or poem on some mythological subject was the goal of their literary labour. The following list of works of a rather prolific writer who lived in Bengal about 1830 will convey some idea of the nature of their writings :*—

"1. A commentary on the *Chhandomanjari*, a treatise on prosody, so framed as to express the praises of Krishna.

2. A commentary on *Santi Sataka*, a work on abstraction from the world.

3. *Sadachara Nirnaya* a compilation from the laws on the Vaishnava ritual, containing 140 leaves or 280 pages in prose and verse.

4. *Dhatu Dipa*, a metrical explanation of Sanskrit roots in the order of the ten conjugations, containing 500 slokas.

5. *Annadika Kosha*, a metrical dictionary of works comprising the Unadi postfixes in two parts, of which one contains words having more meanings than one, and the other words of only one meaning, 300 slokas.

---

* Adam's "Reports on Vernacular Education" edited by J. Long Calcutta (1886) pp. 187-189.

6. *Rogarnava Tarini,* a compilation from various medical works on the treatment of disease, containing 174 leaves or 348 pages, part being in verse, extending to 6,000 slokas.

7. *Arishta Nirupana,* a description of the various signs or symptoms of approaching death, a compilation in verse of 400 slokas, contained in 14 leaves or 28 pages.

8. *Sarira Vivritti,* a treatise on the progress of gestation and on the seats in the human body of the various humours, &c., in prose and verse, comprised in 22 leaves or 44 pages.

9. *Lekha Darpana,* on letter writing, principally in prose, 15 leaves or 30 pages.

10. *Dwaita Siddhanta Dipika,* a defence of the distinction between the human and divine spirits in opposition to pantheism, contained in 71 leaves or 142 pages.

11. *Hariharastotra,* the praises of Vishnu and Siva, in nine slokas, so composed that every sloka has two senses:—of which one is applicable to Vishnu and the other to Siva.

12. *Siva Sarmadastotra,* 8 slokas, containing a double sense, one expressing the praises of Siva and the other some different meaning.

13. A commentary on the preceding.

14. *Yamakavinoda,* 8 slokas, containing the praises of Krishna, written in a species of alliteration by repetition of the same sounds.

15. A commentary on the preceding.

16. *Bhavanuprasa,* eight slokas, containing the praises of Krishna, in a species of alliteration.

17. *Antaslapika,* four slokas, in question and answer so framed that the answer to one in question contains the answers to all the questions in the same sloka.

18. *Radha Krishnastotra,* eight slokas, containing the praises of Radha and Krishna, and so framed that they may read either backward or forward.

19. A commentary on the above, consisting of two leaves or four pages.

20. A specimen of *Alata Chakra Bandha,* two slokas, so framed that each sloka contains materials for sixty-four slokas by the transposition of each letter in succession from the beginning to the end,—first the

thirty-two syllables from left to right, and afterwards the thirty-two from right to left.

21. *Sansaya Satani,* a commentary on the Bhagavat Purana now in progress of composition.

22. A commentary on Yama Shatpadi, which contains the praises of Narayana by Yama.

23. *Stavakadamba,* seventy-six slokas, containing the praises of Saraswati, Ganga, Yamuna, Nityanand, Chaitanya, Vrindavana, Krishna, and Radhika.

24. *Govindarupamriti,* forty-one slokas, containing a description of the qualities of Krishna.

25. *Krishna Keli Suddhaka,* four hundred slokas, on the loves of Radha and Krishna, principally occupied with the period extending from the jealousy of Radha to her reconciliation with Krishna

26. A commentary on the above, of thirty-seven leaves or seventy-four pages.

27. *Govinda Mahodaya,* 800 slokas, containing the history of Radha's eight female friends or attendants.

28. *Govinda Charita,* 350 slokas, containing the lamentation of Radha on account of her separation from Krishna.

29. *Bhakta Mala,* 5,000 slokas, explanatory of the different forms in which Krishna has been propitious to his votaries, translated from Hindi into Sanskrit.

30. *Durjana Mihira Kalanala,* a defence of the doctrine of the Vaishnavas.

31. *Bhakta Lilamrita,* a compilation from the eighteen Puranas of every thing relating to Krishna.

32. *Parakiya Mata Khandana,* an attempt to establish that the milk-women of Vrindavana with whom Krishna disported were his own wives, and not those of the milkmen of that place.

33. A commentary on Kavi Chandra's praise of Hara and Gauri (Siva and Parvati), consisting of 10 leaves or 20 pages.

34. *Desika Nirnaya,* a compilation on the qualifications of a spiritual guide and on the tests by which one should be selected.

35. A commentary on Srutyadhyaya, one of the books of the Bhagavata Purana on the history of Radha and Krishna, consisting of 22 leaves or 44 pages.

36 *Krishnavilasa*, 109 slokas, on the amours of Krishna The preceding works are written in Sanskrit; the following chiefly in Bengalee viz.

37. *Rama Rasayana*, the history of Rama, written on 889 leaves or 1,778 pages, containing 30,000 slokas.

38 *Patra Prakasa*, 8 leaves or 16 pages, on letter writing, the example in Sanskrit and the explanation in Bengalee."

There is undoubtedly good deal of originality in the commentaries such as those of Sáyanáchárvya or Raghunáth. Throughout the Mahomedan period there were at such places as Benares and Nadiyá great Sanskrit scholars with keen intellects. But the intellect was usually exercised, it might almost be said in many cases wasted, upon barren though subtle disputations about knotty points of law, logic or metaphysics.

The sense of individuality fostered by the English environment has been a fruitful source of important changes. In religion, it first created a somewhat chaotic confusion, but later on led to rationalistic Hinduism ; in social polity, it has diminished the stringency of caste rules. But its effect upon literature has been far more remarkable than upon religion or society. The Hindu cannot break through his social bonds without exposing himself to penalties which cannot always be regarded lightly. But there are no such restrictions upon independence of thought in literature. Educated Hindus who hold aloof from reforms which would subject them to the penalties of excommunication, have no hesitation to exhibit their individuality in literature. Vernacular literature in all parts of India has made rapid strides towards progress within the last fifty years; and that this progress is attributable to English influence is inferable from the fact, that the progress is greatest where English education has spread most, and least where it is most backward. Purely vernacular or purely Sanskrit education has done little for the improvement of vernacular literature. In the North-Western Province and in the Bombay Presidency, the educational policy of Government was for a long time to encourage vernacular education almost exclusively in the former, and mainly in the latter. In Bengal, on the other hand, the policy has been, at least from 1835, to encourage English education; and Bengali literature has grown to be much richer than either Hindi or Márátḥi, though before the establishment of the British rule the Hindi literature was far superior to, and the Márátḥi literature by no means inferior to the Bengali literature. The most eminent writers in vernacular literatures within the last fifty years have all been English-educated men.

CHAPTER III.

INFLUENCE OF ENGLISH INDUSTRIALISM.

About the beginning of the last century, the civilisation of England cannot be said, on the whole, to have been superior at least decidedly, to that of India. This is true not only with regard to spiritual and intellectual development, but also with regard to the outer forms of civilisation, the comforts and conveniences of civilised life. Even in her manufactures, England had not yet exhibited any signs of that supremacy which she now enjoys. Her roads were no better than those of India. Traffic was generally impossible during the winter months as it was in India during the rains. The food of London had mostly to be carried on pack horses. In the country, the fields were not drained, and intermittent fevers caused sad havoc among the rural population of England as of India. Epidemics were frequent in both the countries. The cities of England were not,

Industrial condition of England and of India about the middle of the eighteenth century.

less full of filth, than those of India. Calicoes had long been exported from India before they could be manufactured in England. English cloth had to be sent to Holland to be bleached or dyed, while dyeing was a flourishing industry in India. The silk-trade of England had to be protected in 1765 by the exclusion of the French silk from English markets. The English were indebted for the finer varieties of linen to Germany and Belgium, while India manufactured muslins of such exquisite fineness, that a piece could be made, fifteen yards wide, weighing only 900 grains. England imported nearly two thirds of the iron and much of the salt, earthen ware &c. used by her. Until 1774, the weaving of a fabric composed entirely of cotton was considered penal in England. Cotton manufactures were largely imported from India ; in the seventeen years ending 1808-1809,their annual average was £1,539,478.*
It was only towards the close of the eighteenth century that the spinning wheel was introduced into England.

But England made rapid strides towards Industrial progress while India remained stationary. In 1769, James Watt got his patent " for a method of lessening the consumption of steam and fuel in fire-engine," and in 1787, Mr. Cartwright invented the power-loom. The cotton manufacture of England grew with wonderful rapidity. About the middle of the eighteenth century her export of cotton manufactures

Industrial expansion of England in the beginning of this century.

---

* See Vol. I. p. LXXV.

amounted only to £45,000. In 1833, the amount was no less than £46,000,000. In 1830, the first railway was constructed between Liverpool and Manchester; seven years later, the first line of telegraph was constructed; and the Atlantic was crossed by steamers about the same time.

While England was being modernised—if we can so express ourselves—India remained in the old-world condition. She was too far from Europe to feel the quickening impulse of progress which transformed that continent; and centuries of slow evolution had given the social structure of the Hindus a rigidity which unfitted it for the ready reception of a sudden impulse. The caste system had long restricted industrial occupations to low illiterate castes. The higher classes looked down upon such occupations. In the Manu Samhitá, one of the most ancient and authoritative of the Hindu codes of Law, such respectable people as physicians, goldsmiths, carpenters, vocalists, tailors, blacksmiths and dyers are classed with regard to the purity of food prepared by them, with perjurers, thieves, and adulteresses.* In a community where industries were held in such low estimation, it was not to be expected that their improvement would all of a sudden engage the attention of the only classes which could effect it. And the marvellous quickness and suddenness of the

Side note: Effect of the expansion upon Indian industries.

* Manu, IV. 84, 210-16.

Industrial Revolution did not give the Hindus any time to adapt themselves to the new order of things. English manufactures poured in, like an avalanche, and swept the indigenous industries before them. The day of manual skill, in which the Hindu artisans excelled, was over. Hand-made manufactures could no longer compete with machine-made manufactures. Hindu artisans had neither the time nor the education to assimilate the mechanical skill of modern Europe. It was not to be expected that illiterate weavers, or illiterate dyers, or illiterate miners would apply the scientific methods of modern industries to their occupations. If India had her own way, she would probably have protected her industries, as England had protected hers in the eighteenth century, and as most civilized countries protect theirs at the present day. But India could not have her own way; and a protective tariff, was not to be thought of.

Thus the first effect of the industrial expansion of England in the beginning of the present century was the ruin of the artisan population of India. The introduction of the power loom caused great distress among the weavers of England. They invoked the help of Parliament. "They begged to be sent to Canada. They proposed that the terrible power loom should be restrained by law; and when that was denied them, they rose in their despair and lawlessly overthrew the machines which were devouring the bread of their children."* But, the distress of the English weavers was

* "The 19th century" By R. Mackenzie (1892) p. 72.

only temporary. They soon had a share in the wealth created by the expansion of the cotton industry. It was not till the middle of the present century* that the mechanical skill of modern Europe was transported to India by enterprising Englishmen: and the mills and factories on modern methods started by them found employment for a portion of the artisans who were thrown out of work by the importation of the English manufactures. But, the number of such mills and factories, even after nearly half a century of growth, is comparatively very small; and the greater portion of the displaced artisans have been thrown upon agriculture for subsistence. Besides, the foreign proprietors of the mills and factories not being settled in the country their profits instead of benefiting the Indian community only swell the annual drain to Europe.

Recent growth of industrial enterprise and technical education.

Thus the immediate effect of the growth of English industrialism was to reduce the artisan class of India, to the condition of agricultural labourers, at least to a very great exent; and as the former have a more cultivated intellect than the latter, this was certainly a step backward in the intellectual movement of the Indian community. But, the mills and factories started by the English in India have served as models of what English enterprise and modern science can do: and modern industrialism has been penetrating, though very

---

* The first cotton mill in India is believed to be the Bowrea mill near Calcutta which was started in 1817. But it stood alone until 1851, when the first mill was started in western India at Broach.

slowly, into Hindu society. Within the last twenty years many new industries conducted entirely by Indian agency on modern methods have been started by the Hindus.* Technical education has also, as we shall presently see, made some progress within that period, though the progress is very small. The aversion of the upper classes for industrial occupations is gradually disappearing. Members of the highest caste are beginning to engage in industries such as tanning, oil-pressing, soap-making &c. which have hitherto been confined to the lowest castes. The Victoria Jubilee Technical Institute of Bombay was attended in 1893 by 119 students of whom no less than 70 were Bráhmans. Hindu society is adapting itself gradually to its new environment.

The progress, however, is very slow. It is only this year that the first railway line† due to purely Indian enterprise has been opened. In their competetion with the British, the advantages which the Indians have of a low standard of living and of local knowledge are more than counterbalanced by the disadvantages of want of capital and want of mechanical and scientific knowledge. There is such a superfluity of capital in Great Britain that it seeks investment in enterprises offering no higher return than that of 4 or 5 per cent. In India, on the other hand, capital is so scarce, that double this rate

<small>Difficulties of industrial progress.</small>

---

* See Book IV, chapters III and IV.

† Between Tárakesvar and Magrá in Bengal, a distance of 31 miles. The line is narrow-gauge.

of interest is hardly sufficient to attract its investment in enterprises of a risky nature. The competition of a community, the average income of whose members is not more than £2 with one the average income of whose members is not less than £33, in undertakings one of the essential conditions of the success of which is large capital is indeed very difficult. Besides, the physical environment of the Briton has favoured the development of industrial qualities, whereas the physical environment of the Hindu has favoured the development of quietism. The fact that the education which the Hindus have hitherto received is of a literary character also explains to a great extent their want of industrial enterprise. They can not very well develop the resources of their country before they know what those resources are, and how they can be developed. They have not had the necessary training.

The subject of technical education has however, during the last decade attracted some attention. There are some whose idea of technical education does not soar beyond such handicrafts as carpentry, tailoring, &c. Others there are who want art-work. A third class, more aspiring, wishes for the large manufacturing industries. Not a little confusion is frequently caused by jumbling all these up. It behoves us, therefore, to see what it is that the country more particularly requires. We are disposed to think there is not much room for expansion at present in the petty industries, such as carpentry, tailoring, shoemaking, &c. It is not the

Technical education.

making up of cloth or leather, but the manufacture of cloth or leather that is more particularly wanted in this country. Few people are in a position to use made up clothes at all, far less clothes of fine cut or nice fit, or boots and shoes of approved shape and fashionable make. Of furniture of any kind there is but little demand. Our wants in these directions are extremely limited; and they are, we think, well enough supplied at present. Besides, such technical training as is needed for the handicrafts could, we believe, be best obtained at the existing shops. Whatever field there is for enterprise in them is being occupied. It is necessary to bear this in mind in order to understand the relative importance of the different grades of technical education which we notice below.

Industrial schools.
The first school of Industry in India was established at Jabalpur in 1837 for the benefit of the Thugs and their children. In 1850, Dr. Hunter, a Surgeon in the East India Company's service at Madras, founded, at his own cost, a school of fine arts; and in the following year, be founded a school of industry for "improving the manufacture of various articles of domestic and daily use." Both of these schools were taken over by Government in 1855.

A number of industrial schools has, sprung up of late in different parts of the country, in which trades such as those of the carpenter and the blacksmith are taught. There were twentysix such schools in Bengal in 1894 divided into (*a*) three Government schools with 33 pupils; (*b*) nine Board schools with 283 pupils; (c) eight aided schools with 236 pupils; (d) six unaided schools with 213 pupils. Speaking generally, the object of them all is to teach such subjects as carpentry, blacksmith's work, mensuration, engineering, estimating, drawing, surveying by chain and compass, trigonometry, and the plane-table; together with engraving, electro-plating, tinsmithy, clock-making, embroidery or *bidri* work; not all in one school, but some in one and some in another.

In 1882, there were in the whole of India 44 industrial schools attended by 1,509 pupils. In 1892, the number of schools rose to 69, and that of pupils to 3,860.

Art schools. There was, in 1884-85, an Art school at the capital town of each of the provinces, Madras, Bengal, Bombay and the Punjab. They were attended by 655 pupils. In 1891-92, the number of Art schools rose to 6, and that of pupils attending them to 1,048. The Art schools train general and engineering draughtsmen, architects, modellers, wood-engravers, lithographers &c. With regard to the Calcutta school of Art, "the general character of the work done in the school will compare favourably with that of any Art school in the United Kingdom; and outside evidence has testified to the high class character of the students' performances, in illustrations of zoology, in modelling, wood-engraving, lithography, and illustrations of the Annals of the Royal Botanic Garden."*

---

* Resolution of the Govt. of Bengal on the report of the Education Department for 1893-94.

ART SCHOOLS.

The following extract from the Madras Education Report for 1883-84, will give an idea of the nature of the training given in the Madras School of Art:

"A pleasing and novel feature in the year's history is that the Institution is beginning to fulfil its chief object—the supply of skilled labour for various arts in districts—some students having obtained suitable employment. The engagement of one as a designer of textile fabrics is specially gratifying, for it is in relation to improved design that the school is calculated to benefit the industries of the country. Instruction in freehand was more successful than that in geometrical drawing, the failure in the latter subject being probably due to the low general educational standard of most of the students.

Useful instruction has been given and progress made in wood-carving, engraving, metal-work, and in the manufacture of stained glass windows, the students having been instructed in the process of execution as well as of design.

The Institution seems to have been very active in its manufacturing branch, turning out a quantity of high class work. Experiments too have been made in various directions as regards pottery, and valuable information collected. The discovery of superior kaolin, uncontaminated by iron, near Salem, will, it is hoped, prove an important one."

The following extracts from the annual report (for 1883-84) of Mr. Kipling, Principal of the Mayo School of Art at Lahore, will be found interesting:

"The most important work of the year and the most complete in point of accomplishment was the drawing done for the illustration of the Journal of Indian Art, including architecture, Mooltan pottery, ivory-carving, and other subjects. Drawings were also made for carpets, screens in carved wood, for choice examples of Koft work, Hoshiarpur inlay and wood-work, most of the latter being given out for execution to artizans in the districts for exhibition at the Indo-Colonial display in London. The most important piece of original design was the billiard-room for His Royal Highness the Duke of Connaught at Bagshot Park. This was begun by Ram Singh and myself during the last vacation; and we succeeded in satisfying our patrons with a project for lining the new billiard-room with an elaborate arrangement of carved wood in the style of the last century of Punjab wood decoration. These designs and drawings, though chiefly the work of myself and Ram Singh, Assistant Master, were worked upon by the younger students, who made full size experimental drawings, models, &c.—perhaps the most instructive practice that can be found. The actual work is too large and heavy to be undertaken in the school, and it is given out on contract to a carpenter at Amritsar who works under the direction of Ram Singh; while some of the choicer panels, &c., are reserved for the practice of the wood-carving class in the school. In addition to the lining of the billiard-room, all the furniture for the apartment was designed in the school, so as to be in keeping with the rest. In a similar way the design for a carved screen, the gift of the Punjab Government to the Indian Institute at Oxford, was elaborated in the school on lines suggested by Mr. Basil Champneys, the Architect of the Institute, and actually carried out at Amritsar."

Institutions for higher technical education.
But, the fate of Indian art is doomed. The demand for it is daily decreasing, and will continue to decrease as the price of labour rises. In these days of cheap imitation things, genuine art productions requiring a vast amount of labour are not likely to hold their own. It is the larger industries involving scientific methods and appliances, such as cotton manufactures, iron-smelting, paper-making, &c, which are most likely to develop the resources of the country and make it rich, and which are, therefore specially needed. There is also considerable scope for the application of the methods and results of modern science in agriculture. The skilled labour needed for the manufacturing and agricultural industries which are dependent more or less upon science is of various grades. The training

required for the operatives would manifestly be best given in primary schools. But for teachers of such schools, chemists and others under whose direction large industries, manufacturing and agricultural, are carried on, a superior degree of scientific training is required which may be called Higher Technical Education. Besides the Engineering Colleges in the different provinces, and the chemical and physical laboratories of the Medical Colleges and of such institutions as the Presidency College of Calcutta, and the Elphinstone College of Bombay there are but few institutions where higher technical education is now imparted in India. There is a class of scientific agriculture at the Poona College of Science ; and the Bombay University encourages its study by conferring a diploma in agriculture. There has been an Agricultural College at Madras for some years. The course of instruction comprises agriculture, practical farming, surveying, veterinary, geology, physical geography and physics. In 1892, the college was attended by 45 students. The Victoria Jubilee Technical Institute was founded in Bombay in 1888. In 1893 it was attended by 119 Hindu students. Instruction is given in Physics, Mechanics, Drawing, and Technological cotton manufacture and mechanical Engineering.

The following statement shows the condition of Technical Education in British India in 1884-85 :—

INTELLECTUAL CONDITION.

	University Education.		School Education.								Classes in High Schools in.			
	Engineering.		Schools of Art.		Engineering and Surveying Schools.		Industrial Schools.		Schools of Agriculture.		Art.		Agriculture.	
	Number.	Attendance.	Number.	Attendance.	Number.	Attendance.	Number.	Attendance.	Number.	Attendance.	Number.	Attendance.	Number.	Attendance.
Madras	1	19	1	162	1	106	6	249	1	96	...	...	...	...
Bombay	1	102	1	251	2	98	7	307	1	46	36	2,713	8	289
Bengal	1	42	1	157	5	278	5	172	...	...	...	...	...	...
Punjab	...	...	...	85	...	...	4	93	...	...	...	...	...	...
North-Western Provinces.	1	55	...	...	...	...	2	186	...	...	...	...	...	...
C. Provinces	...	...	...	...	7	163	19	316	...	...	...	...	...	...
Assam	...	...	...	...	...	...	1	18	...	...	...	...	...	...
Burma	...	...	...	...	5	110	1	38	...	...	...	...	...	...
Total	4	218	4	655	20	755	45	1,379	2	142	36	2,713	8	289

The following is a comparative statement showing the progress in some branches of technical education between 1882 and 1892:

CLASS OF INSTITUTION.	1881-82.		1886-87.		1891-92.	
	No.	Pupils.	No.	Pupils.	No.	Pupils.
Schools of Art	5	439	4	763	6	1,048
Industrial Schools	44	1,509	68	3,030	69	3,860
Total	49	1,948	72	3,793	75	4,908

CHAPTER IV.

INFLUENCE OF MODERN NATURAL SCIENCE.

Education in India until recently literary.
From the brief survey which we have taken of the history of the Hindu intellect in ancient times it will be seen that its progress had chiefly been in the fields of literature and philology, and of the mathematical and mental sciences. They had made great progress in medicine and surgery; and works like those of Charaka and Susruta may still be read with interest, and even with profit. They had studied the properties of numerous plants and minerals, but only so far as was necessary for medical purposes. Natural science as such was not cultivated by the Hindus or any of the other great nations of antiquity. It is essentially of recent growth. It was only towards the latter half of the last century, that those discoveries were made in Europe, especially in France, which laid the foundation of modern science; and it is only within the last fifty years that it has made the greatest progress. When schools for English education were

established in this country (about 1820) natural science had scarcely been grafted upon the curriculum of education in England ; and though one of the main objects of English education was to teach modern science, very little of it was actually taught until quite recently. The elements of optics, hydrostatics, and mechanics comprised the entire course of natural philosophy, and these subjects too were taught as branches rather of mixed mathematics than of experimental physical science.

Until lately, the Indian educational authorities were not at all favourable to the teaching of natural science. We shall give an instance by way of illustration. The Directors of the East India Company wished to institute a chair for Geology at the Presidency College of Calcutta soon after its establishment in 1855 ; and it seems that Dr. Oldham, Superintendent of the Geological Survey of India, offered to undertake the duties of the professorship in addition to his own work. The Directors, however, sent out Dr. Liebig as professor of natural history and geology in 1856.* But the services of Dr. Liebig were transferred temporarily to the mint before he had entered on the duties of his professorship, and an assistant of the Geological Survey was engaged to give a course of lectures on Geology and Mineralogy during the session 1856-57. The course was attended by a very small number of students ; the authorities thought

* Selections from the Records of the Government of India, Home Department No. LXXVI. p. 61.

that a larger number was not to be expected in future, and the lecturership was abolished. The Directors, however, were not satisfied of the propriety of this decision:

"In any case" say the directors "provision must be made for affording instruction in practical geology to the students of the College of Civil Engineering at Calcutta, a knowledge of the subject being essential to an efficient course of instruction at that institution. The fact that candidates for the degree of B. A are not required to undergo an examination in geology, is not, in our opinion, a sufficient reason why the opportunity of becoming acquainted with that science should not be afforded at an institution which professes to afford the means of a liberal education of the highest order. And as regards the assumed failure of the experiment, we cannot think that a fair trial would, under any circumstances, have been afforded by the delivery of a single course of lectures; and in the present case it may be presumed, without the risk of injustice to Mr. * *, that the attendance would have been much larger had the lectures been delivered by Dr. Liebig.

It is accordingly our desire that the professorship of geology should be re-established and that the services of Dr. Liebig should be made available for the office, an arrangement which we think may be carried out at once, without prejudice to the duties entrusted to Dr. Liebig at the Mint."*

Nothing further was heard about the Professorship of geology at the Presidency College for a long time, and it was established only three years ago.

There are obstacles in the way of scientific education of the Hindus which are of a serious nature. Scientific education offers openings in Europe which may as yet be said to be almost absent in India, at least for the Indians. Scientific research is liberally

<small>Difficulties of scientific progress among the Hindus.</small>

---

* Letter from the Court of Directors dated 28th April, 1858.

endowed in Europe, so that specialists may devote themselves to their favourite subjects with their animal wants fairly supplied ; and there are influential societies which watch over their interests. In India, there are under the Government a few small departments which are maintained chiefly for scientific research, and a few larger departments for which a scientific training is necessary. Both these classes of departments are almost exclusively officered by Europeans. With regard to the departments for scientific research, * it is sometimes argued as if as Orientals, the Hindus were incapable of it, whatever their education might be. It is true, the ancestors of the modern Hindus had made but little progress in Natural Science ; but, the ancestors of the modern Europeans had not made any better progress. Modern Natural Science does not date back earlier than the middle of the last century. The Hindus successfully cultivated Astronomy which requires observational powers of no mean order. They also made valuable observations on plants and minerals.† In their conceptions of the duration and mutability of our planet ; ‡ of the gradual evolution of the organic world ; of an ethereal substance, infinite and eternal ; of material substances as aggregates of atoms ; and of light and heat as different forms of the same substance,§

---

* Research is carried on by these departments in Botany, Geology, Zoology, Meteorology &c.
 † See Book V. Ch. I.
 ‡ See Lyell's "Principles of Geology."
 § Colebrooke's " Philosophy of the Hindus—Vaisesika."

they had anticipated some of the fundamental principles of modern science. The facts, that they have done this in the past, that they have made some contributions* to science, however humble, in the present, that an Oriental nation like the Japanese has, within so short a space of time as a decade or two, risen to scientific eminence, show that the mere fact of his being an Oriental does not argue an inborn incapacity for scientific research in the Hindu. If it were so, if science had been the exclusive prerogative of the Western nations, the Government would scarcely be justified in maintaining scientific research, which benefits only a few members of the European community which can well enough bear the expense of such research, with the money of the poverty-stricken people of India. A civilized Government has certain well recognized responsibilities towards its subjects, one of which is to spend the revenue derived by taxing them upon objects which are calculated to conduce, at least principally, to their good. We see no reason why with an improved system of scientific education, and with just and sympathetic treatment of the young men trained in science, they will not be able to take that place in the modern scientific world which they may be expected to do under the rule of one of the foremost nations of that world. The reason of the recent success of the Japanese in the field of science is, that their young men, trained under Western scientists, instead of being thwarted,

---

* These will be noticed in a subsequent chapter.

discouraged, and set down as incapable, have been aided, encouraged, and stimulated by their Government to pursue science.

Government has within the last decade done much to improve the condition of scientific education. In the Presidency College of Calcutta, a lecturership of Geology has been instituted, and the physical and chemical laboratories have been greatly improved. A great deal still remains to be done to bring up the education to the Western level. But, what has been done already may be taken as an earnest of more to be done in the future. With regard, however, to the employment of Indians in departments requiring scientific training, whatever the intentions* of the Government may be, they are not likely to bear any fruit if they have to be carried out by heads of departments such as the Surveyor-General of India who in a memorandum submitted to the Public Service Commission said: "It is suicidal for the Europeans to admit that Natives can do any thing better than themselves. They should claim to be superior in *everything*, and only allow natives to take a secondary or subordinate part .... In my old parties I never permitted a Native to touch a theodolite or an original computation, on the principle that the triangulation or scientific work was the prerogative of the highly-paid European; and this reservation of the

---

* For an instance of the manner in which the good intentions of the Government may be frustrated by departmental opposition, see "Proceedings of the Sub-Committee, Public Service Commission, Survey Department," pp. 6-7.

scientific work was the only way by which I could keep up a distinction, so as to justify the different figures of pay respectively drawn by the two classes, between the European in office time and the native who ran him so close in all the office duties. Yet I see that Natives commonly do the computations now-a days, and the Europeans some other inferior duties." *

It is but seldom, however, that we have such frank admission. The reason usually assigned for keeping the Hindu down at the low level of routine drudgery is his alleged incapacity for higher work. He is judged incompetent before he is allowed an opportunity to show that he is competent. †

The departments under the Government of India for which some amount of scientific training is required are the Survey, the Telegraph, the Forest, the Medical and the Public Works. In 1886 there were in the

---

* Memorandum by Col. De Pree, Proceedings of the Sub-Committee, Public Service Commission, Survey Department, p. 23

† With regard to the recruitment in India of the Geological Survey of India, the Government of India says in a resolution dated March, 1893: "It has been found, however, owing to the difficulty which is experienced in obtaining Asiatics with pronounced talent for geological research, that the system of appointing natives as probationary Sub-Assistants is not likely to be successful." Considering that there was no lectureship of Geology in any institution in the Bengal Presidency until 1893, that there is even now no adequate provision for the teaching of geology in any part of India, and that there is scarcely any opening for geological knowledge is the absence of a "pronounced talent for geological research" to be wondered at ? Scientific research under present conditions, which require previous assimilation of what has been done in the West, is quite different from what it was a century ago.

Survey of India Department, 146 Europeans, 34 Eurasians and only 2 Indians, and these in the very lowest grades of the junior division; in the Public Works Department, there were 810 Europeans, 119 Eurasians and Europeans domiciled in India, and only 86 Indians of whom not one was in the highest grades.

' The heads of scientific, no less than the heads of political and other departments, not unoften appear to consider the suppression of the educated Indian essential for the maintenance of British prestige. " Both classes of Europeans [official and non-official]" observes a writer holding a high position under the Government of Bengal " are equally reluctant to admit the natives to equality, and the official class is especially aggrieved, because the natives are invading preserves which have hitherto been free from any intruder.......... This is the result of education which has tended to equalise the races, and the nearer the equality the stronger the dislike. .... They [the Englishmen] are more pleased with the backward Hindu than with his advanced compatriot, because the former has made no attempt to attain equality with themselves." *

* H. J. S. Cotton, " New India," pp. 40-41.

Radhanath Shikdar was for sometime chief computer in the Survey of India Department. The following mention is made of him in the preface to the first edition of the "Manual of Surveying" by Smyth and Thuillier:—

"In parts III. and IV. the compilers have been very largely assisted by Babu Radha Nath Shikdar, the distinguished head of the Computing Department of the Great Trigonometrical Survey of India, a gentleman, whose intimate acquaintance with the rigorous forms and

The extreme poverty of the people is a serious obstacle in the way of scientific education, or scientific research. In Bengal, there is only one college, the

mode of procedure adopted on the Great Trigonometrical Survey of India, and great acquirements and knowledge of scientific subjects generally, render his aid particularly valuable. The chapters 15 and 17 up to 21 inclusive, and 26 of part III, and the whole of part V. are entirely his own, and it would be difficult for the compilers to express with sufficient force the obligations they thus feel under to him, not only for the portion of the work which they desire thus publicly to acknowledge, but for the advice so generally afforded on all subjects connected with his own Department."

The acknowledgment of valuable scientific work done by a "native" was probably considered by the editors of a later issue of the work inconsistent with British prestige, and Radha Nath Shikdar's name was omitted. Col. Sherwill thus wrote in the " Friend of India" (1876) :

" A friend has just sent me a copy of the *Friend of India* of the 24th June, all the way from Germany, in order that I might be made acquainted with the *sad fact* that, when bringing out a third edition of "Smyth and Thuillier's Manual of Surveying for India," the much respected name of the late Babu Radhanath Shikdar, the able and distinguished head of the computing department of the Great Trigonometrical Survey of India, who did so much to enrich the early editions of the "Manual," had been advertently, or inadvertently, removed from the preface of the last edition; while at the same time all the valuable matter written by the Babu had been retained, and that without any acknowledgment as to the authorship.

As an old Revenue Surveyor who used the "Manual" for a quarter of a century, and as an acquaintance of the late Radhanath Shikdar, I feel quite ashamed for those who have seen fit to exclude his name from the present edition, especially as the former Editors so fully acknowledged the deep obligations under which they found themselves for Radhanath's assistance, not only for the particular portion of the work "*which they desire thus publicly to acknowledge* —so runs the preface of the 1851 edition,—*but for the advice so generally afforded on all subjects connected with his own department.*"

(" Reminiscences and Anecdotes " by Rámgopál Sányal, p. 25).

Government Presidency College of Calcutta, which has laboratories worth the name. Private colleges which have to charge very low fees * cannot afford expensive apparatus for the purposes of demonstration or experiment. The consequence is, that though scientific subjects have been introduced into the University Examinations, they are generally taught theoretically rather than practically.

Considering these difficulties in the way of scientific education the way in which it has spread within the last decade is rather hopeful. We do not place any exaggerated value upon natural science. As an educational agent we do not consider it in any way superior to general literature (including mental philosophy). There is as much of culture as of narrow-mindedness, as much of angelic as of the reverse disposition among scientists as among literary men. But natural science has of late come into prominence, as the intellectual basis of Western civilization. Without it, it is impossible for a nation at the present day to hold its own, let alone progress. The cultivation of natural science and the adoption of the means and appliances which it has given rise to is a question not of education but of existence. The fate of China in her recent war with Japan shows this plainly. Her discomfiture is due

<small>Recent progress of scientific education.</small>

---

* The monthly fee for all the courses of lectures usually charged by the private colleges in Bengal is three rupees (not four shillings at the present rate of exchange).

to her excessive conservatism. The Hindus have of late begun to perceive the necessity of scientific education for their very existence. They cannot engage in any industry, mining, manufacturing or agricultural, without it; and without such industries there is scarcely any hope for them in the future. An association for the cultivation of science in Calcutta has, for sometime past been trying to spread scientific education by popular lectures on physics, chemistry, geology and biology. All the Universities have now science-courses for their B. A. degrees which are yearly increasing in popularity; and the Bombay University grants degrees in science. The courses for the degree examinations of the different Universities comprise all the branches of natural science.*

---

* The B. course for the B. A. degree of the Calcutta University is:

Pass Subjects.	Honours Subjects. B. *
I.—English.	I.—In addition to the pass subjects, a further course in English and the history of the English language and literature, and an original English essay.
II.—Mathematics. Statics. Dynamics. Hydrostatics.	II.—In addition to the pass course, Analytical Plane Geometry and the Differential and Integral Calculus.

And one of the following:—

III.—Physics and Chemistry.	III.—A fuller course in Physics and Chemistry together with the Doctrine of Scientific Method.
IV.—Physiology and either Botany or Zoology.	IV.—Physiology, Botany and Zoology, together with the Doctrine of Scientific Method.

But though the training in natural science required by these degrees is of a fairly comprehensive character, the provisions made for the teaching of science in the colleges affiliated to them are generally of a very unsatisfactory character. There is only one Arts college, the Government Presidency College

Condition of general scientific education still unsatisfactory.

V.—Geology and either Mineralogy or Physical Geography.	V.—Geology, Mineralogy and Physical Geography, together with the Doctrine of Scientific Method.

Candidates in Natural and Physical Science for the M A. degree of the Calcutta University are allowed to select alternatively one out of the following subjects.

(A) Chemistry.

(B) Heat, Electricity and Magnetism, as principal subjects. with Light and Sound as subsidiary subjects.

(C) Light and Sound as principal subjects, with Heat, Electricity and Magnetism as subsidiary subjects.

(D) Botany.

(E) Physiology and Zoology.

(F) Geology and Mineralogy.

(A) The course in chemistry is both theoretical and practical. In the practical examination candidates ought to show a good knowledge of chemical manipulation and ought to be able to qualitatively analyse complex inorganic substances. They should also be acquainted with the principles of quantitative analysis.

(A) and (C) Candidates have to show a thorough knowledge of the principal subjects and a general acquaintance with the subsidiary subjects, treating the subjects, mathematically and experimentally.

(D) Botany includes the following :—

(a) General and Special Morphology and Physiology.

(b) Systematic Botany.

(c) Palæobotany.

of Calcutta, where there exist chemical and physical laboratories worth the name. This is also the only college in the Bengal Presidency where geology has been taught for the last three years, as yet, however, without that amount of practical work which is essential for a sound knowledge of the subject. Except the Medical College of Calcutta, there is no institution in the Bengal Presidency where Zoology or Botany is taught. And at the Medical College, these subjects are still taught very nearly on the methods adopted half a century ago. Comparative anatomy, histology and physiological botany which have advanced in Europe so rapidly within that time are scarcely touched. The Medical College is administered by men who have spent a good portion of their lives in the practice of medicine and surgery; and it is probable that they set but little value upon subjects which are of so little use to them in their practice. Anyhow, Botany and Zoology are taught in the only institution where those subjects are taught

---

(d) Practical knowledge of indigenous Indian plants, and identification of specimens of them by Roxburgh's *Flora Indica* (Clarke's edition).

(E) Zoology * shall include the subjects (a) Comparative Anatomy and Physiology, (b) Distribution, and (c) Evolution.

(F) Geology and Mineralogy includes the subjects of (a) Stratigraphical Geology, (b) Palæontology, (c) Mineralogy, (d) Crystallography (e) Elementary Inorganic Chemisty.

The Bombay University grants a degree in Science (B. Sc.) the course for which corresponds to the B. course for the B. A. degree of the Calcutta University, but the examination is of a more searching character.

in Bengal without any practical laboratory work worth the name.*

We are not aware that the teaching of general natural science has kept much better pace with modern progress in other parts of India, than in Bengal. In the Madras Presidency, besides the Medical College, there appears to be only one college, the Presidency College, where there is a chair for Biology, and their is no institution where geology is systematically taught. Science appears, however, to be in greater favour in the Western Presidency than in Bengal or Madras, there being chairs for Biology in addition to those of Chemistry and Physics in the Poona College of Science and in the Elphinstone, Wilson, Baroda & Fergusson colleges.

Medical education. We have already noticed the remarkable progress which the ancient Hindus had made in Medical Science. But with the decay of their civilization, it, like the other sciences, attained a stereotyped form in which the British rule found it. Its surgery has been superseded by the more scientific

* Surgeon-Col. Harvey in his presidential address at the Indian Medical Congress held in Calcutta last year (December, 1894) said:—

"The Medical College of Calcutta the parent of all subsequent medical schools, is most miserably and inadequately housed. It has but two poor theatres in which lecture has to succeed lecture without intermission, so that the professors have neither the time nor the opportunity to prepare for their demonstrations, and the rooms are poisoned by the mephitic air of a succession of audiences. The laboratories, dissecting room, anatomical and other departments are all cramped for room, and so damp and dark and ill-arranged that effective teaching is very difficult."

The Medical College building, however, is now being improved.

surgery of the West; but as a system of medicine, it still enjoys a high reputation among all classes of the Hindus, and is widely studied.* Attempts are now being made to improve and systematise its instruction, but they have not yet taken shape worthy of record.

Under British Rule, medical education was imparted from 1822 to 1835 through the Indian classics in special classes attached to the Arabic and Sanskrit Colleges at Calcutta. There was also a separate institution which trained up assistants to the medical officers of the Government. The institution had only one lecturer who delivered his lectures in Hindusthani. The books which the students read were Hindi abridgments of English works, and dissection was practised upon inferior animals. In 1835, Lord William Bentinck proposed the establishment of a Medical College on European principles, and appointed a Committee to report upon the subject. The educationists of the time were ranged in two parties, of which one, called the Anglicist, favoured English education, and the other, known as the Orientalist, advocated Oriental education. The proposal of Lord William Bentinck led to a controversy between the two parties. But the weakness of the Orientalists rendered the contest a very unequal one; and the Anglicists won an easy victory. Dr. Tytler, Superintendent of the Medical

* In Bengal, in 1837, Mr. Adam found one medical school in Rajshahi containing 7 students taught by 2 professors; in Birbhum, one school attended by 6 students; and in Burdwan 4 medical schools with 45 students (Adam's "Reports on Vernacular education," p. 322).

institution and an orientalist of some distinction, denied " that a system of educating the natives through the medium of English would be in the least more comprehensive, or by any means so much so, as one carried on in the native languages," and considered it wholly "inexpedient as a general measure." The committee, however, came to the conclusion, "that it was perfectly feasible to educate native medical men on broad European principles," and that a knowledge of the English language was to be a *sine qua non* in the pupils. The Medical College fulfilled the most sanguine expectations which had been entertained of it. "The pupils" wrote Trevelyan two or three years after its establishment "are animated by the most lively professional zeal, and they evince a quickness and intelligence in the prosecution of their studies which has perhaps never been surpassed." James Prinsep, who examined the chemical class in 1837, reported officially as follows :

" In the first place, I may remark generally, that all the essays are extremely creditable. Indeed the extent and accuracy of the information on the single subject selected to test the abilities of the pupils has far surpassed my expectations ; and I do not think that in Europe any class of chemical pupils would be found capable of passing a better examination for the time they have attended lectures, nor indeed, that an equal number of boys would be found so nearly on a par in their acquirements."*

* Quoted by Trevelyan, "Education of the people of India," p. 32

The progress of medical education in India since 1835 has been immense. Speaking of the "remarkable success achieved by Natives of India whose professions have a more or less scientific, exact, and practical basis," Sir John Strachey says, that "this is especially the case with those who have devoted themselves to the study and practice of European Surgery."* The courses of instruction at the Indian Medical Colleges are similar to those of the medical institutions in the West. †

---

* "India" p. 214.
† The following was the course at the Calcutta Medical College, in 1894:

1st year.	2nd year.	3rd year.
Descriptive and Surgical Anatomy. Chemistry. Botany. Dissection.	Comp. Anatomy, Comp. Physiology, and Zoology. Descriptive and Surgical Anatomy. General Anatomy and Physiology. Chemistry. Practical Chemistry. Materia Medica. Botany. *2nd year.* Dissections. Pharmacy—three months.	Materia Medica. Dissections. Physiology. Hospital practice—one year.

A medical school established in Madras in 1835 was raised to the status of a college in 1851, and affiliated to the Madras University in 1877. The Grant Medical College of Bombay was established in 1845 as a tribute to the memory of Sir Robert Grant, who was for some time Governor of Bombay. It was affiliated to the Bombay University in 1860. Quite recently medical colleges in which a complete education is given in English have been opened at Lahore, Allahabad, Tanjore, and Nellore. The course of studies pursued at these institutions is similar to that of the Medical College of Calcutta.

The attendance at the Medical Colleges of Calcutta, Madras and Bombay in 1885 was 132, 124, and 277 respectively. By 1893, the number of medical colleges had increased to four attended by 811 students.

4th year.	5th year.
Medicine.	Medicine and Clinical Medicine.
Surgery.	Surgery and Clinical Surgery.
Midwifery.	Midwifery and six labour cases.
Medical Jurisprudence with demonstrations.	Medical Jurisprudence with demonstrations.
Hospital practice—twelve months.	Pathology with demonstrations.
	Ophthalmic Medicine and Surgery.
	Hygiene.
	Dentistry.
	Post-mortem records.
	Hospital practice—six months.
	Out-door and Eye Infirmary practice—three months each.

During the five years between 1888 and 1892, 2288 candidates appeared at the medical examinations of the different Indian Universities, of whom 1,058 were successful. Medical education is greatly more valued in Bombay, than in Madras or Bengal. About 26 per cent of the candidates who passed the matriculation of the Bombay University between 1886 and 1890, went up for its medical examinations, the percentage in Bengal and Madras being 4·83 and 5·64 respectively.

Besides the medical colleges preparing for the University Examinations (L. M. S. and M. B.), of which the medium of instruction is English there were in 1884-85, 17 Government vernacular medical schools attended by 1,403 pupils. A school of medicine has recently been established in Calcutta which is independent of Government aid.

Engineering education. Remains of temples, roads, bridges and reservoirs testify to the engineering skill of the Hindus in pre-British times.* But, though some Sanskrit books on engineering subjects † have come down to us, they had long before the establishment of British rule ceased to be taught in schools. Engineering instruction on modern methods commenced in India only about half a century ago.

---

* See "Ways and Works in India" by G. W. Mac. George, pp. 70-72, 108-120, &c.

† Such as measures for villages, and rules for laying out towns and villages, directions for laying out squares, octagons &c. ; and architecture Rájendralálá Mitra "Indo-Aryans," vol. I pp. 37-40.

The Thomason College of Civil Engineering was opened at Rurki in 1849. Its success led the Court of Directors to recommend the establishment of similar institutions in other parts of India. "The success of the Thomason College of Civil Engineering at Rurki" say the Directors "has shown that for the purpose of training up persons capable of carrying out the great works which are in progress under Government throughout India, and to qualify the natives of India for the exercise of a profession which, now that the system of railways and public works is being rapidly extended, will afford an opening for a very large number of persons, it is expedient that similar places for practical instruction in civil engineering should be established in other parts of India."*

The Seebpore Engineering College near Calcutta was opened in 1880. The course of instruction at this institution is adapted to the requirements of civil engineers and of foreman mechanics. The course in the Engineering department, which is adapted to the requirements of the examinations for the Engineering degrees† of the Calcutta University is completed in five years of which the last is spent on works in progress.

The Madras Civil Engineering College consists of

---

* Despatch of 1854, para. 80.

† These degrees are Licentiate in Engineering, Bachelor in Engineering and Honours in Engineering. The subjects for the degree examination are, Civil Engineering, Mathematics, Natural Science, Engineering, Construction and Drawing.

two departments—the collegiate and the school departments. The course of instruction in the collegiate department (which was established in 1862) is adapted to the standard of the degree of B. C. E. in the Madras University. There is also a mechanical engineer class.

Engineering, like medicine, absorbs a much larger proportion of students in Bombay, than in Bengal or Madras. During the five years between 1888 and 1892, no less than 484 candidates presented themselves for the Engineering Examinations of the Bombay University, whereas the Engineering degrees of the Calcutta and Madras Universities attracted 137 and 59 candidates respectively.

Engineering instruction of a more elementary character than that given by the institutions mentioned above is given by a number of Engineering and Surveying Schools of which there were in 1884-85, seven in Assam with 163 pupils; 5 in Bengal with 278 students; 2 in Bombay attended by 98 boys; and 1 in Madras with 106 Students.

Forest School. The Imperial Forest School at Dehra Dun intended for the technical training of officers in the Forest Department was established in 1878. The first theoretical course was held in 1881 when 30 students arranged in two classes attended lectures on forestry, botany, forest law, surveying, mathematics and natural science. Since then the arrangements have been greatly improved. There are now two courses, one in English, and the other in the Hindusthani language. In the English course, students are prepared for the certificate in Forestry by the "Higher Standard"; in the Hindusthani course, for that by the "Lower Standard." In addition to the subjects mentioned above, they are now taught Zoology, Forest Engineering, Forest accounts &c. The Provincial Forest Service can only be entered through the Imperial Forest School. The Poona College of Science has a Forest branch to which appointments are guaranteed by the Bombay Forest Department.

The results of University Examinations in Medicine and Engineering for the five years from 1887-88 to 1891-92 were :

University.	Medicine.		Engineering.	
	Candidates.	Passed.	Candidates.	Passed.
Calcutta.	568	351	137	61
Allahabad. *	117	50	700	306
Punjab	131	78	11	3
Madras.	520	159	59	17
Bombay.	952	420	484	267
Total	2,288	1,058	1,391	654

Professional education in medicine and engineering has now been imparted for nearly two generations, and

* The results are for three years, only ((1889-90 to 1891-92) in Medicine, & two years (1890-91 to 1891-92) in Civil Engineering.

Hindus are distinguishing themselves as doctors and engineers. General scientific education, however, has not been imparted long or thoroughly enough, nor are the conditions favourable enough to lead us to expect original contributions of any great value. What has been done in the West must be assimilated, before any thing strikingly original can be reasonably expected; and that would be a work of time. Hindu scientific works with any pretension to marked originality are comparatively rare. They are mostly school-books, and are chiefly translations or adaptations from English. Such contributions as have more than a fleeting interest will be noticed when we come to treat of modern Hindu Literature.

CHAPTER V.

INFLUENCE OF THE ADMINISTRATIVE POLICY OF BRITISH RULE.

British Rule has introduced conditions some of which are as clearly promotive of progress as others are antagonistic to it. The internal tranquillity maintained by British Rule is beyond question favourable to intellectual development. Its importance, however, as a factor of progress must not be exaggerated. There are well known cases of nations having risen to intellectual eminence notwithstanding political convulsions of a serious nature; there are countries, on the other hand, which notwithstanding long periods of internal tranquillity have scarcely kept pace with modern progress though in immediate contact with it. In pre-British India, owing chiefly to the military occupation being restricted to certain castes, the great majority of the people had generally not been much disturbed by

Tranquillity maintained by British Rule favourable to intellectual progress.

wars. However, even though war does not necessarily hinder progress, nor peace necessarily promote it, it is undeniable that the latter is far more favourable to it than the former.

Economic influence of British administration. But the tranquillity under British rule is maintained by an administration which is essentially foreign. Economically, the effect of such an administration has been prejudicial to material progress, and we have the curious spectacle of the richest nation of Europe governing for a century a country with vast natural resources and with a people not very low in the scale of civilisation, without advancing its material condition to the standard of even the poorest and most backward in Europe.* The higher appointments in the military departments are exclusively, and in the civil departments almost exclusively filled up by Europeans. A large portion of the army is also composed of British soldiers. The standard of living of the European soldiers and officers (civil and military) being much higher than that of the Indians their scale of pay is proportionately higher. From a parliamentary return issued in 1891 it appears, that there were then 28,000 Europeans holding posts worth Rs. 1000 a year and upwards, directly or indirectly under Government, their emoluments amounting to no less than $15\frac{1}{2}$ crores of rupees a year. On the other hand, the number of natives of India drawing a pay

---

*The average income per head of population in India in 1882 was ascertained to be not more than Rs. 27 ; in Turkey it was £4

of Rs. 1000 or upwards a year is given as 11,000, their total pay aggregating only 3 crores of rupees, that is, about one-fifth of the total pay received by the corresponding European element in the service of Government.*

" The cost of British officers," says Mr. H. J. S. Cotton " is too great ; their salaries are too high ; and the blessings of European civilisation that they introduce are luxuries beyond the means of the people. India can no more afford the privilege of being governed by foreigners, can no more pay for her gigantic system of railways, her palatial barracks and other public buildings, than English farmers can afford to plough with race horses, or the Indian ryot with elephants."† In active service, a good portion of the pay received by the European employès of Government is remitted to Europe, or is spent upon objects which benefit European industries. In retirement, large remittances have to be made to Europe from the Indian revenue for their pensions. Large remittances have also to be made to pay for interest on debt which India has been made to contract in England for objects many of which, under present conditions, conduce but little to her good. A portion of the administration (the India Office) is also permanently located in England for which India has to make heavy contributions annually.

---

* Proceedings of the House of Commons, 15th August 1894. Speech of Mr. S. Keay.
† "New India" p. 68.

The annual drain due to these and other causes is considerable, and may be said to be so much capital taken out of India, capital which, under normal conditions, would promote the material development of the country.

"It must be remembered" says Sir G. Campbell "that we give neither our services nor our capital for nothing. Much of this is paid for by remittances to Europe. The public remittances are now £16,000,000 per annum, and it is estimated that the private remittances would be almost as much more if the flow of British capital to India were stopped, and the transactions showed only sums received in England. As it is, the continual addition of fresh capital invested in India about balances. The private remittances, and the balance of trade show only about the same amount as the public drawings, to be depleted from India—that is, about £16,900,000 per annum. This is what is sometimes called the "tribute" paid to England. Well, it is not tribute, but it is paid for civil and military services, loans, railways, industrial investments, and all the rest; and the result is that a large part of the increased production is not retained by the Indian peasant."*

Opinions about the impoverishment of India under British rule. There are authorities who have held that the drain has actually been impoverishing the people. Mr. Montgomery Martin writing at a time when the drain was considerably less than what it is now says :

"The annual drain of £3,000,000 on British India has amounted in thirty years at 12 per cent (the usual Indian rate) compound interest to the enormous sum of £723,900,000 sterling! So constant and accumulat-

---

* "The British Empire." p. 70.

ing a drain, even in England, would soon impoverish her. How severe, then, must be its effects on India where the wage of a labourer is from two pence to three pence a day."*

Sir John Shore writing in 1787 says: "Whatever allowance we may make for the increased industry of the subjects of the state, owing to the enhanced demand for the produce of it (supposing the demand to be enhanced) there is reason to conclude, that the benefits are more than counterbalanced by evils inseparable from the system of a remote foreign dominion." Mr. Frederick John Shore of the Bengal Civil Service writing in 1837 says : "The English Government has effected the impoverishment of the country and people to an extent almost unparalleled." Mr. Saville Marriot, who was for sometime one of the Commissioners of Revenue in the Deccan, and afterwards a member of Council says speaking of the drain about 1845 when it was considerably less than it is now : "It will be difficult to satisfy the mind that any country could bear such a drain upon its resources without sustaining any serious injury. And the writer [Mr. Marriot] entertains the fullest conviction that investigation would effectually establish the truth of the proposition as applicable to India.

---

* "The History, Antiquities, Topograply and Statistics of Eastern India" by M. Martin (London, 1838) Vol. I. Introduction p. xi. Mr. H. J. S. Cotton, at present Chief Secretary to the Government of Bengal, says :

"There is no great harm in saying that the land belongs to the 'State,' when the State is only another name for the people, but it is very different when the state is represented by a small minority of foreigners, who disburse nearly one-third of the revenues received from the land on the remuneration of their own servants, and who have no abiding place on the soil and no stake in the fortunes of the country. It is because we have acted on this principle all over India, with the exception of the permanently settled districts, that we have reduced the agricultural classes to such poverty."

"New India" p. 54.

He has himself most painfully witnessed it in those parts of country with which he was connected, and he has every reason to believe, that the same evil exists, with but slight modification, throughout our eastern empire." Again: "Most of the evils of our rule in India arise directly from, or may be traced to, the heavy tribute which that country pays to England." [*]

Data for the ascertainment of the material condition of India not satisfactory.

Notwithstanding these and other apparently pessimist views the question whether the material condition of India is improving or not is one for a satisfactory discussion of which we have not the necessary data. And the Government do not appear to be at all desirous of collecting such data. Sir Louis Malet who was for a long time permanent Under-Secretary of State for India says in a minute: "If there is any one thing which is wanting in any investigation of Indian problems it is an approach to trustworthy and generally accepted fact. Now I am compelled to say that since I have been connected with the India office I have found a strong repugnance to the adoption of any adequate measures for the collection of a comprehensive and well digested set of facts." This repugnance is likely to be attributed—as it has, in fact, been so attributed—to the great probability of such facts showing "an appalling

---

[*] Quoted by Dadabhai Naoroji in his pamphlet on "The Poverty of India."

picture of poverty and misery." † Even such facts as are in the possession of Government, they appear to be unwilling to make public. In 1876, Mr. Dadabhai Naoroji made some elaborate calculations from which he deduced the average income of an Indian to be Rs. 20. In 1882, Lord Cromer calculated the average income to be Rs. 27 from data collected in a minute by Sir David Barbour the then finance minister. Mr. Naoroji after repeated attempts failed to secure the publication of the data. Last April he put the following questions in the House of Commons:

"Whether as Lord Cromer had stated with regard to his statement of 1882 about the annual average income per head that although he was not prepared to pledge himself to the absolute accuracy of a calculation of this sort, it was sufficiently accurate to justify his conclusion that the tax-paying community was exceedingly poor, and as the calculation was thus accurate, he would grant the return......as such return was the only means of forming a fairly correct idea of the material condition of British India:

And, whether if he were unwilling to grant as a return the details of Lord Cromer's calculations, as asked in the first part of the motion he would give an opportunity to the honourable member for Finsbury of personally inspecting them."

Mr. George Russell replied:

"Considering that the statement to which my honourable friend refers was confessedly founded upon uncertain data, and that any similar calculation which might now be made must be founded on equally uncertain data, and might probably be misleading, the Secretary of State is unable to agree to my honourable friend's motion."

† Report of the tenth Indian National Congress. p. 52.

We have admittedly not got a body of well-ascertained, well-digested facts on which calculations with regard to the material condition of the people could be based. In fact, a member of the House of Commons of some thirty years' Indian experience, who had occupied the high posts of the Governorship of Bengal and of Bombay,* went so far as to declare on one occasion, in reference to the figures published by the Indian authorities, that they are "simply tabular statements of particular theories," and that "they are in fact shams, delusions and snares."

The average income which Lord Cromer allows the people of India is small enough. But it is curious that a civilised and highly expensive Government should not possess or publish reliable data for judging accurately whether that income had been larger or smaller before 1880, and whether it has been increasing or diminishing since. Yet it is certainly very important that we should know this.

We have, on the one hand, rose-coloured descriptions of the continued material prosperity of the people, and, on the other, heart-rending pictures of their poverty and gradual impoverishment. There are, however, certain facts periodically published by Government which throw some light upon material condition. The average monthly wage in rupees of unskilled labour in

---

* Sir Richard Temple at the debate on the motion of Mr. Samuel Smith for an inquiry into the condition and wants of the Indian people, and their ability to bear their existing financial burdens (August 1894).

certain selected stations roughly representing the provinces in which they are situated, between 1876 and 1890, was as follows: *

| | Bengal Presidency. | | N. W. Prov. and Oudh | Punjab | Bombay Presidency | Central Provinces | Madras Presidency |
	Bengal	Behar					
	Bakhergunj R	Patna R	Cawnpore R	Delhi R	Amritasar R	Ahmedabad R	Raipur R	Salem R
Triennial average † 1873 1875	7·5	3 to 4	3·75	5·41	5·95	5·9	3·7	2·5
Quinquennial average 1876 to 1880	7·5	3 to 4	3·85	5	6	6·9	4	2·6
Do. 1881 to 1885	7·5	3·75	3·8	5·12	6	7·39	4·1	2·3
Do. 1886 to 1890	7·7	4·55	4·09	5·79	6·62	7·5	4·5	3·53

* Compiled from the tenth issue of "Prices and Wages in India" (Calcutta, 1893).

† Wages previous to 1873 are not given in the publication to which I have had access.

The average annual prices of staple food grains at these stations between 1871 and 1890 is shown by the following table (in *seers* per rupee) : *

		Bengal Presidency.		N. W. Prov.		Punjab.		Bombay Presidency.	Central Provinces.	Madras Presidency.
		Bakhergunj Rice.	Patna Rice.	Cawnpore Wheat.	Delhi Wheat.	Amritsar Wheat.	Ahmedabad Wheat.	Raipur Rice.	Salem Jawar.	
Quin-quennial average	1871-1875	21.71	20.45	20.12	27.1	23.86	13.44	34.33	32.1	
Quin-quennial average	1876-1880	15.87	16.83	17.5	17.78	19.46	11.04	25.58	14.78	
Do	1881-1885	21.99	18.76	20.48	19.89	24.25	14.66	31.61	26.87	
Do	1886-1890	16.23	18.44	16.88	16.43	18.56	12.02	18.07	25.55	

It will be seen from the figures given above, that except in such places as Patna † and Salem where the wages were abnormally low, the rise in wages in the

* Compiled from the tenth issue of "Prices and Wages in India," Calcutta, 1893.

† With regard to the rise in wages in the Patna Division, however, the annual resolution of Government on the administration report of the Patna Division for 1893 says :

other places has not kept pace with the rise in the prices of the staple articles of food, so that generally the condition of the labourer in 1890 was worse than in 1886. At Raipur his monthly wages would, during the period 1886 to 1890, buy him only 81 seers of rice instead of 127 seers as in the period 1873 to 1875; at Delhi it would buy him 95 seers of wheat instead of 146; at Amritsar 122 instead of 141; and at Bakhergunj 124 seers of rice instead of 162. The discordance between wage and price of staple food appears strikingly great when compared with what they were two or three centuries ago. In the time of Akbar the monthly wages received by an unskilled labourer would have bought him 192 seers of wheat. *

The difficulties, however, in the way of arriving at a true picture of the material condition of India are so great that we shall not attempt it. But whether the annual drain referred to above has caused actual impoverishment or not, there can be no doubt, that by taking away from India what should have added to her capital, it has retarded her material development, and, therefore indirectly, her intellectual development also.

"Though the price of food-grains has owing to the opening out of railways and roads and other causes, risen greatly in this division in the past twenty years, there yet appears to be no corresponding rise in the wages of unskilled agricultural labourer. The wage of a common cooly is said to be now as it was eighty years ago 1½ to 2½ annas a day."

* See Vol. I. Introduction, p. lxxxv.

The evils of an alien rule are in the case of the British greatly aggravated by absenteeism. Had the British settled in the country the evils would have been minimised, if not counterbalanced, by the benefits resulting from their integration in the Indian community, and from consequent identification with the interests of that community.

Hindu ascendency in pre-Mahomedan times.

The moral effect of nearly all the responsible posts under the English Government being held by Europeans has been no less injurious than the economical effect. For the first time in their long history, the Hindus have come into contact with a people who have treated them as intellectually incompetent even to manage their own affairs, and who have excluded them from high positions of trust and responsibility. From remote antiquity India has been subject to invasions from beyond her north-western frontier. But, excepting the Mahomedans, whenever the invaders established themselves in India they could not resist the moral influence of the superior civilisation of the Hindus, and were sooner or later absorbed into the Hindu community. The Scæ or Sakas, who made repeated incursions into India for several centuries before and after the Christian era, and who ultimately became ascendant over parts of Northern India, preserved their individuality but for a short time. The Huns, who repeatedly invaded India from the fifth century after Christ, and who established a separate kingdom in the

Punjab in the sixth, soon lost their national individuality and were merged in the Hindu nation. Even the Mahomedans, who when they occupied India had a civilisation scarcely inferior to that of the Hindus of the time, and a religion one of the most uncompromising that the world has ever seen gradually succumbed to Hindu influence. Throughout the Mahomedan period, Hindus occupied the highest posts under Mahomedan sovereigns both in the military and civil departments. The Hindus did not sink into political nonentity even in those parts which directly owned Mahomedan sway. They were admitted into situations of trust and responsibility. They commanded armies, governed kingdoms, and acted as ministers under Mahomedan kings. Ibrahim the fourth king of Golconda, had Jogadeo, a Hindu, for his prime minister. Mahomed Shah Sur Adil, who occupied the throne of Delhi about the middle of the sixteenth century, committed the conduct of his Government to one "Hemu, a Hindu who had once kept a retail shop, and whose appearance is said to have been meaner than his origin. Yet with all these external disadvantages, Hemu had abilities and force of mind sufficient to maintain his ascendency amidst a proud and martial nobility, and to prevent the dissolution of the Government, weighed down as it was by the follies and iniquities of its head."*

_{Hindu influence in Mahomedan period.}

---

* Elphinstone's History of India. Cowell's Ed.—pp. 460-3.

During the reigns of the Emperors Feroksir, Rafi-ud-Darját, Rafi-ud-Doula, and part of the reign of Mahomed Shah, Rattan Chand, formerly a retail shopkeeper, enjoyed uncontrolled influence all over Hindusthán. He was deputy to Abdulla Khan, Vizier of the Empire. It was through his influence and that of Raja Ajit, that the poll tax upon the Hindus re-established by Aurangzeb was abolished. "He interfered," complains the Mahomedan historian, "even in judicial and religious concerns, in a way that reduced the crown officers to the condition of ciphers. It was impossible to become a Kazi of any city, without the consent of this Hindu being previously taken."*

When Alivardi Khan became prime minister of Shúja Khan, he called to his councils Raja Aalem Chánd and Jagat Set, the former of whom, says Golam Hussein Khan, "possessed great merit, and deserved all the confidence reposed in him." When Alivardi Khan became Governor of Bengal, he appointed as his prime minister Jánkírám, "who was a man of merit, and figured among the trustiest and most zealous of the Viceroy's friends."

Mohanlála was the minister of Surája-ud-Dowla, Governor of Bengal; amongst his other officers who held positions of trust, were Durlavrám and Rámnáráyan.

The Ain-i-Akbari gives a complete list of the high

---

* *Siar-ul-Mutakharin* (Briggs' Translation), pp. 89, &c.

officers during the reign of Akbar.* The following is the number of Hindus amongst them :—

I. Commanders of Five Thousand

1. Raja Bihari Mall.
2. Raja Bhagwan Das.
3. Raja Man Sing. He was for some time Governor of Bengal. Akbar promoted him to a full command of seven thousand ; hitherto Five Thousand had been the limit of promotion. It is noticeable that Akbar in raising Man Sing to a command of seven thousand, placed a Hindu above every Mahomedan officer.

II. Commanders of Four Thousand

4. Raja Todar Mall. Though often accused of headstrongness and bigotry by contemporaneous historians, Todar Mall's fame as general and financier has outlived the deeds of most of Akbar's grandees ; together with Abul Fazl and Man Sing, he is best known to the people of India at the present day. One of the most important reforms associated with Todar Mall's name is, the substitution of Persian for Hindi as the Court language.
5. Rai Rai Sing. He was promoted by Jehangir to be a commander of Five Thousand.

III. Commander of Three Thousand—Jagannath.

IV. Commanders of Two Thousand.

Raja Bir Bal. An entirely self-made man. He was very poor when he came to Akbar's court. Akbar conferred on him the title of Rai Kabi (or Poet Laureate) and had him constantly near himself.

8. Raja Ram Chandra Baghela.
9. Rai Kalyan Mall.
10. Rai Surjan Hada.

V. Commanders of One Thousand and Five hundred—2.
VI. Commander of Twelve Hundred and fifty—1.
VII. Commanders of One Thousand—3.
VIII. Commanders of Nine Hundred—3.

---

* *Ain-i-Akbari* (Blochmann's translation) pp. 308-526.

IX. Commanders of Eight Hundred—2.
X. Commanders of Five Hundred—12.
XI. Commanders of Four Hundred—5.
XII. Commanders of Three Hundred—6.
XIII. Commanders of Two Hundred—8.

The total number of Commanders in the various grades from Seven Thousand to Two Hundred was 415, so that the Hindus filled twelve per cent. of the most responsible political posts under Akbar. The Commanders named above all saw active service. Several governed important provinces; one (Todar Mall) occupied the high post of Vizier or Minister of Finance; and one (Man Sing) was raised to a distinction, which up to his time had been reserved only for Princes of the royal blood.

Mahomedan princes sometimes took Hindu wives, and several of the Emperors of Delhi were descended from Hindu mothers. It is said of Akbar, that from his youth he was accustomed to celebrate the *Hom* (a Hindu ceremony) from his affection towards the Hindu princesses of his harem.* Two of Akbar's wives were Hindus; and Jahangir was the son of one of them. Jahangir had ten wives, of whom no less than six were of Hindu descent. Shah Jahan was the offspring of one of these.† He had more of Hindu than of Mahomedan blood in him.

The Indian Mahomedans gradually became partially Hinduised. Their zeal for the propagation of Islam

---

* *Ain-i-Akbari*, Blochmann's translation p. 184.
† *Ain-i-Akbari*, Blochmann's translation pp. 308-9.

abated. The blind bigotry of the Moslem was gradually tempered by the philosophic culture of the Hindu ; and Hindu influence on the religion and government of the Moslem, gradually became more and more marked.

The brightest period of the Mahomedan Empire was unquestionably the period between the accession of Akbar and the deposition of Shah Jahan, and it was during that period that the Hindu influence was the strongest. Akbar and his most cultured Mahomedan courtiers—the brothers Faizi and Abul Fazl,—were greatly under Hindu influence. Abul Fazl was, in fact, held by some of his contemporaries to be a Hindu.* Akbar held the Hindu belief that it was wrong to kill cows and interdicted the use of beef.† The Hindu princesses of the harem gained so great an ascendency over him, that he not only foreswore beef, but also garlic, onions and the wearing of a beard. "He had also introduced," says Badaoni, "though modified by his peculiar views, Hindu customs and heresies into court assemblies, and introduces them still in order to please and gain the good will of the Hindus." Raja Bir Bar is said by some historians to have influenced Akbar in abjuring Islam. Bir Bar was the special favourite of Akbar. Badaoni says, "His Majesty cared for the death of no grandee more than for that of Bir Bar." The jealousy which the

---

* *Ain-i-Akbari*, p. 27.

† The Emperor Nasiruddin forbade the killing of oxen. Ferishta speaks of him as practising idolatry like the Hindus, so that the Koran was occasionally placed as a stool and sat upon.

pro-Hindu policy of Akbar excited amongst bigoted Muslims was intense, and finds expression in such passages as the following from Badaoni : *

"As it was quite customary in those days to speak ill of the doctrine and orders of the Koran, and as Hindu wretches and Hinduizing Mahomedans openly reviled our Prophet, irreligious writers left in the prefaces to their books the customary praise of the Prophet...........: It was impossible even to mention the name of the Prophet, because these liars [Abul Fazl and Faizi] did not like it.

"The Hindus, of course, are indispensable ; to them belongs half the army and half the land. Neither the Hindusthanis (Mahomedans settled in Hindusthan) nor the Moguls can point to such grand lords as the Hindus have among themselves."

The Hindu Man Sing, Todar Mall and Bir Bar, and the practically Hinduised Abul Fazl and Faizi were amongst the most, if not the most, trusted of Akbar's councillors. They probably contributed more to build up the Mogul Empire on a sound basis of liberal and enlightened policy than all the other officers of Akbar put together. The pro-Hindu policy of Akbar was continued by Jahangir and Shah Jahan. The contest between Dara and Aurangzeb was really a contest between enlightenment and bigotry, between a pro-Hindu and an anti Hindu policy. Dara belonged to the school of Akbar. He wrote a book attempting to reconcile the Hindu and Mahomedan doctrines. He had translations made of fifty *Upanishads* into Persian. Like Akbar, he was considered an apostate. He is said to have been constantly in the society of Bráhmans, Yogis and Sannyásis, and to have considered the Vedas

* *Ain-i-Akbari*, pp. 185, 204.

as the word of God. Instead of the Mahomedan, he adopted the Hindu name (*Prabhu*) for God, and had it engraved in Hindi upon rings. "It became manifest," says the author of Alamgir-námá, " that if Dara Sukoh obtained the throne and established his power, the foundations of the faith would be in danger." Aurangzeb was a bigot such as orthodox Mahomedans had long been looking for; they advocated his cause, as the Hindus did that of the elder brother. The cause of orthodox Islam triumphed. But the triumph was only temporary, ending with the reign of Aurangzeb.

Intellectual effect of the exclusive policy in military and political departments. Under British rule, the Hindus are not *en rapport* with the governing class, at least to the extent they were under Mahomedan rule.* The military and political services except in the very lowest ranks are closed against the Hindus.† Opinions differ with regard to the wisdom of such exclusion. The policy of the Roman Empire was different as the following extracts from Gibbon's "Decline and Fall of the Roman Empire" shew :

"The grandsons of the Gauls who had besieged Julius Cæsar in Alesia, commanded legions, governed provinces, and were admitted into the senate of Rome. Their ambition, instead of disturbing the tranquillity of the state, was intimately connected with its safety and greatness."

* "The belief, then," says Sir C. Dilke of foreign observers, "is that our Indian Government.........needs to places itself in closer sympathy with the natives."

"Problems of Greater Britain" p. 124.

† "The officers of our native army are only superannuated old pri-

"Domestic peace and union were the natural consequences of the moderate and comprehensive policy embraced by the Romans."

"The obedience of the Roman world was uniform, voluntary, and permanent. The vanquished nations, blended into one great people, resigned the hope, nay, even the wish, of resuming their independence, and scarcely considered their existence as distinct from the existence of Rome. The established authority of the emperors pervaded without an effort the wide extent of their dominions, and was exercised with the same facility on the bank of the Thames, or of the Nile, as on those of the Tiber. The legions were destined to serve against the public enemy, and the civil magistrate seldom required the aid of a military force."

"The empire of Rome was firmly established by the singular and perfect coalition of its members. The subject nations, resigning the hope and even the wish of independence, embraced the character of Roman citizens, and the provinces of the West were reluctantly torn by the barbarians from the bosom of their mother country."

"The narrow policy of preserving, without any foreign mixture, the pure blood of the ancient citizens had checked the fortunes, and hastened the ruin of Athens and Sparta. The aspiring genius of Rome sacrificed vanity to ambition, and deemed it more prudent, as well as honourable, to adopt virtue and merit for her own wheresoever they were found among slaves or strangers, enemies or barbarians."[*]

Commenting on the exclusive policy of the British administration, Sir C. Dilke says: "To those who take a purely selfish view it may be urged that we can hardly vates, who in virtue of their longer services draw larger pay, and are permitted to sit down in the presence of an English subaltern......The Russians can get from the territories they have absorbed in Central Asia an Alikhanoff or a Louis Melikoff. We can only produce men who rise to the rank of Naik, Havildar, or Resaldar, or to some other subordinate post, the name of which perplexes the English public." "New India." (pp. 118-119).

[*] "Decline and Fall of the Roman Empire." ch. II.

long go on as we are, refusing to proceed further in the direction of the employment of natives in high office, with the Russians at our door pursuing the other policy, although pursuing it in a less degree than is commonly believed. The unshared rule of a close bureaucracy from across the seas cannot last in the face of widespread modern education of a people so intelligent as Indian natives."*

We do not consider war or politics to be a good school for progress, intellectual or moral. The less need there be for war or political strife the better would it be for humanity. But constituted as the world is now, and as it will probably be for many generations to come, the military and political types of intellectual progress must be valued, and their want in any people must be deprecated. The British system of administration, however, renders the development of such types, among the Hindus an impossibility, though there are apparently men who, if they had the opportunity, might have become highly capable generals and statesmen. The late Raja Mádhava Rao† may be cited as an instance of the latter. Many native statesmen have been pro-

---

* " Problems of Greater Britain" pp. 145-146.

† Mádhava Rao was born in 1828. He became Dewan of Travancore in 1858, and between that year and 1872, the Government of Travancore was virtually in his hands. He removed various fiscal restrictions and revised the system of administration On his retirement from the service of the Travancore State he was for sometimes Prime Minister to the Maharaja of Holkar. Between 1875 and 1883, he administered the Baroda State. The late Mr. Fawcett called him the Turgot of India.

duced" says Sir Richard Temple " of whom the Indian nation may be justly proud"; and among them he mentions, besides Mádhava Ráo, Dinkar Ráo of Gwalior, Kirparam of Jammu, Pandit Manphul of Alwar, Madho Rao Barve of Kolhapur, and Purnia of Mysore *

In the Civil departments of administration, the Hindus are practically, if not theoretically, almost excluded from the higher posts; as will be apparent from the following return furnished in 1891 by the then Under-Secretary of State for India in the House of Commons: " The proportion of Europeans, Eurasians and Indians in the covenanted and uncovenanted services [civil?] of India on March 31, 1886 at salaries varying from 50,000 and more rupees to 1000 rupees were as follow: Salaries of 50,000 rupees and upwards, 26 Europeans, 1 native; 40,000 Rs. to 50,000 Rs., 47 Europeans, 3 natives; 30,000 Rs. to 40,000 Rs., 125 Europeans; 20,000 Rs., to 30,000 Rs. 346 Europeans, 3 Eurasians, 2 natives; 10,000 Rs. to 20,000 Rs., 951 Europeans, 12 Eurasians, 40 natives: 5,000 Rs. to 10,000 Rs., 2078 Europeans, 111 Eurasians, 446 natives; 2,500 Rs. to 5,000 Rs., 1,334 Europeans, :,647 Eurasians, 545 natives; 1,000 Rs. to 2,500 Rs., 2097 Europeans, 1,963 Eurasians, 6,915 natives."

Exclusion in civil departments.

In 1892, the covenanted Civil Service was composed of 939 members of whom only 21 were Indians.† The

---

* " India in 1880." p, 76.
† Strachey's "India," 1894, p 58.

following table compiled from the report of the Public Service Commission (1886) exhibits the proportion of the higher grade appointments held by the Indians (Hindus, Mahomedans, Parsis &c.) in some of the minor departments :

Name of Department	Non-domiciled Europeans.	Domiciled Europeans.	Eurasians.	Indians.	Remarks.
Accounts Department	25	8	3	6	*"Domiciled Europeans" include Eurasians.
Customs	13	60	117	12	
Jails	60	15	13	16	
Opium	49	13	8	1	
Police	315	33	5	17	
Public Works	810	119*	—	86	
Salt	35	32	10	7	
Survey	108	103	38	2	

Policy of the exclusion

With reference to the exclusive policy of the British administration Mountstuart Elphinstone wrote as long ago as 1850 :

"I conceive that the administration of all the departments of a great country by a small number of foreign visitors in a state of isolation produced by a difference in religion, ideas, and manners, which cuts them off from all intimate communion with the people, can never be contemplated as a permanent state of things. I conceive also that the progress of education among the natives renders such a scheme impracticable, even if it were otherwise free from objection. It might perhaps, have once been possible to have retained the natives in a subordinate condition (at the expense of national justice and honour) by studiously repressing their spirit and discouraging their progress in knowledge ; but we are now doing our best to raise them in all mental qualities to a level with ourselves, and to instill into them the liberal opinions in government and policy which have long prevailed in this country, and it is vain to rule them on principles only suited to a slavish and ignorant population." *

A writer quoted by Mr. H. J. S. Cotton in his "New India"† says :

"Repress educated natives, distrust them, let them see that the policy of India for the Indians and of training them to administer their own country is a fiction, and you weld them all into a solid phalanx' united by the common bond of despair and hatred towards Europeans. Can any policy be more insensate than this ? But open the door to their ambitions, and you at once let in all the emulations, class interests, sectional friction, which, if not in themselves good, are at any rate a necessary element in a healthy state of society, and instead of a solid phalanx you have a crowd of aspirants competing with one another under conditions which the Government will prescribe, and in a race of which it will be the umpire and distributor of the prizes."

Divergence of opinion with regard to the admission of Indians into responsible administration.

The Hindu is often authoritatively declared to be incapable of any work which is likely to exercise or develop his higher faculties ; and it is but seldom that he is allowed opportunities to rise above the routine work of clerkship. It is true the authorities sometimes differ very markedly in their estimates of the capabilities of Indians, though the facts on which the estimates are based may be the same. The proceedings of the Public Service Commission furnish curious instances of such divergence. Mr. J. Westland (now Sir J. Westland) said :

" A native will not bear the personal responsibility of going out of routine, and will be apt to break down when urgent work must be

---

* C. H. Cameron, "The duties of Great Britain to India" pp. 173-174.
† *Op. cit.* pp. 78-79.

done. One Native did very well in such employment; but he was altogether an exceptional man, and no system of recruitment would bring half a dozen Natives equal to him into the department. A Native is not equal to a man bred and trained in European ways in the work of organisation and management of a large office. A Native Superintendent can rarely get over the fact that he belongs rather to the side of the clerks than of the masters. You cannot trust him to the same extent to work his clerks, and the work is not so efficiently turned out as under a European. . . .

"Some of the thirty-four appointments might be filled by Natives, but not one-third or anything approaching one-third, could be so filled with any advantage to the public service."

On the other hand, Mr. H. Cotterell Tupp, Accountant General, N. W. Provinces, held almost diametrically different views regarding the comparative merits of Europeans and Indians :

"We have already in our Accounts offices a class of officers called Chief Superintendents, who are the backbone of these offices; they are selected for merit from among the Superintendents, and it is so essential that they should be men of ability and energy that very little favouritism is shown in their selection. They are almost entirely Natives or Eurasians, and are fit for any work below the grade of Deputy Accountant-General; indeed it is upon them, and not on his European assistants, that an Accountant-General now depends for the carrying out of any really difficult task. . . . Besides the Chief Superintendents, there are in each large Accounts office ten or twelve Superintendents, most of whom are quite fit to do the work of an Assistant Accountant-General. From this large class we could at once recruit the forty Native and Eurasian assistants we require, and I would make Europeans unless domiciled, ineligible for these appointments. They have hitherto been appointed by nomination after a limited competition (which has been very nominal), and they have not been a success. A few good officers have entered in this way, but the majority are of very average ability and industry, and do not do their work in any way better than Natives of India, while they cost much more. On the other hand, a few are much worse and more useless than Native officers would ever be, for the natives would be turned out, whereas the Europeans are allowed to remain out of pity for the fate that would befall them if they were dismissed."*

The Director General of the Post Office of India considered natives of India to be not well suited for the post of Superintendent ; the Post Master General of Bombay, on the other hand, gave his evidence that they were.†

* Proceedings of the Sub-Committee of the Public Service Commission, Accounts Department.

† The Director General said :

"The recruitment of the Department is practically limited to domiciled Europeans or Eurasians, and to natives by race and blood. Comparing these classes as respects efficiency of service I would remark that the pure Native is usually specially qualified for sedentary occupation, such as the charge of a post office while the European or Eurasian is better fitted for work of a more active character. A native is trustworthy in money matters, obedient to rule, extracts hard work from subordinates, rarely objects to long office hours, is not addicted to exercise, and if employed near his home will work for a small salary. He therefore usually makes a good Post-master. For the position of Divisional Superintendent, which entails duties of inspection and supervision there is a general preference for Europeans on the part of heads of postal circles."

The Post-master General of Bombay, on the other hand, after describing the duties of the Superintendent, which are certainly not of a sedentary nature says :

"These duties are being efficiently discharged at the present time by Natives of India—Brahmans, Parbhu, and Parsi—in this circle who rank among the best Postal Superintendents in India; and so far as the ordinary postal administration of the circle is concerned, European agency in the Superintendent's grade is not, in my opinion, required so long as men of the same character and ability as the best of the present Native Superintendents can be obtained. There are,

There are it is true, a few Europeans, official as well as non-official, who have borne emphatic testimony to the fitness of the Indians for high positions of trust and responsibility. Sir Charles Turner remarked in his convocation address delivered before the University of Madras in 1887 said:

"Modern India has proved by examples that are known to, and honoured by, all in this assembly that her sons can qualify themselves to hold their own with the best of European talent in the council chamber, on the bench, at the bar, and in the mart."

We need scarcely make any apology for making the following rather long extract from the evidence of Mr. A. O. Hume before the Public Service Commission:

"The fact is—and this is what I, who claim to have had better opportunities of forming a correct opinion than most men now living, desire to urge—there is no such radical difference between Indians and Britons, as it too generally flatters the latter to suppose. The colour of the skins differ, and the ways and methods of thought of the two races, both descended from the same ancestral stock, have also come under the pressure of different environments to differ during the lapse of long ages, but at the bottom their hearts are much the same. Each race exhibits in a greater degree of development, virtues and vices, which are less prominent in the other; but if both races be judged impartially, and all *pros* and *cons* be fairly set down on both sides, there is very little ground for giving preference to either. If you compare the highest and best of our Indians with the ordinary of the rabble in England, these latter seem little better than monkeys beside grand men. If you compare the picked Englishmen we often get in India, trained and elevated by prolonged altruistic labours, and sobered and strengthened by weighty responsibilities, with the ordinary however, outside demands to meet, for which it is essential that there should be some European Superintendents "* (Proceedings, Sub-Committee of the Public Service Commission, Postal Department.

rabble of India, the former shine out like gods amongst common mortals. But if you fairly compare the best of both, though each class will exhibit excellencies and defects less noticeable in the other, neither can as a whole be justly said to be better or worse than the other. No doubt amongst India's 250 millions there are too many of whom no good report can be made, these being the men who chiefly fawn upon, and strive to curry favour with Europeans, and those by whom these latter mostly guage the national character, but, may I ask, are there any lack of similar n'er do weels, even amongst the 30 millions of Britons.

This whole misconception arises from the habit Englishmen in India have acquired, of regarding only the blackest side of the Indian and the brightest side of the English character, and from their theories as to the capacities of the two races being based on a consideration of the worst specimens of the one and the best specimens of the other.

If only they could free themselves from race and class bias, and consider the two races as a whole with absolute impartiality, then all their honest, though erroneous, apprehensions as to the results of much more extended employment of Indians in even the highest offices of the state would disappear, and all the best men among them, at any rate would be as eager to promote as they are now to prevent this necessary and just measure."[*]

Mr. Routledge in his "English Rule and Native opinion in India" says:

"Again I have heard it said that a native of India goes as far as he is taught, and can go no farther. I deny this thoroughly and entirely. It is a gross misrepresentation. The native of India is an essentially capable man, and he is often badly used. I have seen Englishmen going through crowds of the people of India, as at the Calcutta and Howrah landing-stage, elbowing their way as through a herd of cattle, and the people, as a rule, falling back on all hands. Sometimes the rule is broken, and the brutality meets with its match;

---

[*] For some of the facts upon which the opinion of Mr. Hume is based, see Appendix.

but as a rule it selects the poorest people, and rarely is met with real determination. We count them as of inferior race, deny them careers, and then talk of them as incapable of higher life. When the Catholic in England was shut out from public life, what did he become? Some sank, for want of society, to a low state; some went abroad; some, like Mr. Charles Waterton, the naturalist, found a need for all their innate gentlemanliness and loyalty to preserve them from intense hatred to the nation that had proved to them so hard a step-mother. Yet no Roman Catholic ever knew aught so disheartening as the lot of the native of India." *

But the great body of Anglo-Indian opinion, official and non-official, is more or less antagonistic to the employment of Indians in high positions of trust and responsibility. The source of this incompetency is not always exactly indicated, and often not indicated at all. According to Sir George Campbell, "they [the literary Indians] have all the intellectual power and ability of the European, but have not always his courage and resource."† On some ground or other—on the ground of policy if not on that of qualification—the path to higher employment is practically closed against the Hindus. There is now almost a consensus of opinion as to their fitness for the highest grades of the judicial service. Sir C. Trevelyan said :

"There are whole classes of employment for which the natives are specially qualified. The natives are specially qualified for revenue functions. The whole of the appointments in the Customs might be filled by natives. Then there is the great judicial department. It stands that if they are fit to be judges in the High Court, surely they are *a fortiori* fit

---

* *Op. cit.* p. 277.
† "The British Empire" p. 84.

J

for all inferior appointments. The native judges are fully up to the mark not only in point of ability but in point of integrity likewise."

Mr. H. J. S. Cotton says:

"The intellectual attainments and moral virtues of Dwarkanath Mitter sufficiently vindicate the competence of natives to exercise the most responsible judicial functions. He sat for many years upon the Bench of the High Court of Judicature in Bengal. Other native gentlemen might also be mentioned who before and after him have occupied the same post and acquitted themselves with credit. In the highest departments of the Judicial Service, as well as in the lowest, the employment of natives is admitted to be a successful experiment " *

Sometimes, indeed, reasons are assigned for keeping the Indians down at a low level which would not at all harmonise with the declared principles of British Rule. "I hold" said the Conservator of Forests, Berars Division, in his evidence before the Public Service Commission "that the highest posts in the department—those of administration—should always be held by Englishmen. It is right and proper, as well as necessary, that they should in India be at the head of all departments." †

It is the opinion of Sir John Strachey, that "in some branches of the service there is almost no limit to the share of public employment which they may properly receive. This is especially true of the Bench, for the performance of the judicial duties of which Natives have shewn themselves eminently qualified, and in which the higher offices are equal in importance and dignity and emolument to almost any of the great offices of the state."

* "New India" pp. 72-74.
† Proceedings of the Sub-Committee, Public Service Commission, Forest Department.

" Even on the Bench, however," adds Sir John Strachey " there are important administrative duties for which some degree of English supervision is necessary, nor would it be politically wise to place this great department of the Government altogether in Native hands."*
Notwithstanding the admitted competency of the Indians for the highest judicial posts, it is probably on grounds of policy that they are still so largely kept out of them.

Colonel De Pree, Surveyor-General of India, said in a memorandum submitted to the Public Service Commission :

"I may here remark incidently, that my numerous late inspections show me that the tendency of the European Surveyors is to stand and look on, while the Natives are made to do the drawing and hand-printing as if they thought themselves quite above that sort of thing. This is a mistake, and it cannot be permitted for the future. Besides, it is suicidal for the Europeans to admit that Natives can do any one thing better than themselves. They should claim to be superior *in everything* and only allow Natives to take a secondary or subordinate part. . . .

" In my old parties I never permitted a Native to touch a theodolite or an original computation, on the principle that the triangulation or scientific work was the prerogative of the highly-paid European ; and this reservation of the scientific work was the only way by which I could keep up a distinction, so as to justify the different figures of pay respectively drawn by the two classes, between the European in office time, and the Native who ran him so close in all the office duties as well as in field duties.

" Yet I see that Natives commonly do the computations now-a-days, and the Europeans some other inferior duties." †

---

* " India," p. 389.

† Proceedings of the Sub-Committee, Public Service Commission, Survey Department.

But instances of such indiscreet plain-speaking are rare. The moral effect of the exclusive policy has been no less disastrous than the economic effect. At every step the Hindu cannot but feel his degradation. If a man, though healthy, be repeatedly told that he is unhealthy, at least be treated as such, he will, very likely come in time to believe that there is really something wrong ; even so, the Hindu, systematically treated as if he were unfit, is apt to lose his faith in his capacity, which, within proper limits, is essential for sound, intellectual development. The circumstances under which he is placed tend to make him morbidly timid and diffident. If his good fortune has carried him into the higher ranks of any of the services, his actions are subjected to a watch and a criticism to which those of his European colleagues would never be subjected ; as a consequence errors which would be scarcely noticed in the case of the former, become prominent in his case and are pointed out as establishing his own unfitness and that of the race he represents.

Moral effect of the exclusive policy.

It is not necessary to suppose that his actions are intentionally subjected to exceptional criticism. The prejudiced eye sees faults and shortcomings where none exist, at least to the extent imagined. Besides, a community has usually a keener sight for the errors and failings of another community than for those of its own, especially when the relations between the two communities are such that the suppression of the one tends directly or indirectly to the elevation of the other.

Adverse criticism constantly repeated tends to create diffidence and want of boldness. These are however, not the only undesirable traits of character fostered by the exclusive system of British administration. The patronage of kings has since time immemorial, been the principal nursery of genius and talent in India. Literature, science, and art flourished mainly under the fostering care of some court or other. The British Government now occupies the position of these Hindu courts. The Government not only legislates, administers justice, and collects revenue, but also constructs railways, roads and buildings, and prosecutes scientific and literary research. Government service offers the best scope for ambition. It is preferred to such professions as law and medicine, because of the certainty of its prospects, and consequently absorbs as a rule the best talent of the country. Though this is not a desirable state of things, under present conditions it may be said to be almost unavoidable. The community is too poor to support literary or scientific work on Western conditions. But the Indian's scope for ambition in Government service is very limited. There are no great prizes for him, and consequently no great exertions are made. The tendency of the present exclusive system of the Government is to make him discontented and apathetic. There is no stimulus to call forth extraordinary energy and extraordinary vigour of mind, and consequently these qualities are not generally found well developed in him. We have already seen how the physical environment of the Hindu has been detrimental to the development of industrial qualities; the tendency of the British rule has been not to counteract but to aid the action of the physical causes and to reduce him to a condition of lifeless mediocrity.* As is well observed by Major Evans Bell, "the natives of India, of every caste and creed, are men of like powers and passions with ourselves; and in obedience to the universal law—as true in social science as in physiology—the healthy development of their civilisation cannot proceed without space and range for the exercise of all their faculties. Too much constraint, too much assistance, however benevolently intended, will but distort the phenomena of progress, disturb its steady course, and drive the stream into dangerous channel."†

<small>The injurious effect of the exclusive policy upon intellectual progress.</small>

The exclusive system of British rule tends to make the educated Hindu either diffident, and apathetic, or to embitter his feelings deeply towards the Government. Neither frame of mind is favourable to intellectual development. The Indian feels as if he were something apart from the British administration. He takes but little interest in it; he feels no enthusiasm for it. He is not sobered and strengthened by the weight of responsible administration. He is not elevated by the prospect of doing something great. Treated like a

---

* A few years ago, Sir John Gorst (then Under-Secretary of State for India) said: 'Government had alays discouraged independent and original talent, and had always preferred docile mediocrity. This was not a new policy.'

† "Retrospects and Prospects of Indian Policy," Preface p. vi.

child, it is no wonder that he often remains one. Without any outlet for his ambition, it is no wonder he gradually ceases to have any ambition at all. "A gentleman," observes Mr. Henry George "who had taught a coloured school once told me that he thought the coloured children up to the age of ten or twelve, were really brighter and learned more readily than white children, but after that age they seemed to get dull and careless. He thought this proof of innate race inferiority, and so did I at the time. But I afterwards heard a highly intelligent Negro gentleman (Bishop Hillery) incidentally make a remark which to my mind seems a sufficient explanation. He said, our children, when they are young, are fully as bright as white children, and learn as readily. But as soon as they get old enough to appreciate their status—to realise that they are looked upon as belonging to an inferior race * * * * they lose their ambition and cease to keep up."* The case of the Hindu is a somewhat analogous one. He has seldom any expectation of any thing higher than a mere subordinate position and his ambition, and along with it his energy, seldom rises above the level of such position. Recent changes in the administrative policy of British Rule have certainly not tended to enlarge the scope of his ambition. There are now in all the civil departments (to which alone Hindus eligible) are two sharply defined services—the Imperial and the Provincial. The pay and prospects of the former

---

* "Progress and Poverty," Book X, Ch. II.

are much higher than those of the latter. But the Imperial Service is recruited only in England. Such recruitment would not, perhaps, have been very unjust, had not the people of India been so miserably poor. There are but few among them who can afford to send their boys for education to England. Practically, therefore, the sphere of their ambition in the administration of their country is restricted to comparatively subordinate positions under the usually unsympathetic supervision of foreign taskmasters. The effect of the exclusive policy is not only to make them unaspiring and apathetic but also helpless to a degree. They can hardly move a step even in the matter of social reform without the guidance of high-placed officers of Government. The European officers also strive to retain and exercise as much power and influence as they possibly can. They are sometimes looked upon probably not without a substratum of reason—as if they were the sole dispensers of all earthly blessings not only by the subordinates under them, but also by Zamindars and others in no way connected with Government service; and the habits of subserviency thus engendered must be prejudicial to sound progress.

The traits of character created and fostered in the Hindu by the exclusive policy of the British Government are reflected in the Hindu literature. There can be no doubt, that the English contact, especially English education has remarkably stimulated intellectual progress among the Hindus. Their literature has been immensely enriched within the last fifty years. The novel, which now forms an important branch of vernacular literature, is altogether a creation of the English contact. Though Sanskrit boasts of dramas of exceptional merit, the vernacular literatures did not possess any dramas worth the name until recently. History, archæology, biography, and natural science are also new subjects in vernacular literature. But the extension has been more in surface than in depth. Vernacular literature is generally wanting in that boldness of conception, that originality and vigour of thought which invariably accompany healthy progress. This is no doubt partly due to the fact, that the progress effected in the West during the more or less stationary period of Hindu civilisation must be assimilated before any new path can be struck out. But the administrative policy of the British Government is also partly accountable for this serious defect in the recent renaissance of Hindu literature. For its tendency has been to keep down the material condition of India at a level lower than that of the poorest and most backward country in Europe; to suppress the natural aspirations of the flower of Hindu manhood; and to foster in them habits of thought and traits of character which are detrimental to sound progress.

CHAPTER VI.

EDUCATION UNDER BRITISH RULE— ENGLISH EDUCATION.

High Education in pre-British times. The vehicle of higher Hindu education in pre-British times was mainly Sanskrit.* It was imparted in private schools, and in Parishads, the latter resembling the Universities of the West. We are not aware that there are any Parishads now in any part of India.† But private Sanskrit schools (*tols*) have survived to the present day; and the methods of instruction and discipline pursued in them now are not much different from what they were three thousand years ago. The Mahomedan conquest, the destruction or decay of Hindu courts, and the rise of

---

* From the time of Akbar until about 1835, Persian was also largely studied.

† The *Maths* or monasteries of Southern India resemble the Parishads so far, that instruction is imparted in them by a number of teachers in the Vedas, Upanishads, logic, philosophy etc.

INDIGENOUS HIGH EDUCATION.

the vernacular literatures, no doubt affected them seriously. Still there was at the establishment of the British rule, and there is still a good number of *tols* scattered all over the country. In 1801, Mr. Hamilton reckoned 190 such seminaries in the district of Twenty-four Pergunnas in Bengal. In 1818, Ward found 28 of them with 173 scholars in the city of Calcutta, and 31 schools with 747 students at Nuddea, which for, several centuries past, has been the principal seat of Sanskrit learning in Bengal. At a more accurate enumeration, in 1829, by H. H. Wilson it was found that there were then at Nuddea 25 Sanskrit schools with from 5 to 6 hundred pupils. In 1837, Mr. Adam found in the districts of Murshidabad, Bírbhúm, Burdwan, South Bihar and Tirhut, some 353 Sanskrit schools [*] with 2555 students. He calculates that there were about 1830, in Bengal, some 10,800 students of Hindu learning, and some 1800 teachers.[†] In 1881, there were in Bengal no less than 1010 *tols* with 7680 scholars ; in the North-West Provinces and Oudh, 235 *tols* with 4,100 students ; and in the Bombay Presidency 48 Hindu Vedashalas and Sanskrit schools. [‡]

---

[*] Adam's Reports, edited by the Rev. J. Long Calcutta, 1868, page 197. Adam's figures would give 353 teachers. But as there is scarcely ever more than one teacher to a school, we may construe them to mean as many schools.

[†] Adam's Reports, page 27.

[‡] Report of the Education Commission of 1882 pp. 59-60. With regard to Madras, the report states that " in every large town containing Brahman residents and in every Hindu *Mathum*, instruction in the

The following extracts relating to the *tols* from Mr. Adam's reports will give a fair idea of their educational system :

"The Hindu colleges or schools in which the higher branches of Hindu learning are taught are generally built of clay. Sometimes three or five rooms are erected, and in others nine or eleven, with a reading-room which is also of clay. These huts are frequently erected at the expense of the teacher, who not only solicits alms to raise the building, but also to feed his pupils. In some cases rent is paid for the ground; but the ground is commonly, and in particular instances both the ground and the expenses of the building are, a gift. After a school-room and lodging-rooms have been thus built, to secure the success of the school, the teacher invites a few Brahmans and respectable inhabitants to an entertainment, at the close of which the Brahmans are dismissed with some trifling presents. If the teacher finds a difficulty in obtaining scholars, he begins the college with a few junior relatives, and by instructing them and distinguishing himself in the disputations that take place on public occasions, he establishes his reputation. The school opens early every morning by the teacher and pupils assembling in the open reading-room, when the different classes read in turns. Study is continued till towards mid-day, after which three hours are devoted to bathing, worship, eating, and sleep; and at three they resume their studies which are continued till twilight. Nearly two hours are then devoted to evening-worship, eating, smoking, and relaxation, and the studies are again resumed and continued till ten or eleven at night. The evening studies consist of a revision of the lessons already learned, in order that what the pupils have read may be impressed more distinctly on the memory. These studies are frequently pursued especially by the students of logic, till two or three o'clock in the morning.

There are three kinds of colleges in Bengal—one in which chiefly

Vedas, Upanishads, the Indian system of logic and philosophy, the grammar of Panini, rhetoric, the Hindu epic poems and dramas and Hindu Law, has been given from the earliest period."

grammar, general literature, and rhetoric and occasionally the great mythological poems and law are taught; a second, in which chiefly law and sometimes the mythological poems are studied; and a third, in which logic is made the principal object of attention. In all these colleges select works are read and their meaning explained; but instruction is not conveyed in the form of lectures. In the first class of colleges, the pupils repeat assigned lessons from the grammar used in each college, and the teacher communicates the meaning of the lessons after they have been committed to memory. In the others the pupils are divided into classes according to their progress. The pupils of each class having one or more books before them, seat themselves in the presence of the teacher, when the best reader of the class reads aloud, and the teacher gives the meaning as often as asked, and thus they proceed from day to day till the work is completed. The study of grammar is pursued during two, three, or six years, and where the work of Panini is studied, not less than ten, and sometimes twelve, years are devoted to it. As soon as a student has obtained such a knowledege of grammar as to be able to read and understand a poem, a law book, or a work on philosophy, he may commence this course of reading also, and carry on at the same time the remainder of his grammar-studies. Those who study law or logic continue reading either at one college or another for six, eight, or even ten years. When a person has obtained all the knowledge possessed by one teacher, he makes some respectful excuse to his guide and avails himself of the instructions of another. When a student is about to commence the study of law or of logic, his fellow students, with the concurrence and approbation of the teacher, bestow on him an honorary title descriptive of the nature of his pursuit, and always differing from any title enjoyed by any of his learned ancestors. In some parts of the country, the title is bestowed by an assembly of Pundits convened for the purpose; and in others the assembly is held in the presence of a raja or zemindar who may be desirous of encouraging learning and who at the same time bestows a dress of honor on the student and places a mark on his forehead. When the student finally leaves college and enters on the business of life, he is commonly addressed by that title." *

* Adam's Reports pp. 27-29.

Sanskrit lore even such as was imparted at these schools, could not fail to impress favourably upon the minds of the more cultured and thoughtful among the servants of the East India Company. Sanskrit science and Sanskrit literature came almost like a revelation to them, and men like Sir William Jones, Horace Hayman Wilson, and Henry Thomas Colebrooke, devoted their lives to Sanskrit research. Even a politician like Warren Hastings caught the enthusiasm of the Orientalists. While recommending the translation of the *Bhagavatgítá* by Charles Wilkins, Hastings says: "With the deductions or rather qualifications which I have thus premised I hesitate not to pronounce the *Gítá* a performance of great originality; of a sublimity of conception, reasoning, and diction, almost unequalled; and a single exception among all the known religions of mankind of a theology accurately corresponding with that of the Christian dispensation, and most powerfully illustrating its fundamental doctrines."* Sir William Jones used to study Sanskrit with the image of a Hindu god placed on his table.

Sanskrit influence upon British Scholars.

The first step taken by the British Government towards the education of the Hindus was inspired by a desire for the promotion of Sanskrit scholarship. The Sanskrit College founded at Benares in 1791, at the recommendation of Jonathan Duncan, an Oriental

Foundation of Sanskrit College at Benares.

---

* *Calcutta Review*, Vol, III. p. 234.

scholar, was based upon the indigenous Sanskrit school, such as has been described above. Its organisation was essentially Bráhmanical ; and in its schemes of instruction and examination even the prejudices of the Bráhmans were respected. The object of the institution is stated to have been "the preservation, and cultivation of the laws, literature, and religion of the Hindus (and more particularly their laws) in their sacred city." All the professors, except the professor of medicine, were to be Bráhmans. "The scholars were to be examined four times a year in the presence of the Resident, in all such parts of knowledge as are not held too sacred to be discussed in the presence of any but the Bráhmans. The discipline of the college was to be conformable in all respects to the Dharma Shastra in the chapter on education." * The course of studies in the college included theology, ritual, metaphysics, logic, law, grammar &c.

The educational minute of Lord Minto.

The Sanskrit College of Benares costing Government twenty thousand rupees a year was for a quarter of a century the only institution through which the East India Company discharged their educational responsibilities towards their Hindu subjects. The college, however, does not appear to have been successful ; and the Earl of Minto, in a minute dated the 6th of March, 1811, gives the following reasons :

* Kerr's "Review of Public Instruction in the Bengal Presidency" quoted in "Indian Year Book for 1861" by John Murdoch (Madras, 1862) p. 140. *Calcutta Review,* vol. III. pp. 215-216.

"1st. A prejudice appears to exist among the Hindus of that city (Benares) against the office of professor, considered as an office or even as a service; and the most learned pundits have consequently refused the situation, although the salary attached to it is liberal.

2nd. The feuds which have arisen among the members of the college and which may be ascribed chiefly to the avarice and malversation of the former native rector, entrusted with authority over the rest, and with the payment of their allowances have tended materially to defeat the objects of the institution.

3rd. That part of the plan which supposes the attendance of teachers and students in a public hall, appears to be inconsistent with the usages of the Hindus. It has not only never taken effect, but has tended to prevent the professors from giving instruction in their own house."

The minute goes on to propose the establishment of Sanskrit Colleges at Nuddea and at Bhar in the district of Tirhut, guarding, of course, against the defects just mentioned. The minute was evidently inspired by the Oriental scholars, and it bears the signature, among others, of Colebrooke. The following extract from it will show to what extent the authorities of the time were actuated by a desire to revive Sanskrit learning:

"It is a common remark that science and literature are in a progressive state of decay among the natives of India. From every inquiry which I have been enabled to make on this interesting subject, that remark appears to me but too well founded. The number of the learned is not only diminished, but the circle of learning, even among those who still devote themselves to it, appears to be considerably contracted. The abstract sciences are abandoned, polite literature neglected, and no branch of learning cultivated but what is connected with the peculiar religious doctrines of the people. The immediate consequence of this state of things is the disuse, and even actual loss, of many valuable books; and it is to be apprehended that, unless Government interfere with a fostering hand, the revival of letters may shortly become hopeless from a want of books, or of persons capable of explaining them.

The principal cause of the present neglected state of literature in India is to be traced to the want of that encouragement which was formerly afforded to it by princes, chieftains, and opulent individuals under the native governments. Such encouragement must always operate as a strong incentive to study and literary exertions, but especially in India, where the learned professions have little, if any other, support. The justness of these observations might be illustrated by a detailed consideration of the former and present state of science and literature at the three principal seats of Hindu learning, viz., Benares, Tirhoot, and Nadiya. Such a review would bring before us the liberal patronage which was formerly bestowed, not only by princes and others in power and authority, but also by the zemindars, on persons who had distinguished themselves by the successful cultivation of letters at those places. It would equally bring to our view the present neglected state of learning at those once celebrated places; and we should have to remark with regret that the cultivation of letters was now confined to the few surviving persons who had been patronized by the native princes and others under the former Government, or to such of the immediate descendants of those persons as had imbibed a love of science from their parents. It is seriously to be lamented that a nation particularly distinguished for its love and successful cultivation of letters in other parts of the empire should have failed to extend its fostering care to the literature of the Hindus, and to aid in opening to the learned in Europe the repositories of that literature." *

The educational clause in the Charter of 1813. It was apparently with reference to this minute, that it was enacted in the Charter of 1813 :

"That it shall be lawful for the Governor-General in Council to direct that out of any surplus which may remain of the rents, revenues, and profits arising from the said territorial acquisitions after defraying

---

* The minute is partly quoted by Adam from the records of the General Committee of Public Instruction, Adam's Reports, p. 398. It is also quoted in the *Calcutta Review* vol. III. pp. 255-257.

the expenses of the military, civil, and commercial establishments, and paying the interest of the debt in manner hereinafter provided, a sum of not less than one lakh of rupees in each year shall be set apart and applied to *the revival and improvement of literature and the encouragement of the learned natives of India,* and for the introduction and promotion of a knowledge of the sciences among the inhabitants of the British territories in India ; and that any schools, public lectures or other institutions for the purposes aforesaid, which shall be founded at the Presidencies of Fort William, Fort St. George, or Bombay, or in any other part of the British territories in India in virtue of this Act, shall be governed by such regulations as may, from time to time, be made by the said Governor-General in Council, subject nevertheless to such powers as are herein vested in the said Board of Commissioners for the Affairs of India respecting Colleges and Seminaries : Provided always that all appointments to offices in such schools lecturerships, and other institutions, shall be made by or under the authority of the Governments within which the same shall be situated."

The Directors Communicated with the Governor-General as to the best way of spending the lakh of rupees thus set apart for educational purposes. With regard to the educational policy that was to be pursued, they wrote :

"We are informed that there are in the Sanskrit language many excellent systems of ethics with codes of laws and compendiums of the duties to every class of the people, the study of which might be useful to those natives who may be destined for the judicial department of Government. There are also many tracts of merit, we are told, on the virtues of drugs and plants, and on the application of them in medicine, the knowledge of which might prove desirable to European practitioners ; and there are treatises on Astronomy, mathematics, including Geometry and Algebra, which, though they may not add new lights to European science, might be made to form links of communication between the natives and the gentlemen in our service, who are attached to the observatory and to the department of Engineers, and by such intercourse the natives might gradually be led to adopt the modern improvements in these and other sciences." *

Establishment of Oriental Colleges at Calcutta, Agra and Delhi 1824-25.

But no steps were taken to carry the educational provision of the charter into effect until 1823, when a Committee of Public Instruction was formed. One of its very first acts was the establishment of a Sanskrit College at Calcutta, which opened in 1824, with 7 teachers and 50 pupils. We have already referred to Lord Minto's minute of 1811, which recommended the establishment of Sanskrit Colleges at Nadiyá and at Bhár (Tirhut). The proposal, though it appears to have been sanctioned was not carried into effect. A modified scheme was submitted to the Court of Directors in 1821, which suggested the establishment of a Sanskrit College at Calcutta instead of either at Nadiyá or Bhár. The scheme evoked a despatch from the Court of Directors believed to have been penned by James Mill the tone of which was as hostile to the revival of oriental learning as that of 1814 which we have referred to above was favourable to it, as the following extracts will show:

"With respect to the sciences, it is worse than a waste of time to employ persons either to teach or to learn them in the state in which they are found in the oriental books.......We wish you to be fully apprized of our zeal for the progress and improvement of education among the natives of India, and of our willingness to make con-

---

* Quoted in "The History and Prospects of British Education in India" by F. W. Thomas, p. 24.

siderable sacrifices to that important end, if proper means for the attainment of it could be pointed out to us ; but we apprehend the plan of the institutions [The Sanskrit College at Benares and the Madrassa at Calcutta], to the improvement of which our attention is now directed, was originally and fundamentally erroneous. The great end should not have been to teach Hindu learning or Mahomedan learning, but useful learning........In professing, on the other hand, to establish seminaries for the purpose of teaching men Hindu or Mahomedan literature, you bound yourselves to teach a great deal of what was frivolous, not a little of what was purely mischievous, and a small remainder, indeed, in which utility was in any way concerned." *

The Agra and Delhi Colleges were founded, between 1824 and 1825, on an oriental basis like the Sanskrit College. English education, however, was soon grafted upon the original plan. In the Sanskrit College, at Calcutta European medicine and anatomy supplanted the Hindu system. At Agra and at Delhi, Geography and Mathematics were included in the college curriculum. English classes were also attached to the Sanskrit College of Calcutta and to the Agra College, while at Delhi and Benares distinct schools were formed for the teaching of the English language. †

In Bombay, as in Bengal, the first British attempt at higher education was a Sanskrit College which was opened at Puna in 1821. In this case, however, there was scarcely any choice.

Sanskrit College at Puna, 1821.

---

* Quoted by C. E. Trevelyan, "The Education of the people of India" pp. 74-77.

† Report of the Committee of Public Instruction (1831).

The Peshwa had annually distributed large sums of money among learned Bráhmans. The practice was continued for a time when his territories came into British possession. But Mr. Chaplin, Commissioner of the Deccan, proposed, in lieu of such distribution, the establishment of a college for "the encouragement and improvement of the useful part of Hindu learning." After several years' trial the Government found that the institution had "fulfilled no purpose but that of perpetuating prejudices and false systems of opinions." *

Educational Policy of Elphinstone. The government policy of education adopted in Western India was quite different from that of Northern India. The central idea of the former was to work through the vernaculars, as that of the latter was to work through the classical languages. In 1823, the Hon. Mountstuart Elphinstone submitted his scheme to the Court of Directors, the principal object of which was the encouragement of vernacular education. English was to be taught, but only as a classical language; and provision was made for the translation of English books on moral and physical sciences. Higher education was to be imparted through the vernaculars; and an engineering and a medical school were started at Bombay about 1825, in which instruction was imparted by means of translations of standard English works.

---

* "Oriental Christian Spectator" quoted in the "Indian year Book for 1861" p. 142.

Early educational measures in Madras.

In Madras, a Board of Public Instruction was appointed in 1826. Under its auspices a central school was established at Madras in which the Hindus were to be educated in Sanskrit and the vernaculars, and about one hundred schools were started in the rural districts. The central institution, though at first far from a success, formed in 1841, the basis of the Madras High School; the rural schools, however, were abolished after a few years as failures.

Indigenous efforts to spread English Education : Rámmohan Ráya.

While the authorities were trying to spread classical education in Bengal, vernacular education in Bombay, and a mixture of both in Madras, the Hindus themselves were expressing their eagerness for English education in no uncertain tone. When Government proposed to apply a portion of the funds set apart for education to the foundation of a Sanskrit College in Calcutta, they loudly protested against it. Rámmohan Ráya, the most cultured Hindu of the time addressed a letter to Lord Amherst in which he earnestly pleaded the cause of English education :

"We find" says Rámmohan Ráya "that the Government are establishing a Sanskrit school under Hindu pundits, to impart such knowledge as is already current in India. The seminary (similar in character to those which existed in Europe before the time of Lord Bacon) can only be expected to load the minds of youth with grammatical niceties and metaphysical distinctions of little or no practical use to the possessors or to society. The pupils will there acquire what was known two thousand years ago, with the addition of vain and empty subtleties since produced by speculative men, such as is already

THE HINDU COLLEGE. 167

commonly taught in all parts of India." "If it were thought necessary" he goes on to observe "to perpetuate this language for the sake of the portion of the valuable information it contains, this might be much more easily accomplished by other means than the establishment of a new Sanskrit College; for there have been always, and there are now numerous professors of Sanskrit in the different parts of the country engaged in teaching this language as well as the other branches of literature which are to be the object of the new seminary. Therefore their more diligent cultivation if desirable, would be effectually promoted by holding out premiums and granting certain allowances to their most eminent professors, who have already undertaken on their own account to teach them, and would by such rewards be stimulated to still greater exertions. From these considerations, as the sum set apart for the instruction of the natives of India was intended by the Government in England for the improvement of its Indian subjects, I beg leave to state, with due deference to your Lordship's exalted situation, that if the plan now adopted be followed, it will completely defeat the object proposed; since no improvement can be expected from inducing young men to consume a dozen years of the most valuable period of their lives in acquiring the niceties of Byakaran or Sanskrit Grammar."

Indigenous efforts to spread English education: the Hindu College of Calcutta.

The enthusiasm of the Hindus for English education was not confined to such protests. Finding that Government was but little inclined to adopt efficient measures for the spread of English education, they took steps independently to secure it for their boys. The Hindu College of Calcutta was founded in 1817 for imparting English education, mainly through the exertions of David Hare, a retired watch-maker of a very benevolent disposition.* The leading Hindus

* The following interesting account of the establishment of this college was given by Dr. Duff in his evidence before the Select Committee of the House of commons previous to the East India company's

of Calcutta contributed liberally towards its support; and though in 1823, it came under the control of the Committee of Public Instruction, its management continued in Hindu hands. The institution was very successful; and its success showed the real want it supplied. The number of its pupils rose from about 70 in 1819 to above 400 in 1830. The Committee of Public Instruction speaking of the Hindu College in 1831 observe: "The consequence has surpassed our expectation. A command of the English language and a familiarity with its literature and science have been acquired to an extent rarely equalled by any schools in Europe. A

---

charter of 1853 ("The Life of Alexander Duff by George Smith, Vol. I. pp. 99-100):

"The system of English education commenced in the following very simple way in Bengal. There were two persons who had to do with it. One was Mr. David Hare, and the other was a native, Rámmohan Ráya. In the year 1815 they were in consultation one evening with a few friends as to what should be done with a view to the elevation of the native mind and character............Mr. David Hare was a watch-maker in Calcutta, an ordinary illiterate man himself; but being a man of great energy and strong practical sense, he said the plan should be to institute an English School or College for the instruction of native youth. Accordingly he soon drew up and issued a circular on the subject, which gradually attracted the attention of the leading Europeans, and, among others, of the Chief Justice Sir Hyde East. Being led to consider the proposed measure, he entered heartily into it, and got a meeting of European gentlemen assembled in May, 1816. He invited also some of the influential natives to attend. Then it was unanimously agreed that they should commence an institution for the teaching of English to the higher classes, to be designated the Hindu College of Calcutta. A large joint committee of Europeans and natives was appointed to carry the design into effect."

taste for English has been widely disseminated, and independent schools, conducted by young men reared in the Vidyalaya (the Hindu College), are springing up in every direction."

Early Missionary efforts to spread English education. The Jaynarain Charity School, now Jaynarain College providing a secondary training under Missionary management in English, Persian, Bengali and Hindusthani was founded at Benares in 1818 from the munificent bequest of an enlightened Hindu. The Missionary College at Serampore was also projected in the same year.

In 1830, Dr. Alexander Duff, a missionary of the General Assembly of the Scotch Kirk, opened a school in which English was chosen as the principal medium of instruction.

The eagerness for English education was not confined to Bengal. In Bombay the educational policy of Mountstuart Elphinstone was, as we have seen already, to encourage vernacular education. When, however, Elphinstone retired in 1827, a fund raised to perpetuate his memory, was applied to the establishment of a college similar to the Hindu College of Calcutta, which was called the Elphinstone College.

The Elphinstone College of Bombay.

The educational grant made by the Charter of 1833. Thus the cause of English education was gradually asserting itself when an event happened in Bengal which not only assured its existence but secured its future prosperity. In 1833, the grant at the disposal of the Committee of

Public Instruction was increased by an Act of Parliament from £10,000 to £100,000. The committee had on the average been spending more than double the authorised amount.* Still the balance left after meeting all their demands was considerable; and a discussion arose as to how it was to be spent. There were two parties, which were equally balanced, five against five; one in favour of spending it upon oriental education, and the other upon English education.

The Orientalists argued, that the charter grant of 1813 was assigned for "the revival and improvement of literature," which could only mean oriental literature, and for "the encouragement of the learned natives of India; by which oriental scholars alone could have been intended"; that English education meant only a smattering of it, and the question was between "a profound knowledge of Sanskrit and Arabic literature on the one side, and a superficial knowledge of the rudiments of English on the other," that the classical languages were "absolutely necessary for the improvement of the vernacular dialects" and "that the condemnation of the classical languages to oblivion, would consign the dialects to utter helplessness and irretrievable barbarism," that "little real progress can be made until the learned classes in India are enlisted in the cause of diffusing sound knowledge, and that "one able Pundit or Maulavee, who should add English to Sanskrit or Arabic, who should be led

Controversy between the Anglicists and the Orientalists.

------

* Thomas, "History of British Education" pp 28-29.

to expose the absurdities and errors of his own system, and advocate the adoption of European knowledge and principles, would work a greater revolution in the minds of his countrymen than would result from their proficiency in English alone;" and "that as we have succeeded the native chiefs who were the natural patrons of Indian learning, we are bound to give that aid to oriental scholars which they would have done had they never been displaced by us."

To these arguments, the Anglicists replied, that the grant of 1813 was not only for "the encouragement and improvement of literature and the encouragement of the learned natives of India" "but also for the introduction and promotion of a knowledge of the sciences," by which European sciences alone could be intended, that the example of the Hindu College showed, that Indians could acquire a command of the English language and a familiarity with its literature and science "to an extent rarely equalled by any schools in Europe ;" and "the best test of what they can do is what they have done ; that all that is required is to impregnate the national mind with knowledge, but by adhering to oriental education the national mind would for ages be kept " in a state of worse than Egyptian bondage, in order that the vernacular dialects may be improved from congenial, instead of from uncongenial sources" ; that it was quite unnecessary, even if it was practical to have able Pundits and Maulvis versed in English to propagate a taste for European knowledge, as such taste had been created already, and the people were greedy for English education ; and the English Government were not "bound to perpetuate the system patronised by their predecessors, merely because it was patronised by them, however little it may have been caculated to promote the welfare of the people."*

"This fundamental difference of opinion long obstructed the business of the committee. Almost every thing which came before them was more or less involved in it. The two parties were so equally balanced as to be unable to make a forward movement in any direction. A particular point might occasionally be decided by an accidental majority of one or two, but as the decision was likely to be reversed the next time the subject came on for discussion, this only added inconsistency to inefficiency. This state of things lasted for about three years, until both parties became convinced that the usefulness and respectability of their body would be utterly compromised by its longer continuance. The committee had come to a dead stop and the Government alone could set it in motion again by giving a preponderance to one or the other of the two opposite sections. The members, therefore, took the only course which remained open to them, and laid before the government a statement of their existing position, and of the grounds of the conflicting opinions held by them."†

---

* Trevelyan, " Education of the people of India" pp. 95-142.
† Trevelyan, " Education of the people of India" pp. 11-12.

Though the parties were equally balanced, the orientalists in point of distinction, were at first, the stronger, including as they did among them such men as Wilson and Shakespeare. But the arrival of Macaulay in 1834, and his able advocacy of the cause of the Anglicists turned the scale in their favour; and the discussion was at last terminated by his minute in which he thus sums up his arguments:

The controversy terminated by the minute of Macaulay

"I think it clear that we are not fettered by the Act of Parliament of 1813; that we are not fettered by any pledge expressed or implied; that we are free to employ our funds as we choose; that we ought to employ them in teaching what is best worth knowing; that English is better worth knowing than Sanskrit or Arabic; that the natives are desirous to be taught English, and are not desirous to be taught Sanskrit or Arabic; that neither as the languages of law, nor as the languages of religion, have the Sanskrit and Arabic any peculiar claim to our encouragement; that it is possible to make natives of this country thoroughly good English scholars, and that to this end our efforts ought to be directed.

"In one point I fully agree with the gentlemen to whose general views I am opposed. I feel with them, that it is impossible for us, with our limited means, to attempt to educate the body of the people. We must at present do our best to form a class who may be interpreters between us and the millions whom we govern; a class of persons Indian in blood and colour, but English in taste, in opinions, in morals, and in intellect. To that class we may leave it to refine the vernacular dialects of the country, to enrich those dialects with terms of science borrowed from the western nomenclature, and to render them by degrees fit vehicles for conveying knowledge to the great mass of the population."

In March 1835, the following resolution evidently determined by the minute of Macaulay was passed by lord William Bentinck:

The Educational Resolution of Lord William Bentinck, 1835.

"His Lordship is of opinion that the great object of the British Government ought to be the promotion of European literature and science amongst the natives of India, and that all the funds appropriated for the purpose of education would be best employed on English education alone.

"But it is not the intention of his Lordship in council to abolish any college or school of native learning, while the native population shall appear to be inclined to avail themselves of the advantages which it affords; and his Lordship in council directs that all the existing professors and students at all the institutions under the superintendence of the committee shall continue to receive their stipends. But his Lordship in council decidedly objects to the practice which has hitherto prevailed, of supporting the students during the period of their education. He conceives that the only effect of such a system can be, to give artificial encouragement to branches of learning which, in the natural course of things, would be superseded by more useful studies; and he directs that no stipend shall be given to any student who may hereafter enter at any of these institutions, and that when any professor of Oriental learning shall vacate his situation, the committee shall report to the Government the number and state of the class, in order that the Government may be able to decide upon the expediency of appointing a successor.

"It has come to the knowledge of the Governor-General in Council that a large sum has been expended by the committee in the printing of Oriental works. His Lordship in Council directs that no portion of the funds shall hereafter be so employed.

"His Lordship in council directs, that all the funds which these reforms will leave at the disposal of the committee be henceforth employed in imparting to the native population a knowledge of English literature and science, through the medium of the English language; and his Lordship in council requests the committee to submit to

Government with all expedition a plan for the accomplishment of this purpose."

Rapid spread of English education since 1835.

The resolution of Lord William Bentinck gave a great impetus to English education in Northern India. Two of the orientalist members of the Committee of Public Instruction tendered their resignation. New members were elected whose views were more in conformity with those of the Government resolution. The Hindus who had hitherto been unrepresented on the Committee were now allowed a share in their deliberations. The newly organised Committee with Macaulay as their President took very active measures for the spread of English education. Six new schools were established the very year the resolution of Bentinck was passed, and six more were established at the commencement of the next year. A library was attached to each school. Books and scientific apparatus of various kinds were ordered from England. Within three years, between 1835 and 1838, the number of seminaries under the control of the Committee rose from eleven to forty, and the number of pupils from about three thousand and four hundred to six thousand. The Sanskrit Colleges at Benares and Calcutta were open to Brahmans and Vaidyas only ; even the Hindu College of Calcutta would not admit low-caste Hindus. The new seminaries admitted boys irrespective of caste or creed ; and this course does not appear ever to have had any deterrent effect upon the admission of the higher classes. The passion for English knowledge gradually penetrated into the interior.

"The steam boats passing up and down the river" says Trevelyan (1838) "are boarded by native boys begging not for money, but for books." "Some gentlemen coming to Calcutta were astonished at the eagerness with which they were pressed for books by a troop of boys, who boarded the steamer from an obscure place called Comercolly. A Plato was lying on the table, and one of the party asked a boy whether that would serve his purpose. "Oh yes" he exclaimed "give me any book; all I want is a book. The gentleman at last hit upon the expedient of cutting up an old *Quarterly Review*, and distributing the articles among them. In the evening, when some of the party went ashore, the boys of the town flocked around them, expressing their regret that there was no English School in the place, and saying that they hoped that the Governor-General, to whom they had made an application on the subject when he passed on his way up the country, would establish one." *

"The tide" says Trevelyan "had set in strongly in favour of English education, and when the committee declared itself on the same side, the public support they received rather went beyond than fell short of what was required. More applications were received for the establishment of schools than could be complied with; there were more candidates for admission to many of those which were established than could be accommodated. On the opening of the Hooghly College,. in August 1836, students of English flocked to it in such numbers as to render the organization and classification of them a matter of difficulty. Twelve hundred names were entered on the books of this department

* Trevelyan, *op. cit.*, p. 167.

of the college within three days, and at the end of the year there were upwards of one thousand in regular attendance. The Arabic and Persian classes of the institution at the same time mustered less than two hundred. There appears to be no limit to the number of scholars, except that of the number of teachers whom the committee is able to provide. Notwithstanding the extraordinary concourse of English students at Hooghly, the demand was so little exhausted, that when an auxiliary school was lately opened within two miles of the colleges the English department of it was instantly filled, and numerous applicants were sent away unsatisfied. In the same way, when additional means of instruction were provided at Dacca, the number of pupils rose at once from 150 to upwards of 300, and more teachers were still called for. The same thing also took place at Agra." * While pupils had to be paid to enter the Sanskrit Colleges, they were ready to pay to enter the English schools.

The eagerness for English education was also testified by the number of English books sold by the School Book Society of Calcutta. Between January, 1834, and December, 1835, while they sold over thirty one thousand five hundred copies of English books, the number of Arabic and Sanskrit books sold by them amounted only to fiftytwo.

About the year 1837, a step of great importance to the cause of English education was taken by Government.

* Trevelyan, op. cit. pp. 81-83.

L

Persian had hitherto been the official language. It was neither the classical nor the vernacular tongue of the Hindus, but they learnt it as it was the language of the courts, and was absolutely necessary for official employment. But about 1838, the vernacular language was substituted for the Persian as the language of the courts. This measure served as an incentive, though indirectly, to English education. Persian had hitherto been the only language of liberal education to the body of the Hindu community; for all but Bráhmans were debarred from Sanskrit education,* and the vernacular literatures were not yet sufficiently rich to offer anything like a liberal education. With the abolition of Persian as court language the necessity for learning it was gone; and when the choice lay between Persian and English as media for general education, the Hindus could not be long in deciding which to adopt, when they considered that though both were foreign to them, English, besides being the language of their Governors, possessed a literature immeasurably superior to the Persian.

Impetus to English education given by the discontinuance of Persian as official language about 1838.

In 1842-43, the committee of education gave place to a more powerful organisation known as the council of Education. It was chiefly by means of the council's exertions that the following proclamation was issued by Lord Hardinge in 1844, which opened up avenues of respect-

The Educational Resolution of Lord Hardinge, 1844.

---

* The Vaidyas received it to a very limited extent only.

able employment to those who acqitted themselves creditably at the final examinations :—

"The Governor-General, having taken into his consideration the existing state of education, and being of opinion that it is highly desirable to afford it every reasonable encouragement, by holding out to those who have taken advantage of the opportunity of instruction afforded to them, a 'fair prospect of employment in the public service, and thereby not only to reward individual merit, but to enable the State to profit as largely and as early as possible, by the result of the measures adopted of late years for the instruction of the people, as well by the Government as by private individuals and societies, has resolved that in every possible case a preference shall be given in the selection of candidates for public employment to those who have been educated in the institutions thus established, and specially to those who have distinguished themselve s therein by a more than ordinary degree of merit and attainment.

The Governor-General is accordingly pleased to direct that it be an instruction to the Council of Education, and to the several Local Committees, and other authorities charged with the duty of superintending public instruction throughout the Provinces subject to the Government of Bengal, to submit to that Government at an early date, and subsequently on the 1st of January of each year, returns (prepared according to the form appended to this resolution) of students who may be fitted, according to their several degrees of merit and capacity, for such of the various public offices as, with reference to their age, abilities, and other circumstances, they may be deemed qualified to fill.

The Governor-General is further pleased to direct that the Council of Education be requested to receive from the Governors or Managers of all scholastic establishments, other than those supported out of the public funds, similar returns of meritorious students; and to incorporate them, after due and sufficient enquiry, with those of Government institutions; and also that managers of such establishments be publicly invited to furnish returns of that description periodically to the Council of Education.

The returns, when received, will be printed and circulated to the head of all Government offices both in and out of Calcutta, with instructions to omit no opportunity of providing for and advancing the candidates thus presented to their notice ; and in filling up every situation, of whatever grade, in their gift, to show them an invariable preference over others not possessed of similar qualifications. The appointment of all such candidates to situations under the Government will be immediately communicated by the appointing officer to the Council of Education, and will by them be brought to the notice of the Government and of the public in their annual reports. It will be the duty of controlling officers, with whom rests the confirmation of appointments made by their subordinates, to see that a sufficient explanation is afforded in every case in which the selection may not have fallen upon an educated candidate whose name is borne on the printed returns.

With a view still further to promote and encourage the diffusion of knowledge among the humbler classes of the people the Governor-General is also pleased to direct that even in the selection of persons to fill the lowest offices under Government respect be had to the relative acquirements of the candidates, and that in every instance a man who can read and write be preferred to one who cannot."

Progress of English Education in Bengal 1844 to 1850.

In accordance with this Proclamation, the Council of Education organised a system of examinations with scholarship for meritorious students. The proclamation, and the examinations instituted to carry out its principle were objected to by the Court of Directors. The standard of the examinations was high. It required " a critical acquaintance with the works of Bacon, Johnson, Milton, and Shakespeare, a knowledge of ancient and modern history, and of the higher branches of mathematical science, some insight into the elements of natural history, and the principles of moral philosophy and political economy, together with considerable facility of composition, and the power of writing in fluent and idiomatic language an impromptu essay on any given subject of history, moral or political economy." The Court of Directors considered that the standard could only be attained by students in the Government Colleges, which would, therefore, be virtually given a monopoly of public patronage; and that the high test instead of promoting would tend to discourage the general acquisition of the English language, as those who could not hope to pass the test, would not think it worth their while to bestow any time upon the acquisition of the English language; at least with a view of entering the public service. The examinations instituted by the Council were also objected to by the proprietors of Missionary and other private institutions. The Council, however, continued their examinations, though on account of the high test, and the limited number of institutions which sent up candidates, the number of successful students was very small.*

Progress of English Education in the Bombay Presidency to 1857.
The Bombay Board of Education was created in 1840; and Sir Erskine Perry, a strong advocate of English Education, became its President in 1843. During the nine years of his Presidentship (1843 to 1852), the number of English schools under the control of the Board nearly doubled, and nine private English

---

* *Calcutta Review*, Vol. XV. p. 319. Within five years (1845 to 1849) the Council passed only thirty-five students, six in the first class, and twenty-nine in the second division.

schools were started in Bombay. The opening of the Grant Medical College in 1845, the establishment of chairs for Botany and Chemistry at the Elphinstone Institution in the following year, and the amalgamation of the Sanskrit College and the English school at Puna, were some of the more notable among the measures adopted by Sir Erskine Perry to promote English education. In 1850, there were in the Bombay Presidency 10 Government or aided English institutions (including the Grant Medical College) with about 2,000 pupils.*

Progress of English Education in the Madras Presidency to 1857.
In Madras, under the auspices of the committee of Native education a high school was founded, in 1841, for imparting English education. Two schools of a similar character were started at Cuddalore and Rajamahendri in 1853 and 1854 respectively.

In 1837, Mr. Anderson, the first Missionary of the Scottish Church in Southern India, opened an English school in Madras, which is now represented by the Christian College, and the Church of Scotland Missionary Institution. The success of the experiment led the Church Missionary Society to establish their college at Masulipatam in 1841, and the Jesuit Fathers their college at Negapatam in 1846. In Madras, the Wesleyan Mission started an English school in 1851. The London Missionary Society opened their school in 1853. It is estimated that, in 1854, some 33,000 boys were

* Thomas, *op. cit.* p. 50.

receiving English education in schools conducted by Missionary Societies.

The Pachaiyappa's Institution was opened in 1842 from funds derived from a charitable bequest. It was administered by a body of Hindu gentlemen as trustees. Two branch schools were opened after a time in connection with it. In 1854, they were all giving a high class education to about 1,000 pupils.

Thus English education was steadily progressing in all parts of India, when the Court of Directors' despatch of 1854 gave a great impetus to it. Before the renewal of the charter in 1853, evidence on educational subjects was taken by a committee of both Houses of Parliament from such men as Sir Erskine Perry, the Hon. C. H. Cameron, Sir C. E. Trevelyan, Dr. Duff and Professor H. H. Wilson. With the exception of Professor Wilson, they were all ardent Anglicists, and the cause of English education was well represented by them. Some years ago in 1845) the Bengal Council of education had suggested the establishment of an University in Calcutta on the model of the London University. The Court of Directors had then declined to accede to the proposal. The evidence now tendered, however, with regard to the progress of education convinced the Directors of the desirability of an University. "The rapid spread of a liberal education" say the Directors "among the natives of India since that time, the high attainments shewn by the native candidates for Government scholar-

The Education Despatch of 1854.

ships, and by the native students in private institutions, the success of the Medical Colleges, and the requirements of an increasing European and Anglo-Indian population, have led us to the conclusion that the time is now arrived for the establishment of universities in India."*

Another important step taken by the Directors, in 1854, for the spread of education was the creation of educational departments in the several presidencies. "We desire" say the Directors "to express to the present Boards and Councils of education our sincere thanks for the manner in which they have exercised their functions, and we still hope to have the assistance of the gentlemen composing them in furtherance of a most important part of our present place [referring to the University Scheme]; but having determined upon a very considerable extension of the general scope of our efforts, involving the simultaneous employment of different agencies, some of which are now wholly neglected, and others but imperfectly taken advantage of by Government, we are of opinion, that it is desirable to place the superintendence and direction of education upon a more systematic footing, and we have, therefore, determined to create an educational department as a portion of the machinary of our Governments in the several presidencies of India." †

Creation of Education Departments.

* Despatch of 1854, para. 24.
† Despatch of 1854, para. 17.

The systems of grants-in-aid formed one of the salient features of the scheme propounded in the despatch. "The consideration" say the Directors "of the impossibility of Government alone doing all that must be done in order to provide adequate means for the education of the natives of India, and of the ready assistance which may be derived from efforts which have hitherto received but little encouragement from the state, has led us to the natural conclusion that the most effectual method of providing for the wants of India in this respect will be to combine with the agency of the Government the aid which may be derived from the exertions and liberality of the educated and wealthy natives of India and of other benevolent persons. We have therefore resolved to adopt in India the system of grants-in-aid."*

The grant-in-aid system.

The Universities in Calcutta, Bombay and Madras came into existence in 1857. Since then two more Universities have sprung up, the Punjab University in 1878, and the Allahabad University in 1887. All the Indian Universities grant the degrees of Bachelor and Master of Arts ; the Bombay University also grants the degree of Bachelor of science, and the Punjab University the degrees of Bachelor, Master and, Doctor of Oriental learning. All these Universities are based on the model of the University of London and are primarily examining bodies, except the Punjab University

Establishment of the Universities, the results of University education.

---

* Despatch of 1854, paras. 51, 52.

which possesses a teaching branch. The following tables will exhibit the immense progress which University education has made since 1857:

1. Results of Collegiate Education for fifteen years from 1857 to 1871.

Province.	Maximum No. of Arts' English Colleges.	Number of Students who passed the F.A., B.A., and M.A. Examinations.		
		F.A.	B.A.	M.A.
Madras	12	784	152	6
Bombay	4	244	116	28
Bengal	17	1,495	548	112
N.-W. Provinces & Oudh	9	96	26	5
Punjab	4	47	8	......
Total ...	46	2,666	850	151

2. Results of Collegiate Education for ten years from 1872 to 1881 :

Province.	Maximum No. of English Arts' Colleges.	Number of Students who passed the F.A., B.A., and M.A. Examinations.		
		F.A.	B.A.	M.A.
Madras	25	2,032	890	22
Bombay	6	709	340	34
Bengal	22	2,666	1,037	285
N.-W. Provinces & Oudh.	9	365	130	33
Punjab*	2	107	37	11
Central Provinces	1	90	......	......
Total	65	5,969	2,434	385

3. Results of Collegiate Education for five years from 1887-88 to 1891-92 :

University.	Matriculation or Entrance passed.	F.A. Passed.	B.A. Passed.	Honours in Arts and M.A.
Calcutta	9,425	3,810	1,599	266
Allahabad †	2,508	704	291	33
Punjab	1,407 §	466	158	9
Madras	9,457	2,798	1,765	21
Bombay	4,143	1,042	848	19

* Passes in the Calcutta University only are shown in this table. Honours in degrees gained in the Punjab University College and University are excluded.

† For four years only from 1888-89 to 1891-92.

§ For three years only from 1889-90 to 1891-92.

INTELLECTUAL CONDITION.

High class schools & colleges under Hindu management. The appreciation of English education by the Hindus is specially attested by the rapid increase within the last twenty years in the number of high class English institutions under Hindu management. These are now fifteen such institutions in Bengal imparting collegiate instruction. In the entire country, between 1886-87 and 1892-93, the English Arts colleges under public management decreased from 32 to 30, but aided colleges of this description rose from 37 to 46, and unaided ones from 17 to 27. "Colleges of these latter descriptions" observes the Government of India "are, generally speaking, taking the place of Government institutions."* With a view to encourage the growth of local effort in education, the education commission of 1882 recommended : *First*.—That in order to evoke and stimulate local co-operation in the transfer to private management of Government institutions for collegiate or secondary institution, aid at specially liberal rates be offered for a term of years, whenever, necessary to any local body willing to undertake the management of any such institutions under adequate guarantees of permanence and efficiency. *Secondly*.— That in the event of any Government school or college being transferred to local management, provision be also made for the legal transfer to the new managers of all educational endowments, buildings, and other property belonging to such institutions in the hands of

* Resolution issued in the Home Department on the Quinquennial Education Report for 1886-87 to 1890-91.

Government. *Thirdly.*—That all Directors of Public Instruction aim at the gradual transfer to local native management of Government schools of secondary instruction (including schools attached to first or second grade colleges), in every case in which the transfer can be effected, without lowering the standard, or diminishing the supply of education, and without endangering the permanence of the institution transferred.*

* " Report of the Education Commission of 1882 " pp. 465—467.

CHAPTER VII.

Education under British Rule—Vernacular Education.

Indigenous Vernacular Education. The English found a large number of elementary Vernacular schools (*Páthashálás*) all over the country. There is no connection between them and the high class indigenous Sanskrit schools (*tols*, which have been mentioned before. The latter are intended for the highest castes, the former for all but the very lowest. What preparatory training is required by the Bráhman boys for entrance into the tols is generally given at home. The higher castes never appear to have encouraged the education of the lower in any way. Under Hindu kings there were endowmentsf or tols, but never any for Páthashálás. The Bráhman scholars wrote text book after text book, and commentary after commentary for the tols, but never any for the Páthashálás; in fact, they seldom condescended to write in the vernaculars. The lower classes left entirely to their own resources evolved a system of education—if system it can be called—which was suited to their humble requirements.

The following description of Páthashálas in Bengal given by Mr. Adam in 1835 still applies generally to such institutions all over India which have not yet been brought under the operations of the Education Departments:

"The benefits resulting from them are but small, owing partly to the incompetency of the instructors, and partly to the early age at which through the poverty of the parents the children are removed. The education of Bengalee children, as has been just stated, generally commences when they are five or six years old and terminates in five years, before the mind can be fully awakened to a sense of the advantages of knowledge or the reason sufficiently matured to acquire it. The teachers depend entirely upon their scholars for subsistence, and being little respected and poorly rewarded, there is no encouragement for persons of character, talent or learning to engage in the occupation. These schools are generally held in the houses of some of the most respectable native inhabitants or very near them. All the children of the family are educated in the vernacular language of the country; and in order to increase the emoluments of the teachers, they are allowed to introduce, as pupils, as many respectable children as they can procure in the neighbourhood. The scholars begin with tracing the vowels and consonants with the finger on a sand board and afterwards on the floor with a pencil of steatite or white crayon; and this exercise is continued for eight or ten days. They are next instructed to write on the palm-leaf with a reed-pen .. .. and with ink made of charcoal, which rubs out, joining vowels to the consonants, forming compound letters, syllables, and words, and learning tables of numeration, money, weight, and measure, and the correct mode of writing the distinctive names of persons, castes, and places. This is continued about a year. The iron style is now used only by the teacher in sketching on the palm-leaf the letters which the scholars are required to trace with ink. They are next advanced to the study of Arithmetic and the use of the plantain-leaf in writing with ink made of lamp-black, which is continued about six months, during which they are taught addition, subtraction, multiplication, and division, and the simplest cases of the Mensuration of land and commercial and agricultural accounts, together with the modes of address proper in writing letters to different persons. The last stage of this limited course of instruction is that in which the scholars are taught to write with lamp-black ink on paper, and are further instructed in agricultural and commercial accounts and in the composition of letters. In country places the rules of Arithmetic are principally applied to agricultural and in towns to commercial accounts: but in both town and country schools the instruction is superficial and defective. It may be safely affirmed that in no instance whatever is the orthography of the language of the country acquired in those schools, for although in some of them two or three of the more advanced boys write out small portions of the most popular poetical compositions of the country, yet the manuscript copy itself is so inaccurate that they only become confirmed in a most vitiated manner of spelling, which the imperfect qualifications of the teacher do not enable him to correct. The scholars are entirely without instruction, both literary and oral, regarding the personal virtues and domestic and social duties. The teacher, in virtue of his character, or in the way of advice or reproof, exercises no moral influence on the character of his pupils............ On the other hand, there is no text or school-book used containing any moral truths or liberal knowledge, so that education being limited entirely to accounts, tends rather to narrow the mind and confine its attention to sordid gain, than to improve the heart and enlarge the understanding. This description applies, as far as I at present know, to all indigenous elementary schools throughout Bengal." *

---

* Adam's Reports, p. 25.

With regard to the number of indigenous elementary schools, it was reported by Sir Thomas Munro in 1826, as the result of inquiries instituted by him, that there were in the Madras Presidency some 12,000 of them.* He estimated that nearly one-third of the entire male population of the Presidency received school education. "The state of education exhibited" says he "low as it is compared with that of our own country, is higher than it was in most European countries at no very distant times." Investigations made in the Bombay Presidency showed that about 1830, it contained 1,705 schools with 35,143 pupils, of which 25 schools with 1,315 scholars were maintained by Government. The population of the Presidency was estimated about the same time at 4,681,735 souls. Considering that the male population alone received school instruction, and that boys between the ages of 5 and 10 years—which is the period during which Indian boys in general remain at the *páthashálás*—form one-ninth of the total male population, we find that about 13 per cent. of the boys of school-going age were receiving elementary instruction about 1830

Indigenous Vernacular Schools about 1830.

The following tables extracted from Adam's reports will exhibit the state of indigenous education in cer-

---

* The figure given in Munro's minute is 12,498; but, as the schools imparting high education in Sanskrit are included in that number, we have made an allowance of 498 for them.

(Thomas, *op. cit.* p. 3).

tain areas in Bengal and Behar which were studied in detail :

	Total number of children between 14 and five years of age.	Number of children receiving school instruction.	Number of children receiving domestic instruction.	Total number of children receiving domestic and school instruction.	Children receiving neither domestic nor school instruction.	Proportion of children capable of receiving to children actually receiving instruction is as 100 to.
City of Moorshedabad..	15,092	959	300	1,259	13,833	8·3
Thana Daulatbazar ...	10,428	305	326	631	9,797	6·05
,, Nanglia ...	8,929	439	285	724	8,205	8·1
,, Culna ...	18,176	2,243	676	2,919	15,257	16·05
,, Jehanabad	15,595	366	539	905	14,690	5·8
,, Bhawara ...	13,409	60	288	348	13,061	2·5

	Total adult population.	Instructed adult population.	Uninstructed adult population.	Proportion of total adult population to instructed adult population is as 100 to.
City of Moorshedabad ...	97,818	7,355	90,463	7·5
Thana Daulatbazar ...	42,837	1,772	41,065	4·1
,, Nanglia	30,410	1,613	28,797	5·3
,, Culna	81,045	7,308	73,737	9·01
,, Jehanabad	57,573	2,835	54,738	4·9
,, Bhawara	44,416	1,033	43,383	2·3

The earliest attempts to impart vernacular education on more civilized methods than those described in the above extract were made by Christian Missionaries. During the latter half of the eighteenth century the great missionary Schwartz established schools at Madras, Trichinoply, Tanjore and other places; and early in the eighteenth century, the Baptist Mission at Serampur under Carey, Ward, and Marshman did much to extend vernacular education. About 1815, Mr. May a Missionary at Hooghly started a number of vernacular schools which were very successful and which secured from Lord Hastings a monthly grant of Rs. 600.

Spread of Vernacular education by Christian Missionaries.

Mr. Hare, who was the pioneer of English education in Bengal, also did much in conjunction with Raja Radhakant Deva, to improve the indigenous vernacular education. The first systematic effort, however, was made by the Calcutta School Society which was founded in 1818 under the Presidency of the Marquis of Hastings. The objects of the Society were "to assist and improve existing schools, and to establish and support any further schools and seminaries which may be requisite; with a view to the more general diffusion of useful knowledge amongst the inhabitants of India of every description especially within the provinces subject to the Presidency of Fort William, and to select pupils of distinguished talents and merit from elementary and other schools, and to provide for their instruction in seminaries

The Calcutta School Society.

of a higher degree, with the view of forming a body of qualified teachers and translators who may be instrumental in enlightening their countrymen, and improving the general system of education. When the funds of the institution may admit of it, the maintenance and tuition of such pupils, in distinct seminaries, will be an object of importance."

The society carried out its objects by distributing books, and by carrying on examinations through its officers and agents. In 1821, it had under its superintendence 115 schools with 3823 pupils; and two years later it secured a monthly grant of Rs. 500 from Government.

The Committee of Public Instruction in Bengal which **Committee of Public Instruction.** came into existence in 1823 though recognising the importance of vernacular education, did not take any step directly to promote vernacular education.

" We are deeply sensible" say the Committee in one of their annual reports " of the importance of encouraging the cultivation of the vernacular languages..........We conceive the formation of a vernalcular literature to be the ultimate object to which all our efforts must be directed. At present, the extensive cultivation of some foreign language, which is always very improving to the mind, is rendered indispensable by the almost total absence of a vernacular literature, and the consequent impossibility of obtaining a tolerable education from that source only. The study of English, to which many circumstances induce the natives to give the preference and with it the knowledge of the learning of the west, is therefore daily spreading This, as it appears to us is the first stage in the process by which India is to be enlightened. The natives must learn before they can teach. The best educated among them must be placed in possession of our knowledge before they can transfer it into their own language. We trust that the number of such translations will multiply every year."

Progress of vernacular education in Bengal, 1835-1855.

In 1835, Lord William Bentinck appointed Mr. Adam to inquire into the indigenous system of education in Bengal and Behar. The inquiries extended over three years, but they resulted only in reports containing a vast mass of the most interesting information. No action was taken, as the committee of education considered the plan * submitted by Mr. Adam to be almost impracticable. Between 1838, when Adam's inquiries were concluded, and 1855, when the education department was formed, scarcely anything was done directly to promote vernacular education in Bengal.†

Vernacular education in the Bombay Presidency.

Vernacular education made better progress in Bombay and the North-Western Provinces than in Bengal. The Bombay Board of Education, which was created in 1840, divided the educational area of the Bombay Presidency into three divisions each under an inspector, founded stipendiary studentships, and proposed to open a vernacular school in every village containing 2,000 inhabitants provided the people bore a certain share of the cost. In 1842, there were 120 Government vernacular schools with 7,750 pupils.

* Adam's Reports, p 259, *et. seq*.
† In 1844, Lord Hardinge established over a hundred vernacular schools, but they were not successful.

In 1845, Mr. Thomason, Lieutenant-Governor of the North-Western Provinces, issued orders to the Collectors and their subordinates to encourage the indigenous vernacular schools. By 1849, he had elaborated a comprehensive scheme of vernacular education, which consisted in the establishment of a superior school at each tahsil or subdivision of district, and of an elementary 'circle' school in a central situation which was not to be more than two miles distant from any of the villages forming the circle. "For the support of these schools the consent of the land-owners was to be obtained to the appropriation of a small percentage on the amount of the Government revenue one per cent., being the amount paid, of which half was to be contributed by the land-owners and half by the Government."* The scheme was sanctioned by the Court of Directors; and by the end of 1854, there were in the North-Western Provinces 897 schools, mostly of the elementary type, with 23,638 scholars.

Vernacular education in the North-West, 1845—1855.

The Court of Directors' despatch of 1854 gave considerable impetus to vernacular education throughout India. "We desire" say the Directors "to see the active measures of Government more especially directed, for the future, to this object [mass education], for the attain-

State of Vernacular education in 1859.

---

* Despatch from the Secretary of State for India, 7th April, 1859.

ment of which we are ready to sanction a considerable increase of expenditure."

The Education Departments which came into existence soon after the date of this despatch took vigorous measures for the promotion of vernacular education. The steps taken in Bengal, Bombay, and Madras between 1855 and 1859 are thus summarised in a despatch from the Secretary of State for India, dated 7th April, 1859:

"In the Lower Provinces of Bengal, several plans for promoting vernacular education have been simultaneously introduced. In some of the districts, Mr. Thomason's plan, founded on the encouragement of indigenous schools by periodical inspection and by rewards, was brought into operation. In others, it was attempted to accomplish the object under the grant-in-aid rules, and in those districts a considerable number of schools have been established on that principle. Great difficulties, however, were encountered in obtaining local assistance and support; and the conclusion arrived at, after the experience of two or three years, by Mr. Pratt, the Inspector, who most perseveringly followed this course of proceeding, was that it was vain to hope to base any general scheme of popular education, at least in the greater part of Bengal, on the grant-in-aid system under the prescribed rules. The Inspector of the Eastern Education Division, Mr. Woodrow, had *a priori*, arrived at a similar conclusion, and had struck out an altogether different course, to which he had obtained the sanction of Government. The principle of his plan was to make use of the existing indigenous schools, and he proceeded by forming these schools into circles of three, four, or five, and attaching to each circle a well qualified teacher, to be paid by Government, whose duty it would be to go from school to school, instructing village schoolmasters in their duties, and imparting instruction in the higher subjects to the more advanced pupils; encouragement being given to both masters and pupils by the prospect of small pecuniary rewards. This plan has so far been found very successful, and it is proposed to extend it to others of the educational divisions.

"In Bombay, the education officers have continued to prosecute the plan previously in force of forming vernacular schools on a partially self-supporting plan; it being intended, however, to introduce gradually the plan of "circle" schools of a somewhat superior class. One peculiarity of the system pursued at Bombay is, that the schools maintained at the joint expense of Government and of the local community are constituted as Government schools, instead of remaining, like those under the grant-in-aid rules, private schools receiving a grant from Government. The question of a change in this respect has been raised by the Government of India, and is still undetermined. In Madras, a plan of popular education was brought into operation in some of the talooks of the Rajahmundry district, resembling very much the hulkabundee system of the North-Western Provinces; but it is admitted that even if the plan could be maintained in Rajahmundry, and in districts similarly situated, it is inapplicable to districts under the revenue system prevailing generally in the Madras presidency. A system has accordingly been lately sanctioned, as an experiment, in some of the Madras districts, based like the plan of Mr. Woodrow in Bengal, on the improvement of existing village schools, and on the encouragement of the schoolmasters to self-improvement, by the promise of a reward to be given in books or in money at the discretion of the Director."

Primary and secondary education.
The system of vernacular education which has been evolved within the last thirty years comprises primary education, and secondary education. The primary schools may be called improved *páthsálás*. The instruction imparted in both is quite elementary but that in the Government or aided primary schools is of a far superior character. The secondary* or as they are some-

---

* Secondary schools, in the language of the Education Departments, also include high schools which prepare up to the standard of the University matriculation.

times called middle schools, carry vernacular education to a much higher stage, the highest standard including Geometry, Algebra, Elements of Chemistry, Physics, Botany, Physical Geography &c. The vernacular is always the medium of instruction in the middle as in the primary schools ; but there are numerous middle schools where English is taught as a second language.

Primary education in Bengal. In Bengal primary education received a fresh impulse under the Lieutenant Governorship of Sir George Campbell. He assigned an annual amount of four lakhs of rupees to primary education and his successor, Sir Richard Temple, continued his policy. The number of primary schools rose from 2512 with 68,543 pupils in 1871 to 51,778 schools with 898, 389 scholars in 1881-82. In the year 1891-92, there were 62,349 primary schools with 1,280,694 pupils.

In Madras. In the Madras Presidency, scarcely anything was done for primary education before 1868. In that year the imposition of an education cess of one per cent. was sanctioned and district Education Committees were formed. Under the direction of these Committees, primary education was greatly extended, the number of children receiving such education rising from 68, 237 in 1871 to 360,000 in 1882. In 1892, 22,111 schools were imparting primary education to 608, 976 scholars.

In Bombay. In the Bombay Presidency the education cess was introduced in 1864 ; and it greatly contributed to the expansion of primary education. The number of primary schools rose from

2,738 schools with 159,628 pupils in 1871 to 5,338 schools with 332,688 pupils in 1882. In 1892 there were 11,719 primary schools with 584,946 scholars.

The Education Commission and Primary Education.
The Education Commission of 1882 recommended "that while every branch of education can justly clam the fostering care of the state, it is desirable in the present circumstances of the country to declare the elementary education of the masses, its provision, extension and improvement, to be that part of the educational system to which the strenuous efforts of the state should now be directed, in a still larger measure than before." The Commission considered that primary education "possessed an almost exclusive claim upon local funds set apart for education, and a large claim upon provincial revenues." The Government concurred in the recommendations of the Commission; and since 1883, its educational policy has been to carry them out as far as possible. In 1886-87, the total expenditure on primary education from public funds (Provincial revenues, and district and Municipal funds) was Rs.42,07,863; by 1892-93, it had risen to Rs. 50, 45, 513, the ratio of increase being nearly treble that upon high or secondary education. "In addition to the direct expenditure on Primary schools there is the expenditure on training teachers for employment in such schools. The expenditure from public funds on training schools rose from Rs. 4,53,008 in 1886-87 to Rs. 5,12,405 in 1891-92. It is said that the number of students being trained for work in Secondary schools is probably less than one-

fourth of the total number of students, so that the greater portion of this expenditure is devoted to the improvement of Primary education. Measures have been taken in the various provinces to facilitate the conversion of indigenous into aided Primary schools, but this conversion is sometimes retarded by a reluctance on the part of the teachers to submit to departmental rules and methods of instruction and often by want of funds."*

The total number of public Primary Schools for boys rose from 84,673 in 1886-87 to 91,881 in 1891-92.

Secondary Vernacular education. In 1886-87, there were 4,160 secondary schools (including high schools which teach in English up to the matriculation standard) attended by 404,189 students of whom 271,654 were in the exclusively English division. In 1891-92, the number of schools rose to 4,438 and that of pupils to 438,988 of whom no less than 302,019 were in the exclusively English division; so that, whereas the number of boys seeking secondary education in English rose by over 30,000, those seeking secondary education in the vernaculars rose by 5,797 only. The increase in the secondary schools for boys was chiefly in schools teaching English which rose from 2,301 to 2,544 ; 755 of the latter number were high schools and 1,789 middle schools.

* Resolution of the Government of India (Home Department) on the Quinquennial Education Report 1886-87 to 1891-91.

"It seems inevitable that in a grade where English and vernacular education co-exist, the tendency will be under existing influences for the former to oust the latter and accordingly the kind of education in Secondary schools in which the percentage of students shows the largest advance is high English education. In middle English schools in the North-Western Provinces and Oudh, the English language has been substituted for the vernacular as the medium of instruction; and, though opinions on the merits of the two systems are said to be divided in Bengal, it seems clear that students of a course which leads up to the Entrance Examination will, independently of other reasons for preferring English teaching, wish to learn all subjects of general knowledge in the language in which the Entrance Examination is held.

The great majority of the pupils receiving education are instructed in Primary schools, that is in reading, writing, elementary Arithmetic and land measurement; in 1892-93, the percentage was 93·9. In the same year, 5·7 per cent. of the total number of pupils was receiving Secondary education, and only 0·4 per cent. were students receiving high English education, or studying Law, Medicine, or Engineering.

CHAPTER VIII.

EDUCATION UNDER BRITISH RULE—FEMALE EDUCATION.

Indigenous female education. We have already adduced evidence to show, that there were highly educated Hindu ladies in ancient India.* But for many centuries previous to the establishment of British Rule there is no case known of a Hindu lady distinguishing herself in literary pursuits. Highborn ladies among the Rajputs received elementary instruction in reading and writing, and sometimes an exceptionally enlightened Pandit imparted education, though rarely of a very high order, to his daughter. There were some petty sects among the Vaishnavas, the female members of which learned to read and write. But in point of morality they

* Vol. II. p. 107.

were not held in much higher estimation than the class of unfortunates among whom some sort of education has always been prevalent.* With these few exceptions the female Hindu, population, at least just before the establishment of British rule, was absolutely unlettered. Writing of the state of instruction among women in Bengal about 1835, Adam observed that "it cannot be said to be low, for with a very few individual exceptions there is no instruction at all. Absolute and hopeless ignorance is, in general, their lot."†

As in the case of vernacular education, so in that of female education, the missionaries took the lead. In Calcutta, the first attempt to instruct Indian girls, in organised schools, was made about 1821 by the Calcutta Female Juvenile Society which subsequently assumed the name of the Calcutta Baptist Female Society. The Society's schools in Calcutta and its vicinity were, in 1834, imparting elementary instruction to some 200 scholars. About the same time, the Corresponding Committee of the Church Missionary Society and the London Missionary Society also established girl schools in Calcutta and its neighbourhood.‡ But all these schools were attended chiefly, if not exclusively by Christian girls.

Missionaries the pioneers in female education.

---

* Dr. Rajendralala Mitra says, that at Cuttak, in Orissa, he found three schools for the education of the daughters of courtezans, and they were well attended. "Indo Aryans" vol. I. p. 282.

† Adam's Reports, p. 131.

‡ Adam's Reports pp. 34-35.

The first successful attempt to start a school for Hindu girls in Bengal on a secular basis was made by Drinkwater Bethune. On the 7th of May, 1849, the school opened with 21 pupils, placed under the charge of an English lady, who, with the help of a Pandit, was to teach them Bengali, as much English as their guardians might choose, and, in the words of Mr. Bethune's opening address, "a thousand feminine works and accomplishments in embroidery and fancy work, in drawing, and in many other things that would give them the means of adorning their own homes and of supplying themselves with harmless and elegant employment." As is usual in such cases, the school for sometime met with opposition from the orthodox Hindus. But, by the end of May, 1850, the twentyone pupils had increased to thirtyfour. After the untimely death of Mr. Bethune,* it was taken up and supported by the Marquis of Dalhousie ; and when he left India, it became a Government institution. The Court of Directors, when sanctioning the assumption by Government of the charge of Mr. Bethune's School, gave their cordial approval to the order of the Government of India, that female education should be considered to be as much within the province of the Council of Education as any other branch of education ; and the Court's interest in the subject was further

---

* Mr. Bethune by his will left lands and other property in Calcutta for the endowment of the Bethune School in perpetuity. (Education Commission Report, P. 525)

expressed in their despatch of July 1854, in which it was declared that schools for females were to be included in those to which grants-in-aid might be given. *

<small>Progress of female education in Bengal, 1859 to 1893.</small>
By the year 1859 female schools had been established by the local community at Dacca and at Howra. Girls were also reported to be in attendance at a few of the vernacular schools in Eastern Bengal. In 1871, there were, in Bengal, 274 aided girls' schools with 5,910 pupils. Since then there has been a great development of female education upon the grant-in-aid system. In 1882, the number of girls' schools rose to 1,015 containing 41,349 pupils. In 1894 the number of girls' schools was 2,999, and that of pupils, 61,034 besides 33,686 girls in boys' schools. The college department of the Bethune School was opened in 1879. Since then it has sent up candidates for the Examinations of the Calcutta University every year. In 1893, one of its pupils took the degree of B. A. with honours in literature, and six passed the Entrance Examination successfully. There is another high class Government female school in Bengal, the Eden Female School at Dacca. Besides these, there were, in 1893, three high schools for girls in Calcutta with 219 pupils, mostly Anglo-Indian and Eurasian ; one middle English school at Hooghly (Chinsura) with 8 pupils ; and 26 middle vernacular schools distributed over eight.

---

* Despatch from the Secretary of State for India, 7th April, 1859.

of the nine divisions in Bengal. The upper primary schools for girls were 201, and the lower primary 2,766. According to the census of 1891, the proportion of literate females in Bengal was 4 in 1000, an increase of 0.1 per cent. over the number shown by the census of 1881.

In Bombay, the first school for Indian girls was opened by the American Missionary Society in 1824. The Scottish Missionary Society followed; and in 1827, the girl schools of this Society were attended by 300 scholars. In 1840, the Society opened five schools, in the neighbourhood of Puna, for the daughters of the higher classes of Hindus. Since then female education in the Bombay Presidency has made steady progress. In 1851, a private girl school was established at Puna by Jati Govinda Rao Phule which was long held in high repute. In the same year, a munificent endowment of Rs. 20,000 was created by Maganbhai Karamchand at Ahmedabad for the foundation of two girls' schools. The following sketch of the progress of female education in Bombay from 1854 to 1882 is given in the report of the Education Commission.* "The despatch of 1854 found 65 girls' schools (of which we have full returns) in Bombay with about 3,500 pupils. There were also 593 girls attending boys' schools. In 1857, small annual rewards were offered by government to vernacular school masters, who should form girl's classes in their

side note: Female education in Bombay 1824 to 1892.

* *Op. cit.* p. 524.

schools, with the results that in 1864-65, there were 639 girls in such schools. The visit of Miss Carpenter, the interest shown by European ladies at Thana, Dhulia, and elsewhere, and the liberality of certain Southern Mahratta Chiefs and leading Parsis, gave a fresh impulse to the movement. Female Normal Schools were established at Ahmedabad, Bombay and Poona......In 1869, there were altogether 209 girl's schools, in the Bombay presidency, attended by 9,291 pupils. The statistics for 1871 show 218 girl's schools with 9,190 pupils. Since 1871, the Bombay Government has recognised its duty towards female education. Grants-in-aid have been more freely given, and a large number of girl's schools have been founded, with the result of multiplying nearly threefold the number of pupils returned in 1871. It is worthy of remark, however, that the number of pupils (11,238) in departmental girls' schools now exceeds the number (10,621) in aided and unaided institutions, excluding mixed schools for boys and girls. Apart from this, the special features of female education in Bombay seem to be (1) the evidence of a growing desire among the commercial classes for its extension ; (2) the efforts on a large sale made by the natives themselves (Parsis, Marathas, and Gujrathis) to meet this demand ; and (3) the successful endeavours by the Government to create an efficient staff of teachers."

In 1882, there were in Bombay 343 girls' schools attended by 26, 766 pupils. In 1892, the number of institutions rose to 793, and that of pupils to 73,017. The proportion of literate females in Bombay, is much higher than in Bengal, being 10 per thousand according to the census of 1891.

The following sketch of the progress of female education in the Madras Presidency is taken from the report of the Education Commission of 1882.*

Female education in Madras, 1841 to 1892.

"In the Madras Presidency, the first attempt at female education in the modern sense, consisted of the boarding schools maintained by the Church of England Societies in Tinnevelly, but intended almost exclusively for daughters of Christian converts. In 1841, the Missionaries of the Scottish Church commenced the work of educating the Hindu girls of Madras. In 1845, the first girls' school under partial native management was opened. As narrated in Chapter II., of this report, the despatch of 1854 found about 8000 girls in Missionary schools in the Madras Presidency and neighbouring states; 1,100 being in boarding schools. The total number of girls' schools, was 256. The despatch of 1854 led to an increase of effort. In 1858-59, grants-in-aid to the extent of Rs. 1,589 were given to 39 schools attended by 1,885 girls. In 1870-71, aid to the amount of Rs. 25,682 was given to 138 schools, with 7,245 girls. There were, besides, 2,148 girls in 289 mixed schools and 792 in village boys' schools.......In 1858, an annual examination for schoolmistresses' certificates, was instituted, which gradually developed into a general examination for girls' schools,

* *Op. cit.* pp. 522—523.

and exerted a wholesome influence in improving the quality of the teaching. In 1870-71, there were 141 candidates of whom 41 passed. These improved arrangements, together with the increased efforts of the missionary bodies and the native educational agencies which had entered the field, aided by grants and supplemented by Government efforts, produced a great increase during the next ten years." There were in 1882, "according to the departmental return, 557 girls' schools, with 35,042 pupils, aided and unaided institutions forming by far the most important element in the total. Madras has now an organised system of female instruction, from normal or training school for female teachers, down to primary schools, for girls......Besides the Christian zenana mission, there is a zenana agency on a secular basis, conducted by a committee of native gentlemen and English ladies. Zenana education, however, is not so extensively developed, or apparently so much required as in some other provinces ; the seclusion of women of the better classes is less complete, and it is easier for girls to obtain a considerable amount of education at school. Madras ranked highest in the census returns of 1881 among the provinces of India with regard to female education (excepting the little territory of Coorg)......The proportion under instruction is 1 girl in 403 of the female population, and the proportion of those able to read and write, but not under instruction, 1 woman in 166 of the female population."

In 1892, there were in the Madras Presidency 1060 institutions imparting education 98, 471 female scholars.

The proportion of literate females as shown by the census of 1891 is the same as in Bombay, viz. 10 per thousand.

Female education in the North-west 1855 to 1892.
The Secretary of State, in his despatch of 7th April 1859, reviewing the state of female education in the North-Western Provinces says :

"A movement in furtherance of female education in the Agra district Was commenced by the Deputy Inspector of schools, Gopal Sing, in 1855. The expense was in the first instance, defrayed entirely from the public funds; 'the agricultural classes, though quite willing and ready to make use of the schools, were not then prepared to go further and to pay the teacher.' The schools were attended by scholars of all classes of Hindus, including a considerable proportion of Brahmins; and of the girls, the age of some exceeded 20 years, the remainder being from 6 years old to 20. The masters were selected by the parents of the scholars, and committees of respectable native gentlemen were formed to exercise a general supervision over the schools, and to arrange for their visitation. The number of schools in the Agra district had risen in January 1857 to 288 and the attendance of the girls was estimated at 4,927. It being desired at that time to carry out the experiment of female education in a more efficient manner, sanction was sought, and obtained, to the assignment of Rs. 8,000 as a direct grant from Government for female schools in the district, to meet an estimated expenditure on 200 girls' schools of Rs. 13,200 per annum, the balance being provided from the hulkabundee cess and from other sources."

"Mr. Reid and Mr. Kempson, the successive Directors of Public Instruction from 1854 to 1878, were strong advocates of female education, while Sir William Muir who became Lieutenant Governor in 1868, cordially supported the efforts of the education Department. The girls' schools existing before 1857 for the most part disappeared in the Mutiny. In 1859 a fresh start was made. In 1870-71, the number of girls' schools in the North-Western Provinces and Oudh, was 640, with 13,853 pupils. Between 1871 and 1881, a great decrease took place in girls' schools. The total number of girls' schools in 1882 was 308 attended by 8,883 pupils. The census officers in 1881 returned the number of girls under instruction at 9,771 in the British districts of the North-Western Porvinces, being one girl to 2,169 of the female population. The number of females returned by the census of 1881 as able to read and write, but not under instructions in the British districts, was 21,590, or one in 981 of the female population."* The number of girls' schools in 1892 was 467, and that of pupils attending them 12,813. The proportions of literate females is the same as in Bengal, *viz.* 3 per thousand.

In the year 1856-57, there were known to exist in the Punjab only 17 schools for girls with 306 pupils, nearly all Mahomedans. By 1865-66, the number of schools had risen to 1,029, and that of pupils to 19,561. "Although schools were thus opened and scholars enrolled in large numbers without much difficulty, it appears from subsequent official reports, that a large proportion of the schools were merely rudimentary schools which had existed from time immemorial for the purpose of, conveying religious instruction. The character of the education did not seem in 1867-68 to be satisfactory.

Female education in the Punjab, 1855 to 1892.

---

* "Report of the Education Commission of 1882" pp. 526-527.

and in that year, Rs. 10,000 were withdrawn from the grant for girls' schools. The number of schools has gone on steadily decreasing from 1029 with 19,561 pupils in 1865-66 to 317 schools with 9,756 pupils in 1881-82." * In 1892, there were 952 girls' schools attended by 20, 162 scholars. With regard to literacy among the female population Punjab is on the same level with the North-Western Provinces and Oudh.

The following table shows the condition of female as compared with male literacy, and the progress which has been made within the decade between 1881 and 1891† :

Female compared with male literacy.

* "Report of the Education Commission of 1882," p. 527.
† " Census of India, 1891, General Report." p 217.

INTELLECTUAL CONDITION.

Province or State, &c.	Males. No. per 1,000 Males of— Illiterate		Literate, &c.		Variation in Literates in 1891.	Females. No. per 1,000 Females of— Illiterate		Literate, &c.		Variation in Literates in 1891.
	1881.	1891.	1881.	1891.		1881.	1891.	1881.	1891.	
Ajmer	879	867	121	133	+12	994	992	6	8	+2
Assam	953	924	47	76	+29	999	997	1	3	+2
Bengal	913	892	87	108	+21	997	996	3	4	+1
Berar	938	916	62	84	+22	992	998	—	2	+2
Bombay	883	860	117	140	+23	993	990	7	10	+3
Sindh	921	915	79	85	+6	995	995	5	5	—
Lower Burma	539	557	461	443	−18	964	962	36	38	+2
Upper Burma	…	538	…	462	…	…	985	…	15	…
Central Provinces	953	941	47	59	+12	998	998	2	2	—
Coorg	869	844	131	156	+25	990	986	10	14	+4
Madras	862	851	138	149	+11	991	990	9	10	+1
N.-W. Provinces	940	937	60	63	+3	998	997	2	3	+1
Oudh	948	942	52	58	+6	999	998	1	2	+1
Punjab	937	926	63	74	+11	998	997	2	3	+1
Total, British Provinces	…	889	…	111	…	…	994	…	6	…
Haidrabad	937	928	63	72	+9	997	997	1	3	+2
Baroda	894	856	106	141	+38	995	995	2	5	+3
Mysore	888	895	112	105	−7	993	993	4	7	+3
Bombay States	900	887	100	113	+13	998	998	2	5	+3
Bengal States	965	945	35	55	+20	999	998	1	2	+1
N.-W. Province States	963	965	37	35	−2	999	999	—	1	—
Punjab States	947	941	53	59	+6	999	999	4	1	−3
Total, States	…	902	…	98	…	…	993	…	7	…
India	909	891	91	109	+18	996	994	4	6	+2

Appendix A.

I am indebted to Kaviraj Bijayaratna Sen Kaviranjan of Kumartuli, Calcutta, for the following information about the present condition of the study and practice of the Hindu system of medicine in a few districts of Bengal (see Chapter IV. p. 108):

In Calcutta and its suburbs there are some 125 physicians practising the Hindu system. The number in Dacca is about 100, and in the districts of Bankura, Burdwan, Birbhum and Midnapur, about 300. The physicians all spend a part of their time in teaching. The number of pupils receiving instruction in the Hindu system of medicine in the localities just mentioned has been estimated at about 3,150.

Appendix B.

EXTRACT FROM THE EVIDENCE OF MR. A.O. HUME, C.B. BEFORE THE PUBLIC SERVICE COMMISSION—(SEE CHAPTER V. P. 143).

"At the close of December, 1857, under Lord Canning's direct orders, I raised a local force of 500 infantry, 350 cavalry, and five guns (all natives, of course) who thenceforth were continually employed, and so comported themselves as to obtain on two occasions, the battles of Anantram and Harchandpoor, the honour of an entire Gazette to themselves. During the first few months of the year I had the assistance of Colonel (then Lieutenant) Sherriff, and later of Lieutenant Laughlan Forbes, two gallant young officers to whom our great successes, and considering the circumstances they were really great, were due. But I had charge of the whole force, was with them throughout, and was in a better position than even most military men to judge what natives are capable of in the way of pluck and dash. For we were wholly isolated, we were always opposed to great odds, and we had no European troops with us except when Colonel Riddel's column moved down about the time of the taking of Calpee, within seventy miles of us. And it was not only of mere pluck that I had experience but of administrative capacity. In June 1857, after the wing of the 9th Native Infantry had mutinied, the Gwalior authorities being afraid of the first Gwalior Grenadiers, to get rid of them, sent them over to garrison Etawah. There they mutinied also, and I was obliged to leave the station with the officers of that regiment. But let me note, before proceeding further, that during the mutiny of the 9th N. I. my townspeople stood by us to a man.

My life was saved the night of the mutiny when, after getting off the rest of the people of the station, I had remained behind to see if anything could be done, by two natives, who passed me safely through two successive parties of sepoys, who were especially on the look-out to shoot me, they having the idea in those days that they could not safely make off with the treasure without first killing the District Officer. It was a bright moonlight night, my only disguise was a large chudder, over a native pagree—native shoes over dark stockings and my trousers pulled up out of sight. I had no particular claim on these men—one, Gyadeen, was a Chuprassi, one was a townsman. Had I been detected, they, as well as myself, would certainly have been shot and this they perfectly knew, yet they walked with me one on either side, chatting together, through the sepoys, who luckily paid no particular attention to us and answered unconcernedly a question as to whether it was known what had become of the Collector (myself) by the remark, that he was said to have gone into the city to try and rouse the townsmen. I don't think that I am more of a coward than most of my countrymen, but at that critical moment I could not for the life of me have answered in that cheery unconcerned manner.

The sepoys of the 9th Native Infantry, having mostly gone off to Delhi, with the little treasure that remained (the bulk of it I had previously sent safely into Agra, by the aid of my friend Raja—then Kour—Lutchman Singh and Kour Zor Singh of the Chohan House of Pertabnere), order was speedily re-established. I should say, however, that several native officers of the 9th Native Infantry and about twenty sepoys had remained faithful under a good old Ahir (note the caste) Soubadar, and were with and protecting the whole body of the fugitives down at the Jumna Ghat at the time of my own fortunate escape.

On the restoration of order and the advent of the first Gwalior Grenadiers, I found myself with some thirty women and children. All my native friends told me (they were many of them Brahmins and so warmed themselves into the confidence of some amongst the sepoys) that the Grenadiers would certainly soon mutiny, and were only waiting for the word from the rest of the Contingent at Gwalior, to do so. So I determined to send the women and children at once into Agra. By that time things were looking very black, for tidings of disaster on disaster "followed fast and followed faster," till even our most sincere well-wishers believed that our Raj was at an end. But even at that time, though the intervening country was up, and outside my own district villages, where everywhere burning and anarchy prevailed, Rajah Lutchman Singh and our mutual friends, Kours Zor Singh and Anup Singh, volunteered with their own people to escort our ladies and children into Agra Kour Zor Singh was at first. dead against it; he begged and prayed me not to send them to Agra (where he conceived that sooner or later, as at other places, all would be massacred). but to join them myself and let him escort us all through Central India, to the chiefs of every State in which he was in one way or anothers related or connected, safely to the sea. But when he saw that my mind was made up, he fell in with the scheme, and he and his brothers, Anup Singh, and Lutchman Singh personally safely escorted the ladies (this was in June) into Agra, and there is no lady living of this party but will testify to the chivalrous courtesy and watchful care with which these noble gentlemen fulfilled their dangerous and self-imposed task. * * *

Then came the battle of the 5th of July, and it was some little time before anything like order was re-established in Agra. But throughout this time communications were reaching me from my district begging me to make arrangements for its proper administration. Then I devised and Government sanctioned this scheme. The district comprised five very large Tahsils. I constituted each a Soobahship, and appointed one native gentleman, Kour Zor Singh (Chohan Rajpoot) for Etawah; Rajah (then Row) Juswunt Row (Brahmin) for Bhurtenan; Lulla Laik Singh (Senghur Rajpoot) for Bidhona; Chowdhree Ganga Pershad (Kayat) for Puhpoondh; and the Tahsildar of Oreya, an elderly Bania of Muttra, for Dullelnugger as Soobah to each, making them suitable allowances to keep up the necessary armed retainers and establishments—all Government officials (of course many had fled) who had thus far remained at their posts being included in these latter. We had here men of very different castes—Brahmin, Rajpoot, Kayat, Bania, yet each and all rose to the emergency, and during the next troublous five months, in the very centre of the outbreak, maintained order throughout their jurisdictions, and so maintained it that in after times no man ever complained of any injustice, any abuse of power—no man had ever anything but good words to speak of their administration. They kept me informed weekly of all that passed, they kept up for us communication with Cawnpore. Through them we got the first news of Neil's arrival, and more than all, directly he did arrive, they collected 700 camels, and under their own men, the Cawnpore district being " up " like the whole of the rest of the Doab except Etawah, escorted these to Cawnpore, and thus rendered an immediate advance on Lucknow possible, which, but for this, must have been much delayed. Moreover, whilst all over the country Government revenue was being realized by all kinds of pretenders, dacoit leaders and the like, not a rupee was thus made away with. My orders were that every man should retain his revenue until I returned and then to pay it to me, and these orders were carried out to the letter.

I do not know how administrative capacity could have been better demonstrated than it was by these five gentlemen. I doubt if any Englishman living could have administered one of those Soobahships at that time as cleverly and satisfactorily as every one of these native gentlemen did, and I am quite sure that no Englishman could have proved himself more heroically faithful to the trust reposed in him than did the Tahsildar of Oreya. He was only a Bania; an elderly man, very stout and 'good tempered, the last man from whom heroism was to be expected, and yet he gave up his life and underwent torture rather than betray his trust. The facts are these. When the Jhansi Brigade of mutineers were known to be on their way towards Oreya, *en route* I believe to Delhi, the Tahsildar by night removed in small parcels his records and treasure to the forts of certain loyal zemindars whom he could trust in the north of the Pergunnah. Only one or two of his men on whom he could rely were in the secret. The rest of the establishment got to know that the things were gone, but they did not know where they were concealed. It was a small matter, but no Englishman could have managed this much. He reported this to me. At the same time as this Brigade was a powerful military force, against which our people with only matchlock men could do nothing, I ordered him and officers on the line of march, in order to prevent the looting of bazars and murder of villagers, &c, to receive it civilly, furnish the required supplies and keep matters as straight as possible. The Tahsildar remained at his post and did what was necessary. All would have gone well had not some rascal betrayed to the mutineers the fact that the Tahsildar had hid away his treasure and records. They had taken it for granted that like all other Tahsils at that time, it had long since been looted and had made no inquiries, and the Tahsildar passed as being now Soobah on the part of the Maharaja of Gwalior, whose territory marched with the greater part of the Tahsil. When they learnt the truth they seized him and called upon him to tell them where the treasure had been hid. He refused to tell them, making of course all kinds of excuses. Then they threatened to hang him, and when he still remained firm even prepared to do so; but he was a kindly looking old man, and even they, mutineers as they were, seemed to dislike the job, and so they tied him on to one of their brass guns, telling him they would let him go if he chose to tell them. It was in July I think, possibly August. He would not tell and he was dragged on the gun the whole distance to Etawah. When he arrived there, he was insensible. By the intercession of people in Etawah he was released there and carried to his home at Muttra, where he died. He was only a fat old Bania, like thousands of others whom most Englishmen considered the incarnation of selfish cowardice, but he knew how to suffer and be strong and die rather than be faithless to his salt.

I have mentioned already my dear old friend Rajah Lutchman Singh, and I should like to say something more of him. The Commission examined him at Allahabad I think, but none of them probably guessed what a daring and gallant servant of the State that modest little elderly gentleman had shown himself in more stirring times. He is a Rathore Rujput, a distant cousin of the Raja of Awa, and born of parents by no means overburthened with worldly possessions, he entered the office of the Board of Revenue in 1854, or thereabouts, as Translator. Poor Christian there became acquainted with him, and when he took charge of the Etawah district appointed him to a Tahsildarship, in which I found him when in January, 1856, I relieved Christian. There is an idea that Indians are no riders; that they are not active. Now Agra is seventy miles from Etawah, Lutchman Singh's wife and children were in Agra (respectable officials in those days never took their families with them on service), and with my permission, Kour (as he then was) Lutchman Singh used on the Saturday afternoons to ride into Agra, spend the the day there, and on the Monday morning ride back again to his Tahsil, where I always found him fresh and at work by 10 a. m. I don't suppose we have a covenanted Assistant or Joint Magistrate, now-a-days at any rate, who could do as much. Later a specially good Tahsildar being wanted somewhere in the Jhansi Division, he was, much to my regret, transferred thither. Just before the mutiny broke out, he obtained leave in order to visit his family. His only road lay through Etawah, and he halted there to see me. Then came the bad news, and instead of going on he determined to stay with me (he was well known to and greatly respected by the people of Etawah) and endeavoured to assist me. There through all our troubles, he remained, always hopeful, always cheerful, and ready for anything, until I sent him along with Zor Singh in charge of the ladies to Agra.

Of his services in the Civil department to me as regards my Etawah arrangements and the Government generally, during the rest of the year 1857, I need not speak, but one point I must dwell upon. Towards the close of September, and in the beginning of October, Agra was threatened by a large military force from the South; they came within nine or ten miles of Agra, and were encamped just on the other side of Kuary Nandi.

That the force was very large and had many guns was known, but Government could not get particulars. In the Gwalior arsenal were mortars, shells, and all requisites enough to knock the old fort of Agra about our ears in half an hour. Had this force got any of this war material? What guns had they really got? Had any part of the contingent joined them? Government sent out spies in vain; that some had been promptly hung, and that the others had either funked it and abstained from going or been disposed of was known, but this was all. At this juncture Lutchman Singh volunteered to get the required information. The danger of the attempt was extraordinary; he was a native of Agra, known by sight to every one in the place, known too as a faithful Government servant. About 3,000 of the Agra budmashes were in the rebel camp; if one of them detected him, his immediate death was certain. Yet he went, disguised as a fakir, stayed there two or three days and brought back the fullest and most accurate information—information which, but for the marvellous misunderstanding between the Civil and Military authorities, would have rendered impossible the great surprise, a few days later of the 10th of October, of which all that needs now be said is that "All's well that end well." Now I know of no pluckier exploit than this of Lutchman Singh's; no not in those fighting times when plucky deeds were as plentiful as blackberries on a Devonshire hedge.

When in December I was allowed to return to Etawah he accompanied me, and was with me throughout as one of my righthand men and all I can say is that a more *preux chevalier* in the field, or a bolder and yet wiser adviser in Council, never breathed. *   *   *   *

When the news of the destruction of the Tahsil Shamli and the massacre of its defenders reached Muzaffernagger, the head quarters of the district, the Collector, a good little gentleman, but of unwarlike tendencies, was greatly troubled, and in the dusk of the evening, getting into his buggy, he quietly started down the road to Meerut. But his servants guessing what was happening, ran at once to the Serishtadar and Tahsildar, and these being both strong men, and knowing well that if the news of the flight of the Collector got abroad, the budmashes would have the city on fire in a dozen places before dawn, and then all would be anarchy, pursued him on horseback, brought him back, took care he made no further attempt to escape, issued an encouraging proclamation in his name, posted off a special messenger to the Collector of Saharunpur, explaining the circumstances, and begging that some competent officer might be sent to take charge of the district, and till this officer arrived carried on the administration with the utmost vigour. When that officer came, the non-fighting Collector was safely guided to Meerut, whence with the earliest convoy he found his way down country, sailed for England, and India knew him no more.

So it is not always the native gentleman who runs away or shows incapacity in moments of danger for high executive office and it is not always the English gentleman, even when like the officer I have referred to he comes of a blue-blooded stock, who is able to rise to the occasion."

APPENDIX C—EDUCATIONAL STATISTICS.

TABLE I.

RESULT OF EXAMINATIONS AT THE UNIVERSITIES IN INDIA, FOR ENTRANCE, (MATRICULATION) DEGREES, &c.

Year.	Entrance.		First Arts Examination		B. A.		Honours in Arts and M.A.		Law		Medicine.		Civil Engineering.	
	Candidates.	Passed	Candidates.	Passed	Candidates.	Passed	Candidates.	Passed	Candidates.	Passed	Candidates.	Passed	Candidates.	Passed
					Calcutta University.									
1867-68	1,507	814	388	188	212	99	25	15	82	54	64	21	6	6
1877-78	2,720	1,166	791	253	228	68	62	38	62	30	227	118	34	11
1887-88	4,305	1,907	1,241	481	813	323	82	43	356	238	85	41	16	9

APPENDIX C.

Year	Entra. Exam. Candidates	Entra. Exam. Passed	F. A. Exam. Candidates	F. A. Exam. Passed	B. A. Candidates	B. A. Passed	M. A. Candidates	M. A. Passed	Law Candidates	Law Passed	Medicine Candidates	Medicine Passed	C. Engineering Candidates	C. Engineering Passed
					MADRAS UNIVERSITY.									
1867-8	1,069	338	350	117	24	14	—	—	14	10	1	1	—	—
1877-87	2,495	807	516	191	157	52	4	—	26	11	9	8	4	2
1887-88	6,589	1,963	1745	516	831	437	12	4	123	40	125	46	6	4
					BOMBAY UNIVERSITY.									
1867-68	539	163	69	21	40	24	12	6	6	3	9	3	7	—
1877-78	1,049	217	150	61	87	30	6	3	14	4	86	41	45	28
1887-88	3,012	823	519	123	407	176	7	3	63	26	213	106	50	27
					ALLAHABAD UNIVERSITY.									
1891-92	2003	747	529	161	223	112	20	15	37	14	—	—	377	150
					PUNJAB UNIVERSITY.									
1891-92	1161	619	214	109	45	6	2	—	—	—	—	—	—	—

TABLE II.*

Expansion of the different grades of education in India between 1886 and 1892.

GRADE.	1885-86.		1891-92.		Percentage Distribution.			
					Boys.		Girls.	
	Boys.	Girls.	Boys.	Girls.	1885-86.	1891-92.	1885-86.	1891-92.
Collegiate { Arts ...	8,119	8	12,940	45	...	...	...	...
{ Professional	2,384	27	3,261	31	...	...	...	...
High ...	35,290	375	57,462	926	1	2	...	...
Middle ...	109,993	4,348	125,014	6,105	4	4	2	2
Upper Primary ...	321,052	15,641	343,734	19,920	12	11	6	6
Lower Primary { (a) Reading	1,567,944	132,023	1,819,889	178,477	57	60	57	58
{ (b) Not Reading...	691,804	77,444	658,758	100,616	25	22	34	32
Technical...	8,269	234	16,125	461	...	...	...	...
Normal ...	4,289	660	4,327	819	...	...	...	...
TOTAL...	2,749,144	230,760	3,041,510	307,400				

* "Moral and Material Progress and Condition of India" p. 388.

APPENDIX C.

TABLE III.
Progress of education in India between 1855 and 1892.

Province.	Earliest Year.			1870-71.		1881-82.		1891-92.	
	Year.	Institutions.	Pupils.	Institutions.	Pupils.	Institutions.	Pupils.	Institutions.	Pupils.
Madras	1856-7	13,766	204,856	16,749	263,685	18,136	441,659	23,204	693,985
Bombay	1855-6	2,875	106,040	6,134	265,793	9,664	437,746	12,272	634,438
Bengal	1854-5	25,378	527,731	41,430	878,401	59,892	1,099,767	67,824	1,531,965
Assam	1854-5					1,950	56,483	2,800	83,638
North-West Provinces	1854-5	3,920	52,952	10,174	246,424	13,595	292,069	10,862	282,570
Punjab	1856-7	5,621	44,291	16,125	139,039	8,423	195,409	9,408	260,227
Central Provinces	1862-3	1,169	21,353	1,949	83,999	1,430	81,212	1,988	117,483
Berar	1866-7	247	8,644	454	16,441	915	35,840	1,322	51,483

TABLE IV. RESULTS OF UNIVERSITY EXAMINATIONS FOR THE FIVE YEARS 1886-87—1890-91.*

	Universities.		
	Calcutta.	Madras.	Bombay.
A.—Examined for Matriculation †...	100·00	100·00	100·00
{ Failed	52·26	73·13	74·59
{ Passed	47·74	26·87	25·41
Examined for Degree in Arts	20·59	10·37	12·87
,, ,, Law	7·06	1·80	2·44
,, ,, Medicine	2·30	1·52	6·66
,, ,, Civil Engineering	0·55	0·16	2·97
Total examined for Degrees	30·50	13·85	24·94
{ Passed	13·97	6·80	11·78
{ Failed	16·53	7·05	13·16
Total not appearing for Degrees	17·24	13·02	0·47
B.—Passed the Matriculation	100·00	100·00	100·00
Examined for Degree in Arts...	43·13	38·61	50·66
,, ,, Law	14·79	6·68	9·62
,, ,, Medicine	4·83	5·64	26·21
,, ,, Civil Engineering	1·15	0·61	11·67
Total Examined for Degree	63·90	51·54	98·16
{ Passed	29·25	25·32	46·35
{ Failed	34·65	26·22	51·81
Total not appearing for Degrees	36·10	48·46	1·84

* The Census of India, General Report, p. 225.

† The actual figures are, Calcutta, 21,238; Madras, 34,393; and Bombay, 14,774.

END OF VOLUME III.

A HISTORY
OF
HINDU CIVILISATION
DURING BRITISH RULE

BY

PRAMATHA NATHA BOSE, B.SC. *(Lond.)* F.G.S., M.R.A.S., &c
Vols. I & II.

Some Press Notices.

A very interesting and instructive work written with considerable knowledge, and in a liberal and impartial spirit. The author, as a Hindu has practical acquaintance with Indian manners and customs such as could hardly be acquired by a foreigner, and in collecting his information he has drawn equally from native and foreign sources. * * He is careful about his facts, sober and sensible in his judgments, and simple, clear, and direct in his modes of expression.—THE TIMES, *October 4th, 1894.*

These two volumes contain useful and accurate information packed into a moderate compass.—THE SATURDAY REVIEW, *November 3rd 1894.*

The author is a very learned and deeply read man. * * That he writes English perfectly and that he knows his subject well go without saying.—THE ASIATIC QUARTERLY REVIEW, *April 1895.*

A trustworthy and convenient exposition for English readers who may desire to trace the influences of Western contact with Hindu institutions."—THE DAILY CHRONICLE, *May 11th 1895.*

The author has laboured diligently to present an adequate picture of the varied conditions of his extensive subject. He has the great advantage of treating the matters with inside knowledge, and his scientific training has materially helped to give value to his exposition. He writes with simplicity and clearness. His work can not fail to be extremely serviceable to all who wish to understand the conditions of Indian life, and specially to English students of the great problems of modern Indian development.—INDIA, *April 1895*.

This work raises many questions of intense interest for us, and as the expression of the opinions and views of a highly educated Hindu is of special importance we look forward with pleasure to the remaining promised volumes.—The Westminister Review, May 1895

" J'aime mieux remercier M. Bose de out ce qu'il a réuni d'informations utiles dans ces deux volumes. J'ai déjà signalé, celles qu'il a données dans son premier livre sur les movements religieux contemporains. On lira de même avec profit ce qu'il dit dans le deuxième sur les mariages précoces, sur les abus du koulinisme, sur l'abolition du suicide des veuves, sur les aliments défendus, sur el', interdiction, des voyages outre-mer et dans le troisieme livre sur la position faite fair a la femme, sur la famille Hindoue, sur les jeux et divertissements, sur l'alimentation, le mobilier et le costume, Meilleurs encore son les chapitres du quatrieme livre sur l'agriculture, sur les metiers et les arts industriels, sur la grande industrie, sur l'industrie miniére.

A. BARTH IN REVUE Critique *2-9 September 1895.*

Mr. Pramatha Nath Bose has written a book which is in many ways remarkable. In the form of " A HISTORY OF HINDU CIVILISATION UNDER BRITISH RULE" he has given proofs that there are exceptions to the rule that Hindus are incapable of turning out original literary work.* * * Without expressing entire concurrence with all the opinions to which he gives expression, we are free to say that his book reflects laborious research and most painstaking efforts to drag truth up from the bottom of a very deep and dark well.—THE MADRAS TIMES, *Wednesday, October 31st 1894.*

A HISTORY OF HINDU CIVILISATION DURING BRITISH RULE deserves to be read by all those who take the least interest in the progress of the people of this country,—MADRAS STANDARD, *Wednesday, October 17th 1894.*

The work is in two volumes, and exceedingly interesting. It is written in excellent English, and must have cost the writer much time and much research. * * * The work like the one published by Mr. Bose is calculated to attract the attention of all who have the welfare of India at heart—those who wish to see the country improve, whether Natives or Europeans.—THE EVENING MAIL, *Bangalore.*

We most cordially welcome the first two volumes of this work which Messrs. Newman & Co., have just published and which the English-knowing public owe to the patriotic literary efforts of Mr. Pramatha Nath Bose.—THE HINDU, *Friday, September 7th, 1894.*

The chapters on the religious condition of India show a just appreciation on the author's part of the labours of the Sanskritists and Orientalists.—THEOSOPHIST, *December 1894.*

The volumes contain such a valuable collection of useful, interesting, and rare information on a variety of social and industrial topics, that they have a distinct claim on the attention of the educated public. We hope that Mr. Bose's patriotic efforts will receive due appreciation in every way from his countrymen and from those English speaking peoples in other parts of the world, who sympathise with our efforts for an improved national state.—THE HINDU, *September 14th, 1894.*

It is very interesting, and we would strongly recommend all those interested in the welfare of India not to fail to purchase a copy.—THE EVENING MAIL (*Bangalore*) *November 20th 1894.*

His work seems to us to be written fairly and impartially, and in a spirit that must make it most valuable as a work of reference. Not only to Englishmen and to his country-men will it be of interest, but scholars in all lands will be instructed and edified by it.—THE ADVERTISER (*Maulmein*) *20th September, 1894.*

It would be almost impossible to find any author—European or Native—better qualified to undertake the work of describing "HINDU CIVILISATION UNDER BRITISH RULE" than Mr. Pramatha Nath Bose.—THE BOMBAY GAZETTE, *September 1st, 1894.*

This is the title of a remarkable production from Bengal, which is a credit both to the printers and to the author. What Mr. Bose has achieved in the half of his work already published, will, we trust, make the reading public, eagerly desire the early publication of the remaining half. * * * Mr. Bose's work does not confine itself only to chronicling those new ideas and the movements, many of them very short lived, into which they developed. In dealing with every phase of the society and before giving an account of the changes made under British rule, he takes a brief, but masterly review of the India that has passed away, of the India that developed under the Aryans from the Vedic times. and the Indian that deteriorated in the 9th to 11th centuries.—THE INDIAN SPECTATOR, *October 7th 1894*.

Mr. Bose has indeed performed the task, he sets before him, as well as probably it is possible for any one to do in the present state of our knowledge and in the present condition of the country. The work he has given us is a credit to himself and will no doubt be highly esteemed by the literary world.—THE INDIAN SPECTATOR, *October 14th 1894*.

Mr. Bose has brought out all these facts prominently in his book and if we cannot subscribe to everything that he says, we must say that he has put before the readers the forces which are moving the hitherto dormant mass of Hindu social organism. THE INDUPROKASH (*Bombay*) *January 21st 1895*.

The object of the book is to give a history of the changes which our religion, our society and our industries have undergone and are still undergoing, during the British rule, a subject interesting enough but which has been rendered still more interesting by short accounts which the author has given of every subject from the very beginning of civilisation, so that we have in one view, as it were, a history of our institutions from the earliest time, so far, of course, as such a history is available.

The book has been written with singular impartiality. Whatever remarks the author has to make, he has made them in his introduction and they show an originality of treatment and thought. In the body of the book, he has confined himself to merely narrating facts, and there are many interesting anecdotes, related of our last generation, which form delightful reading, but a somewhat disappointing one in as much as there are not more of them.—THE INDIAN MIRROR, *September 4th 1894*.

The book has been written in quite a new and original plan. It professes, as its name implies, to give an account of the changes which our institutions are at present undergoing; but it really gives us much more than that. We have in it accounts, historically drawn up of the several institutions, religious as well as social, from an earlier period, which cannot fail to be interesting. The subjects so treated are so many as almost to give the book an appearance of a cyclopædia.—THE BENGALEE, *September 22nd 1894.*

The subject is a large one, and there is much in these volumes which will be of considerable value to English readers. There is a particularly interesting account of the rise, growth, and the final predominance of caste.—THE INDIAN DAILY NEWS, *September 26th 1894.*

Judging by the two volumes placed before the public credit will be freely given to the author for honest and conscientious work, prolonged and patient labour in the gathering of materials, and in every possible instance to bring the information down to date. * * * The work is deserving of high praise and is an important contribution to contemporary Indian history of the right sort.—THE TRIBUNE, *October 3rd 1894.*

We have now gone—although cursorily—over the whole field of Mr. Bose's two volumes, and shall await the publication of his remaining two volumes with interest. From what we have stated above, our readers will see that Mr. Bose is eminently fitted for the task he has undertaken. He is not a theorist and he is not an enthusiast; he advocates reform, but can appreciate what was good in the past; and above all, he can let facts speak for themselves. A laborious enquirer he is at the same time a pleasant narrator and his style is simple and pleasant, chaste and perspicuous.—CALCUTTA REVIEW, *January, 1895.*

www.ingramcontent.com/pod-product-compliance
Lightning Source LLC
Chambersburg PA
CBHW022041230426
43672CB00008B/1037